The *ABC*'s

of
Languages
&
Linguistics

A PRACTICAL PRIMER TO LANGUAGE SCIENCE

The
ABC's
of
Languages
&
Linguistics

A PRACTICAL PRIMER TO LANGUAGE SCIENCE

CURTIS W. HAYES   *JACOB ORNSTEIN*
WILLIAM W. GAGE

National Textbook Company
NTC a division of *NTC Publishing Group* • Lincolnwood, Illinois USA

1990 Printing

Copyright © 1987, 1977 by National Textbook Company,
a division of NTC Publishing Group,
4255 West Touhy Avenue,
Lincolnwood (Chicago), Illinois 60646-1975 U.S.A.
All rights reserved. No part of this book may
be reproduced, stored in a retrieval system, or
transmitted in any form or by any means, electronic,
mechanical, photocopying, recording or otherwise,
without the prior permission of NTC Publishing Group.
Library of Congress Catalog Number: 86-61183
Manufactured in the United States of America.

0 ML 9 8 7 6 5 4

Table of Contents

Preface to the Second Edition

Much has transpired in the field of linguistic science since the publication of *The ABC's of Languages and Linguistics* (Chilton Books, 1964), and hence the need for revision. A new coauthor, Curtis W. Hayes, has joined us, bringing to the revision a great deal of experience and fresh insight in the realms of both pure and applied linguistics. Great effort by all three of us has been made to incorporate new and significant data into this current book.

There is, by now, such a large number of language texts on the market that it is desirable to offer something quite different, to make a unique contribution, lest our effort be redundant. Through our joint endeavors, it has been possible to retain in the present volume a broadness of scope that has been of note in reviews following the first appearance of the *ABC's*. One indication of such breadth may be seen in the chapters that include discussions of the most dynamic linguistic schools of thought. Recent developments in sociolinguistics and psycho-linguistics are touched upon, and we also direct the reader's attention to a number of topics in the burgeoning and ever-expanding discipline of applied linguistics. For example, in the latter chapters, we introduce the reader to new trends in language teaching; and there, too, we discuss frankly the decline in language requirements and enrollments. The latest enrollment figures have been received from the Modern Language Association of America, as well as from other authoritative sources. At the same time, positive and encouraging developments in the language teaching field are also detailed.

The *ABC's* has been utilized as a broad orientation to the discipline of language study rather than as an introduction to be employed in technical linguistics classes. Our revision attempts to serve in the same capacity as the original *ABC's*. Above all, the *ABC's* is intended to interest students in pursuing the study of language. For this purpose we have at the end of each chapter thought-provoking, purposeful study questions, and a list of texts and articles which may be consulted for further reference.

All three of us have benefited from the suggestions and criticisms of a number of scholars and teachers. We must express appreciation to Professors Carolyn Kessler, Hassan Sharifi, and Archibald A. Hill for their careful reading of the manuscript, and to Mr. Alfred Pietrzyk of the Center for Applied Linguistics for his valuable suggestions in the chapters in which we discuss the political and social ramifications of language. Our profound gratitude goes to Mr. Richard Brod, member of the Association of the Departments of Foreign Languages (ADFL), for furnishing the most recent figures on language trends based upon Modern Language Association surveys. This information has aided us in providing a valid and comprehensive view of the current foreign language teaching practices in the United States. It is also with deep gratitude that we acknowledge the extremely valuable assistance and insights of the following: Dr. Richard E. Wood of Adelphi University and Dr. Margaret Hagler, Lincoln Land Community College, who shared their expertise for "One Language for the World?" (Chapter 10); Professor Edward L. Blansitt Jr., University of Texas, El Paso, on whom we relied greatly; and Mrs. Sarah B. Boyer, Senior Secretary of the Cross-Cultural Southwest Ethnic Study Center, University of Texas at El Paso, for her assistance.

And finally, to our students, who offered judicious criticism, we give special recognition.

The Authors

A Caveat to the Reader

The science of linguistics, particularly "pure linguistics" (as opposed to its applications), is at present in an extreme state of flux. While the ferment is in its way fascinating to professional linguists, it poses real danger of confusion to those less familiar with the field. Despite the zeal and persuasiveness of certain linguistic theoreticians, almost "charismatic" in their approach, there are few if any categorical or indisputable "truths" in linguistic doctrine.

Hence it is the better of sanity for readers to peruse those sections concerning linguistic theory open-mindedly, regarding the theories as essentially successive approximations leading to a more profound and sophisticated understanding of universal principles applying to language systems *as a whole*. In this manner, as in physics, chemistry, botany or another natural science, an ongoing "symbiosis" can be reached; or more simply put, some sort of "consensus" can be achieved, generally acceptable to many, if not all, professional linguists.

Jacob Ornstein, Ph.D.

I. Facts and Fantasies About Language

THE IMPORTANCE OF LANGUAGE

In all probability one of our first actions of the day is to talk to someone. What is so remarkable about that? Most of the other three billion people in the world do the same thing. But suppose a dog, or any animal, awoke one morning and started talking. It would make the front page of every newspaper in the world as well as the evening news.

We are so accustomed to talking, and hearing other people talk, that we occasionally forget what a marvelous attribute language is. Only when we consider the plight of *not* being able to talk do we fully appreciate its importance.

Consider an aphasiac, a person, that is, who has lost the ability to talk. He may still understand what is said and even communicate in writing; but such a person is as badly handicapped as one with the most distressing physical impairment. He needs institutional care in the same way as any disabled person, or special training, at least, to enable him to carry on in the outside world.

One of the authors recently communicated with an aphasiac who could say almost nothing, and even said the reverse of what he meant—an intended "No" coming out "Yes," and vice versa. The man was a wealthy Florida realtor, yet one day he wrote: "Believe me, I'd give all my property and savings if I could only talk again."

By contrast, reading and writing—marks on paper that stand for speech—are much less important. In fact, half the adults on earth, even in this modern and advanced day, are illiterate or unable to read and write. And many of the world's languages, probably a large majority, have no writing system at all.

Although literacy is a tremendous advantage in modern industrialized societies, it is by no means essential. That is, we can still get along without being able to read or write. Of course, this does not alter the fact that illiteracy is one of the world's great social and educational problems. The point is that illiteracy does not incapacitate humans as greatly as aphasia does. People who cannot read and write can still get along reasonably well in our society, but the aphasiac must seek professional help until he is cured or rehabilitated.

There is a well-known story in the Bible that reflects the importance of language in human society. According to the Old Testament, mankind spoke only one language until Nimrod began to build a tower that was to reach heaven. "And the Lord said, 'Behold, they are one people, and they have all one language, and this is only the beginning of what they will do; and nothing that they propose to do will now be impossible for them. Come, let us go down, and there confuse their language, that they may not understand one another's speech.' "

Some scholars attribute the source of this legend to the many languages of the slaves who were gathered together to build the famous "hanging gardens" of Babylon. The name "Babel" is said to be a variation of the word "Babylon," rather than the Hebrew *balal*, meaning "to confuse."

1

Some people believe there is nothing men could not do if they really understood each other's language. Utopia requires far more than that, no doubt, but it is true that a shared language tends to unite people, while different languages divide them. Those of us who have ever lived in an environment in which we did not understand the language know from personal experience how welcome a few words of our native speech can sound. Even in the strange accents of strangers, our native language seems lovely to us, and we have a shared feeling for those who speak as we do.

George Bernard Shaw said that England and America are two countries separated by the same language. The wit of this remark results, partly, from the way it clashes with our conviction that the same language really unites people. A New York psychiatrist's experience corroborates this. By learning the argot of emotionally disturbed hot-rodders, he was able to communicate with them by discussing drag racing and other "tribal customs."

LANGUAGE: AN INFINITE, HUMAN CAPABILITY

While the legend of the Tower of Babel shows how speaking different languages divides people, an even sharper distinction is that between users and non-users of language. The ability to learn languages is, perhaps, the chief difference separating man from all other animals. Let us first briefly approximate what we feel to be the attributes of a language. One traditional (pre-1960) linguistic definition of language is that *a language consists of a structural system of vocal symbols by which a social group cooperates.* But this definition is not too helpful, since animals may have social groups, and they may interact through a system of vocal sounds. A study of porpoises indicates that this interaction may go much further in complexity than we ever imagined. A more recent definition is that *a language consists of a system of rules which relate sound sequences to meanings.* The terms "system of rules," "sound sequences," and "meaning" we will define and discuss later. All languages—it is important for us to point out at the onset—have distinctive sets of sounds called *phonemes*; these sets are grouped together into utterances called *morphemes* (phonemes containing meaning); and morphemes fit into patterns called words, phrases, clauses, and sentences.

The concept of a *sentence* is especially vital in linguistic studies today. Some linguists believe that a language is an unbounded set of sentences. The important term is "unbounded." More specifically, a speaker or hearer has control over and knowledge of an indefinitely large number of sentences. The idea that a set may be indefinite may boggle the mind for the moment; but if we consider that we "know" more sentences than we can hope to hear or speak in our lifetimes, the concept becomes clearer. Many of the sentences that we speak or hear (or even read) are new sentences, never having been spoken or heard before. As a test, how many sentences in this book, or even on this page, are new? And if these sentences are new, consider all of the sentences that we have not heard or spoken that will be new. In fact, tomorrow's sentences are new, as are the next day's. There is the possibility that each sentence represents a creative act. What is basic, however, is that there is no end to the sentences of a language.

If we were to put a limit on the capability of a human being to understand sentences, then we would not have a language. He would not only run out of things to say but the capability to say something new would be absent. Yet a limit is precisely what we have in animal communication. In fact, since the noises that animals make do not constitute an unbounded set, linguists would say that animals do not have language. Animal noises—be they of chimpanzees, porpoises, dogs—are a closed set. Bees have been said to have language. A bee—forgetting for the moment that bees are unvocal—can communicate the direction and distance of nectar to other bees, but that is all the information that it can communicate. It cannot say anything about the weather, flowers, or the presence of animals in the near vicinity, all of which, it would seem, are important for the successful taking of nectar. A chimpanzee may be conditioned to make noises or to move symbols about in response to a number of stimuli, but there is a limit to what a chimpanzee can communicate; and we must *teach* him to communicate. More basically, he cannot understand or speak novel utterances, a capability within the competence of a normal human being. By way of contrast, a child is not taught his language; he has only to be exposed to a language to learn it. In fact, we cannot prevent children from learning the language(s) of their environment.

Except in those cases in which brain damage has occurred, or in which a child is severely retarded, language learning (the more technical term is *acquisition*) occurs. Even in the retarded, as Eric Lenneberg has demonstrated in his study of mongoloid children, language development takes place. If we consider the size of the brain, we find that even nanocephalic dwarfs have the ability to learn language. Language, as far as we can determine, is species-specific. The reason that higher-ordered primates cannot learn language is that they are not human.

THE UNEXPECTED INTRICACIES OF OTHER PEOPLE'S LANGUAGES

At a party recently a linguist was asked whether people like the Eskimos had a "real" language or whether they just communicated through gestures and grunts. The gentleman who asked this question, a well-educated person with a master's degree, was truly amazed when he learned that the Eskimos not only have a real language but that it is very complex in structure from a linguistic point of view. Then the linguist completely overwhelmed the linguistically-naive guest by writing for him a single word in Eskimo which is equivalent to an entire sentence in English or any European tongue. It was *a:slisa-ut-issar-si-niarpu-ba*, which simply means "I am looking for something suitable for a fishline."

There is probably no subject about which there are so many errors and downright misinformation as that of language—even among persons of higher education. One of the most widespread of these misconceptions is that the language of technologically underdeveloped or "primitive" peoples must be very simple and crude. The fact of the matter is that from the standpoint of the speaker of English or a European tongue the languages of such groups often contain subtleties that do not exist in his own.

Although English speakers may think it is unusual that certain languages mark verbs for gender, much stranger features may be found. In the Nahuatl (Modern Aztec) language of northern Mexico, for example, it is necessary in certain verbal forms to express whether the purpose of the action affects an animate being or an inanimate object. In English we say "I *see* the women" and "I *see* the house," but the verb does not change. In Nahuatl, however, in using the verb "to eat" with the root *cua*, the Aztec speaker makes certain to prefix *tla* to indicate that he is not eating a human being. It has been pointed out that this distinction appears most clearly in such words as *tetlazohtlani*, "one who loves (people)," as contrasted with *tlatlazohtlani*, "one who loves (things)."

In Hupa, an Indian language of northern California, nouns as well as verbs are marked for time. Thus one finds the following distinctions:

xonta: house (now existing)
xontate: house which will exist in the future
xontaneen: house which formerly existed

Even speakers of many non-Western languages have convinced themselves that their language has no "grammar," believing that the users merely make up structure as it comes into their minds. The same sort of impression may hold true for a linguistically naive, well-educated speaker of a Western language—our party guest for example—who may believe that he does not know the grammar of English. Linguists, in recent times, have made the useful distinction between "knowledge of language" and "knowledge about language." Our knowledge *of* language is often a tacit or subconscious one that we draw upon when speaking our language. Our knowledge *about* language is usually *taught* knowledge, which makes explicit what we know implicitly. Native speakers of any language, for instance, have knowledge *of* their language, but few have knowledge *about* their language, unless they have taken a course on its structural characteristics.

All languages have structure. The linguist's task has been to describe this structure and to make explicit what the native speaker knows subconsciously about his language.

When we attempt to learn a non-Western language, we are usually confronted by a system with many bewildering intricacies and complexities. There may be the necessity for distinguishing between objects which are in sight and those which are not, as in southern Paiute where *ma avaaniaak'a a* means "He will give something visible to someone in sight."

There is the possibility of having different verb forms, not only to show whether the principal object involved is an agent or something acted on—as with active and passive voice in some familiar languages—but in addition, as in many Philippine languages, to show that it is the instrument or that it is the beneficiary of an action. Thus, in Maranao:

somobali so mama sa sapi ko gelat (emphasis on *so mama*, "the man")	"The man slaughters the cow with a knife."
or	
isomabali o mama so gelat ko sapi (emphasis on *so gelat*, "a knife")	"With a knife, the man slaughters the cow."
begen ian reka	"He'll give it to you." (give-something he to-you)
or	
began ka ian	"You he'll give it to." (give-for someone you-he)

Different verb forms may be used to indicate who does what when relating an incident. In English our use of *he*, *she*, *it*, and *they* is often ambiguous: "When Tom went hunting with Harry, he shot a moose." Who shot a moose? In Cree when the "party of the first part," "of the second part," and sometimes "of the third part" are indicated, one says:

wapamēw (A saw B); *wāpamik* (B saw A); or *wāpamēyiwa* (B saw C)

Returning to Eskimo, which was thought to be so primitive by the aforementioned guest, we ought to point out that its structure does appear formidable to one acquainted with only Indo-European patterns. Eskimo is what is known as a *polysynthetic* language, which means that entire sentences are incorporated into a single word. Each element of the word carries meaning but does not have an independent existence; that is, it cannot be pronounced alone, like such English words as "king" or "banana" can be. The Eskimo elements are more nearly like the "-ness" of "kindness." We see immediately that the traditional parts of speech of Latin or of English grammar become inadequate or actually misleading in describing a polysynthetic language. For example, "Do you think he really intends to go to look after it?" can be expressed in Eskimo by the word: *takusar-iartor-uma-faluar-nerp-a*.

This brings us to the familiar and commonplace notion that all languages can be analyzed as one would analyze Latin, Greek, French, or English. A school of American linguists, those associated with *structural* or *descriptive* linguistics, and who have taken the descriptive label "Bloomfieldian" after Leonard Bloomfield, the eminent and brilliant linguist who gave direction to this school, did extensive research and field work on this subject in such remote areas as Africa and Malayo-Polynesia. Bloomfield also worked on North and South American Indian languages, and helped to dispel a particular version of universal grammar: that all languages were similar to Latin and Greek, a notion which emanated from the 18th century and was based upon the notion of a universal logic. Bloomfield and his fellow structural linguists believed that each language was in a way an island, a unique entity unto itself, and should be approached as such. Any similarity among such diverse languages was purely accidental. They felt that the 18th century tendency to describe all languages as having derived from one source, in this case Latin or Greek, obscured important differences in other, less well-known languages. The tendency to look for logical similarities among diverse languages was misdirected but not, as we shall find, misguided.

Linguists who broke away from the influence of European grammatical practices and models to approach each language without prejudice found that distinctions that are important in one language or group of languages may be insignificant or entirely lacking in another. For example, in Hungarian and the Uralic languages *gender* (masculine, feminine, or neuter), which is so important in the Romance languages and German, is for the most part not signaled. This is carried so far that no separate words exist for "he" and "she," both of which are expressed by *Ö*. Within a sentence, however, it becomes clear that one is talking about a female, of either the human or animal species. While the Romance languages, as well as English, make the distinction between present and past *tense* (time of action), such as "I looked" and "I look," Chinese has basically only one form for the verb, such as *kan*, "look," "looked." However, suffixes may be added to Chinese verbs to indicate various *aspects* (*aspect* refers to distinctions of duration of time, continuity of time, and completion of time). *Kan-le* can mean "had looked," "have looked," or "will have looked." Chinese *aspect* parallels English *aspect*, usually termed *perfective* and signaled by forms of *have*, which may be found in the past ("had looked"), the present ("have looked"), and the future ("will have looked")—though the English speaker, including many who have learned Chinese or have studied Chinese grammar, is inclined to feel that *-le* equates with the English past tense. There are other *aspects* in Chinese, but we leave the analysis of these to those who may wish to study in more detail the grammar of the Chinese language.

In summary, it remains interesting, and even fascinating, to observe the distinctions that some languages make, which in others may be nonexistent. One of the commonest of these is between a "we" that includes "you" and a "we but not you," distinguished in the Maranao tongue:

inclusive	exclusive
tano	*kami*

Let us consider another example of linguistic variety: the Turkish language makes a strict distinction between hearsay and personally observed or attested past. For instance, to express the sentence, "His daughter was very beautiful," one of the two following forms must be used:

hearsay	attested
kiz cok güzel imis	*kiz cok güzel idi*

In the first example *imis* is used because the speaker does not know the statement to be a fact since he has no personal knowledge of it, while in the second *idi* is employed because he has personally verified that the young lady in question was beautiful.

MISCONCEPTIONS ABOUT LANGUAGE

Perhaps we assume that other people must express their thought precisely the way it is done in English, German, or other European languages, because for centuries we have been under the influence of the classical traditions. It was the custom in centuries past to regard Greek and Latin as ideal languages, the *proto*-types (the first or parent) for other languages, and to speak of other languages as being derived, albeit imperfectly, from these two classical languages. It is not difficult to understand the reason for the preeminence of Greek and Latin. Most of the learned manuscripts, including translations of the Bible, were written in Latin and Greek. Implicit was the assumption that, since the Roman Catholic Church used Latin in its liturgy, even God spoke Latin. This particular, biased orientation to language was partially changed with the advent, in the first part of the 20th century, of various modern approaches to the description and analysis of language.

That other people must necessarily express a given thought as we do in English is far from the case. No two languages in the world express all concepts and thoughts in exactly the same way. We say in English "I am hungry," but in French it is *J'ai faim* and in Spanish, *Tengo hambre*—which is more literally in both languages, "I have hunger." All European languages have some way of saying "How are you?", but Burmese has no such expression and one must employ instead one of five or six levels of politeness. We say, "I feel sorry for you," but Japanese renders this expression by *o kinodoku desu*, or literally, "It's a poison for your soul."

Information about the world is organized according to the linguistic patterns of a given language community in ways which, while not totally arbitrary, are not according to the canons of Western logic. All grammars contain a great deal that is contrary to what we would regard as the "sensible" ways of organizing experience, and it would be a mistake to believe that any language is particularly logical or that the more exotic languages are, as a whole, less logical than the more familiar ones.

This divergence in patterns of expression accounts for the fact that many of us "feel" that every language has its own soul or spirit. No matter how well done a translation may be, some meaning will always be lost from the original because every language is inextricably interwoven with the peculiar culture of its speakers. As the late Dr. W. R. Parker of Indiana University remarked, when observing in Goethe's *Faust* that Dr. Faustus stops addressing Margaret by the formal *Sie* (for "you") and uses the intimate *du*, this subtle yet significant change in tone, so much a part of the German language, could not be signaled in English by the same grammatical means. Here again, the individual who in learning a language goes beyond its basic everyday expressions and becomes acquainted with its nuances and fine distinctions is in the best position to analyze what makes its speakers tick linguistically—and perhaps to a large extent, psychologically.

Yet the practice of structural linguists to seek and to emphasize differences between and among languages rather than similarities led to a further misconception: that a language may differ from any other in an infinite number of ways. This view distorted, as it were, an important 17th century notion, expressed by the language philosopher Descartes and his followers, who believed that languages are far more alike than they are different. Since languages are learned by human beings, and since human beings do not appear more predisposed to learn one language than another, and since all human beings seem to be equipped with the same neurological equipment, then it must follow, according to Descartes, that languages share a number of important features (features that are now called language *universals*). Noam Chomsky has resurrected this 17th century notion of universal grammar in his book *Cartesian Linguistics* and has made it a premise of his own brand of linguistic analysis.

It is a sign of a healthy and viable science, surely, that such questions as universal grammar are being reexamined and that earlier theories, such as the theory of innate ideas, are being given explicit characterization. Suffice it for us to say here that languages which appear, upon superficial examination, to be totally different may, upon a closer, deeper analysis, be more similar than different.

Still another misconception is the one regarding the superiority and inferiority of languages. There is in fact a tremendous body of folklore built up about most languages. Regarding French, there is the legend that it possesses special attributes which enable it to express thoughts more clearly than any other language. There is even a saying in French, *Ce qui n'est pas clair, n'est pas français*: "What is not clear, is not French." Nationalistic Germans have attributed to their language mystic qualities that supposedly give it special powers of vigorous expression. About Italian there exist many beliefs regarding its seniority and musicality. Incidentally, in this vein the Spanish emperor Charles V once said that English was the language to speak with merchants, German with soldiers, French with women, Italian with friends, and Spanish with God!

These beliefs have no basis in scientific linguistic fact any more than the assertion that any given language is prettier than another. Like the beauty of a painting or that of a woman, the charm of any language lies solely in the eyes—or ears—of the beholder. One often hears that German is not as beautiful as Spanish or Italian because it is "guttural," and in the aesthetic judgment of some people gutturalness sounds harsh. From the linguistic viewpoint this judgment is meaningless; a linguist would merely say that German has more "guttural sounds" than English, French, or Italian, or in more technical phraseology, that German has a high number of sounds produced with the velum, the flap of soft flesh that is part of the back of the mouth and that cuts off the breath stream between the oral and nasal cavities. Yet to many speakers of Semitic languages, gutturalness is not only not a defect but is a positive virtue. In Israel to speak Hebrew with a markedly "guttural" pronunciation is considered very chic. Arabic has an unusually high number of "guttural" sounds but few persons who claim Arabic as their mother tongue would consider it one iota less beautiful than French or English.

It is equally false to believe that the sounds of a particular language are in themselves easy or difficult to the native speaker, although some sounds encountered by young children learning their language appear to be harder to learn than others. The degree of difficulty is dependent on the language background with which we start, and there are probably no sounds with which the native speakers of other languages would not have trouble. Incidentally, children of, say, a year and a half, who have not yet mastered their own language, often make use of many sounds that the adults of their speech communities would class as extremely difficult. Learning the sounds of a first language is in part a process of eliminating sounds that do not belong to it.

At the root of many linguistic misconceptions is the undeniable fact that many people regard language as static and inflexible rather than as dynamic and ever-changing. It is common to hear and read statements to the effect that a certain language is incapable of expressing the concepts of modern society. This is a fallacy, and from the evidence of linguistic research there does not appear to be any language that cannot be harnessed to serve any verbal communication need. In fact, any linguistic system can be "developed" to accommodate new terminology and concepts by means of its *rule system*. The fact that languages may express concepts through different patterns or rules does not alter this principle at all. When Wycliffe was told that English was too "rude" for the Scriptures to appear in, he retorted, "It is not so rude as they are false liars."

It is, however, undeniable that the Wichita language of an Oklahoma Indian tribe is not suitable in its present state for discussing nuclear physics or celestial navigation. But this is primarily because the speakers of Wichita have never had to cope with such problems. If, however, the roles of Wichita and English were reversed, it predictably would be English that would lack specialized terminology and expressions.

We do not know the details of the origin of language. But we do know that languages have an organic existence, and that they develop semantically according to the needs of the community employing them. The more technologically advanced the speakers are, the more equipped the language will be to cope with science, technology, and the concepts of an industrialized society. Conversely, the languages of such advanced nations as the United States, Germany, and France may and often do lack numerous concepts and nuances referring to the phenomena of nature and to pursuits like herding, hunting, and fishing, which are elaborately present in many languages of people of nonindustrialized cultures. Berber has a far richer vocabulary for discussing camels and livestock and their care than has Danish or Italian.

There are languages in existence in which there is no way of saying *stereophonic playback recorder* or *nuclear warhead* without a lengthy paraphrase, since no such words or compounds as these exist. But this does not mean that the speakers of these languages could not coin such expressions. The coining of new terms—and this important fact is often not realized—is part of the organic development of any living language in a dynamically growing society. For example, the reason that Homer had no word for "motorcar" is simply because he did not have such a vehicle to convey him over the hills of ancient Greece. The modern Greeks, however, have coined a word for this useful vehicle, terming it *autokineto*, composed of *autos* (self) and *kinetos* (moving thing). That, after all, is the way the term *automobile*, used in somewhat varying shapes in most European languages, was also conceived and constructed (*autos* plus an original Latin root *mobilis*, through Old French *mobile*). But tastes vary in languages, and although Czech, for example, uses the word *automobil*, Polish has preferred to express the same concept by the word *samochod* (with *sam* roughly meaning "self" and *chod*, "locomotion").

Thai was not equipped until a few years ago with words for most modern innovations. There was a tradition in Thailand of using Sanskrit roots in technical vocabulary, much as we make use of Greek (*astronomy, epiglottis*, etc.). With modernization the Thais have avidly set about the business of coining new words, even to the extent of having contests for the best word made up to express some new Western-derived concept. Preferably, the new words should include Sanskrit elements already used in Thai and, ideally, should have some resemblance in sound to the term used in European languages.

The growth and development of languages presents still other opportunities for myth-building. It has been difficult for people to realize that every language is in a constant state of flux and is at any period moving in new directions usually considered to be corrupt and decadent by the purists. The constant mutability of language is obscured because of the tendency for people to think in terms of the standardized written form of a language. People believed that classical Latin was perfect and unchanging even while spoken Latin was becoming French, Spanish, Italian, and the other modern Romance languages. Beliefs in immunity to change on the part of any living language are totally without foundation.

Many of the most persistent myths about language occur in speculations concerning the relation of speech to writing. Commonly, people feel that a language which has never been written is not really a language at all. In point of fact, an unwritten language can have all the attributes of any written language and may have a rich literature, although necessarily a literature limited to what is handed down by oral tradition. In the case of languages which have been written for centuries, people often feel that the written language represents the real language and the spoken form only a pale and probably corrupted reflection of it. Linguists, while understanding the great importance of the written form and recognizing the many ways in which writing and speech interact with each other, nevertheless maintain that speaking is the basic symbol-using activity of human beings, with writing being a superstructure built upon it, and that, while spoken language is an attribute of the species, writing is culturally determined.

Facts, fantasies, and even prejudice exist about languages just as they do about individuals and nations. While some of these beliefs are romantic and many appeal to the imagination, it would seem to be far better to know more about the nature of language as a branch of the cognitive and behavioral sciences than to perpetuate old wives' tales about it. We propose in the following chapters to examine what human language is and what general principles apply to its function and use in the world. We can enjoy this excursion all the more if we rid ourselves of our misconceptions before embarking. Even if we find that we cannot easily discuss the bullish and bearish fluctuations of Wall Street ticker tapes in fluent Eskimo, it may turn out that for the fine points of under-ice fishing Eskimo may be superior to English and French combined.

I. QUESTIONS AND ACTIVITIES

1. How do we "intuitively" know that there is no end to the sentences of a language?

2. Some languages have been described as "primitive." What is meant by that term?

3. Is there a social status associated with the particular language that we speak? What accounts for the fact that certain languages are "prestigious" while others are not?

4. Coining of words: we coined a word for the man who traveled around earth in a space module, "astronaut." What does it mean? Are there other words that have "astro" or "naut" within them?

5. Can you list some of your observations about language? For example, is the statement "There is a 'correct' way to talk" a myth? Why or why not?

6. There are a number of vocabulary items that distinguish American English from British English. "Paving," for instance, may refer to either a "sidewalk" or to "street" depending upon whether our speaker is in England or in the United States. "Bonnet," "boot," and "windscreen" are British terms for parts of the automobile. What are their counterparts in American English? What are some other vocabulary differences?

I. FOR FURTHER REFERENCE

Bloomfield, Leonard. 1933. *Language*. New York: Holt.

Carroll, John B., ed. 1957. *Language, Thought, and Reality*. Cambridge, Mass.: The Technology Press of M.I.T.

Chomsky, Noam A. 1966. *Cartesian Linguistics*. New York: Harper and Row.

Fromkin, Victoria and Robert Rodman. 1974. "What is Language," "Animal 'Languages,' " in *Introduction to Language*. New York: Holt, Rinehart and Winston.

Lenneberg, Eric H. 1967. *Biological Foundations of Language*. New York: John Wiley.

Lilly, John C. 1969. *The Mind of the Dolphin: A Non-Human Intelligence*. New York: Avon Books.

Postal, Paul. 1968. "Epilogue," in Roderick Jacobs and Peter Rosenbaum: *English Transformational Grammar*. Lexington, Mass.: Xerox.

Premack, Ann James and David Premack. 1972. "Teaching Language to an Ape." *Scientific American* October, 92-99.

Steiner, George. 1971. "A Future Literacy." *The Atlantic Monthly* August, 41-44.

Von Frisch, K. 1967. *The Dance Language and Orientation of Bees*. C. E. Chadwick, trans. Cambridge, Mass.: Belknap Press of Harvard University Press.

Wang, William S-Y. 1973. "The Chinese Language." *Scientific American* February, 50-63.

II. The Beginnings of Language

HOW DID IT ALL BEGIN?

Before we begin this chapter on the origins of language, perhaps we should point out that there is little evidence available to substantiate any theory on the origin and evolution of language in *Homo sapiens*. Neither is there evidence that language becomes more "effective" or less "effective" with time; nor is there support for the contention that one language is intrinsically better than another, represented by the claim that "French is the most logical language, Italian the most musical, German the most scientific." It has been claimed that languages spoken in primitive societies are less sophisticated, linguistically speaking, than languages spoken in highly developed technological societies. Some have even said that language tends to degenerate through time, from a pure, or standard, language to one that is incapable of expressing subtle nuances. Professor Maynard Mack, a renowned literary scholar, may have had this in mind when, in his presidential address to the members of the Modern Language Association (printed in the May 1971 issue of the *Publication of the Modern Language Association*), he said, "Language is susceptible to pollution, becomes murky, noisome, suffocating. That is the condition we face now. Never, I suspect, has our common tongue been so debased and vulgarized as it is today in commerce, so pretentious, over-blown, and empty as it is in the babble of the learned and bureaucratic jargons, not excepting ours, so tired, mechanical, and unimaginative as it is in the obscenities of the young."

There is no proof that would serve to corroborate Professor Mack's eloquent assertions, just as there is no evidence that would sustain a particular theory on the origin of language. While there continues to be research attempting to distinguish the neural capacities of *Neanderthal* (first man), *Cro-Magnon* (later man), and *Homo sapiens* (modern man), we have no evidence that language has in any sense evolved since the appearance of *Homo sapiens*. Numerous theories have been and continue to be proposed, and, although scholars have debated the issue, sometimes heatedly, we still do not know a great deal about the origin of language. Yet some will likely continue to search for an origin for some time to come.

Many of the books and articles written about the origin of language contain a good deal of fantasy, and occasionally, nonsense. Some linguistic societies will not permit a paper to be read on language origins, believing that any attempt to explain this elusive and frustrating question results in idle speculation and tends to become a vacuous exercise in futility. Yet a few of the theories are interesting, if only for their historical perspective. One of the first Biblical accounts can be found, appropriately, in Genesis, though it does not explain when and how man began to speak, but only that speech (the power to name things) arose through the power of God. The description is an attempt, clearly, to offer an explanation for the unexplainable: "And out of the ground the Lord God formed every beast of the field, and every fowl of the air, and brought them unto Adam to see what he would call them; and whatsoever Adam called every creature, that was the name thereof. And Adam gave names to all cattle, and to the fowl of the air, and to every beast of the field."

Although the Biblical account relates nothing of the origin of speech, nor of the language first spoken by Adam, it does reflect a skill associated with language, especially the young child's capability, that of naming. In the March 27, 1960, *New York Times* Book Review Section, literary critic J. Donald Adams suggested much the same thought: "It is indeed hard to rid ourselves of the idea that the desire to name things lies at the root of language."

There has even been conjecture concerning the language of Adam and Eve. Until very recently the stock answer was that Adam and Eve spoke Hebrew, a Semitic language, from which all others ultimately derived. It is not difficult to see why this notion still persists: the Bible was first written in Hebrew, and Jesus spoke a Semitic dialect. There is, however, no reason to believe that Hebrew even remotely resembles the first language of man since we can prove that most of the languages of the world do not stem from Hebrew. As readers of the Bible know, the Old Testament does not mention specifically which language was spoken by Adam and Eve. But myths seem to propagate others, for as late as the 17th century a Swedish philologist claimed that in the Garden of Eden God spoke Swedish, Adam spoke Danish, and the serpent spoke French.

Furthermore, any attempts to trace all language back to a common source have not been particularly convincing in their conclusions. The 18th century Russian empress Catherine the Great wrote to Benjamin Franklin inquiring of him how American Indian languages showed their relationship to Hebrew. As late as 1934, at a Turkish linguistics congress someone seriously argued that Turkish is at the root of all languages—all words being derived from *günes*, the Turkish word for "sun," very likely the first object to attract man's attention and demand a name.

We know that the origin of language goes so far back in history that any attempt to deduce what actual elements of the first language are found in any known language is bound to fail. We can only surmise from what we know that languages at that time must have resembled those of today, in that each had a *phonological*, *syntactic*, and *semantic* component. Our ability to delve accurately into history is so limited that we cannot yet determine whether there was a single language from which all present languages descended or whether there were several languages. Language changes with time, and dialects become separate languages, obscuring, occasionally, the genetic relationships which sometimes exist between and among diverse languages.

About all we have for any information about the linguistic past are inscriptions on objects and artifacts, and these are from a relatively late period in human history. The written documents that have come down to us in both the Occident and the Orient, dating from 5000 B.C. at the earliest, represent from the historical viewpoint a fairly recent time considering the millennia that man has been known to exist. The British linguist Louis H. Gray wrote in 1939, "If we are unable to affirm that the earliest men could speak (except in the sence that animals and birds can speak), no skeletal remains thus far found show any evidence that they could not. Anthropology throws no light on the problem."

In 1939, linguists could not say much about the appearance of speech in man, except to note, like Gray, that what evidence there was tended to show that man could always speak. In an article, "On the Speech of Neanderthal Man" (*Linguistic Inquiry*, Vol. II, Spring 1971), Professors Philip Liberman and Edmund S. Crelin, both of Yale University and Haskins Laboratories, reported on their extensive anatomical studies of the "vocal" apparatus of the newborn child, the restructured tract of Neanderthal man, and *Homo sapiens*. They found that the vocal tract of Neanderthal man, unlike those of Cro-Magnon and *Homo sapiens*, was similar in anatomical proportion to the tract of the newborn, and that each was incapable of speech because of the high position of the larynx (voice box) in the throat. They concluded that although it was difficult to determine whether Neanderthal man had the mental capacity for articulate speech, it was reasonably certain that he lacked the "anatomical prerequisites" for speech and specifically lacked the ability to make the full range of human speech sounds.

Liberman and Crelin also discovered that non-human primates, such as the ape and the chimpanzee, have anatomical advantages: having a higher larynx greatly reduces the chances of choking to death. "The only function," they say, "for which the adult vocal human tract is better suited is speech." Perhaps the reason for our knowing little about the evolution of speech is that "the intermediate stages in its evolution are represented by extinct species." The disappearance of Neanderthal man "may have been a consequence of his linguistic—hence intellectual—deficiencies with respect to his *sapiens* competitors. In short, we can conclude that Man is human because he can say so." An interesting hypothesis, we might admit, especially when we examine the noises of the animal world.

Although animals and birds can be taught to perform certain feats and even to utter individual words, man is the only *being* who is able to accomplish the act of speaking; that is, to make the complex sequence of organized noises adding up to definite meanings. Just how unique language is we will touch on at a later point.

VARIOUS PAST THEORIES

The ancient Greek philosophers, much given to speculation, theorized considerably about language. Socrates, as recorded in the *Cratylus* of Plato, notes that in Greek the sound *r* often appears in words denoting motion and *l* in those referring to smoothness. (Note in English: *run*, *river*, *ripple*, *ride*, *race*, *rise*.) He submits that *onomatopoeia*, or the imitation of the sounds of actions, was the basis of the origin of language and the reason why the "correct" name was found for all things.

The 18th century German philosopher Leibnitz represented the view that all languages came from a proto- or beginning speech. In the next century Darwin hypothesized that speech originated from "mouth pantomime"—that the vocal organs unconsciously imitated gestures performed by the hands. As recently as 1962, one of the two speakers who dealt with this question at the meeting of the American Anthropological Association presented ideas that followed this general tack.

Many theories of language have been proposed—and nearly all of them have been accorded fanciful names which neatly catalogue them according to the type of words envisioned as forming the first instance of speech. One of these was what the German scholar Max Mueller christened the "bow-wow" theory, which states that language arose in imitation of the sounds of nature, such as the babbling of a brook, the murmur of the wind, and so on. Since a dog barks, for example, and says "bow-wow," man referred to him as a "bow-wow." This theory, however, appears not to hold, since the same noise is often interpreted differently by different language groups. In imitating a rooster, for instance, English speakers say "cock-a-doodle-doo," the Spanish and French "cocorico," and the Chinese "go-go-gooo." Most of the so-called onomatopoeic words are made according to the sound patterns of a particular language system.

The "ding dong" theory tries to establish a mystical and difficult-to-fathom relationship between sound and meaning. This label refers to the notion that the primeval term for an object could represent any noise associated with it, including ones made by hitting it, blowing on it, or the like. The "ta ta" theory, in line with Darwin, holds that language originated from verbal imitation of bodily movements and gestures, gesticulating with the mouth and tongue, so to speak.

We may smile when we consider still other theories. The "yo-he-ho" theory argues that language arose as exclamatory utterances brought about by intense physical effort. When used they presumably meant such things as "Heave on that rock." The "pooh-pooh" theory maintains that language first consisted of exclamations prompted by such emotions as fear, pleasure, pain, and the like. Present-day examples in this classification, like the onomatopoeic words, turn out to be rather closely bound to a particular language.

Interestingly, even the linguist Otto Jespersen formulated a theory of original language. Realizing that the reconstructions of earlier stages of language merely scratch the surface of the long period of human speech, he felt that linguists could work themselves further back into history by observing general tendencies and directions of change. In his work on language history he was impressed by the "breaking-down" processes that are found whenever there is evidence of an earlier and a later stage of a language, for instance, Old, Middle, and Modern English. "We must imagine primitive language as consisting (chiefly at least) of very long words," he writes, "full of difficult sounds, and sung rather than spoken. . . . The evolution of language shows a progressive tendency from inseparable conglomerations to freely and regularly combinable short elements." Yet language has been around too long for this theory to hold. If, for the sake of argument, breaking-down processes took place faster than building-up processes, language would have ceased long ago when the last speaker could say nothing but "Uh." Languages for most of human history must have been much like languages as we now find them.

A few years ago, D. S. Diamond, an English lawyer and sociologist, wrote a book titled *The History and Origins of Language*, in which he attempted to prove that the first words were brief interjections, something like the first instinctive utterances of infants. At first these sounds were made as calls for assistance, accompanied by gestures designed to illustrate the sort of aid desired. To his credit, Diamond seeks empirical evidence in a vast variety of languages, including Hebrew and the African languages, to support his theory. Captivating as his theory may be, however, it does represent, to a large extent, sheer speculation.

G. Revész, late Professor of Psychology at the University of Amsterdam, in his book, *The Origins and Prehistory of Language*, feels that human speech developed through various stages that we may find in animal noises. The ultimate root is to be found in *contact sounds* which merely serve to identify members of the same species and to promote a sense of collectiveness. Communication begins with the *cry* specific to some internal state of the animal, so that the other members can determine whether it is frightened, angry, hungry, or hurt, and can act accordingly. A cry does not need to be anything we would consider a deliberate message. The last stage of pre-speech, believed by Revész to be limited to the most highly developed mammals, such as cats, dogs, and monkeys, is the *call*, a sound addressed to one member of the species. Revész believes that it was specialization in the development of calls that led to the *word*, which in its first unrecoverable rudimentary stage of *imperative language* was most nearly analogous to the imperatives (commands) and vocatives (names called out) of later fully functioning human speech.

A FEW CONCLUSIONS

It would be helpful if we could synthesize, out of the pieces of all the laboriously elaborated theories that have been offered, the genesis of a reasonable or consistent explanation for the origin of language. We do not have to delve deeply, however, to see that the proposals are so disparate as to be virtually unconnectable.

The conclusion is obvious: to paraphrase a German philosopher, "We only know that we don't know." We cannot reconstruct any vestige of original language; we cannot even extrapolate back from recent trends, from a modern language like English to an earlier one like Sanskrit, as Jespersen tried to do. The beginnings—if we can even speak of a beginning—are too far lost in the midst of antiquity.

Neither can we recapture glimpses of the original language from observing children. Children learning their language do not go through its linguistic history all over again. They are immersed in a world of talking from the beginning. Well before they use anything we might want to call words, influences of the language they hear can be detected in their babbling. Gradually, according to a biological schedule, they learn their language, absorbing the particular structures at their own individual and maturational pace.

Earlier scholars even tried experiments with children to determine whether, if left to their own resources, they would develop a language. We must perhaps grant that what would happen would no doubt be interesting to know, and it could at least make a good science fiction plot to have a Mad Linguist abducting babes for his origin-of-language researches. But, since it is "impossible, unnatural, and illegal to try the experiment," as Max Mueller reasonably put it, it would not really be relevant to the beginning of language. In the last analysis, theories on the origin of language may be speculative, but even in this day and age there is a continuing interest in how it all began.

Two points do stand out in the theories we have just discussed. One, to talk about origin means that there *had* to be an origin. No serious thought is given by the various theorists to the notion that there perhaps was no beginning, or that when modern man made his appearance he had language. No invention was involved. As Eric Lenneberg puts it, "Knowledge of language precedes speech and may exist without speech." We know that language is a biological fact, that young children are not "conditioned" to learn a language (being exposed to one is enough), and that differences among languages do not outweigh their similarities. All languages are spoken—each puts words together into phrases, sentences, discourse; and each language has a syntax—no language has a random word order. "Consider," Lenneberg continues, "the vast differences in the forms and semantics of languages (making a common and focal origin of language most unlikely); consider the geographical separation of some human societies that must have persisted for thousands of years; consider the physical differentiation into a number of different stocks and races. Yet, everywhere man communicates in a strikingly similar pattern."

The second point is that some investigators have attempted to correlate the behavior of higher primates with man. No animal has ever attained the mastery of even the rudimentary language skills of a very young child. The difference between man and the higher primates appears not to be one of degree of complexity but one of quality of complexity.

ANIMAL RESEARCH AND ITS IMPLICATIONS

Two avenues of research have appeared in recent times. The first is the classical study of animal behavior, of attempting, for instance, to hypothesize about linguistic skills from observing the behavior of rats and pigeons. The second is *ethology*, the study of instinctive behavior in animals. Revész made certain steps in this direction by endeavoring to investigate the sounds, calls, and cries that animals make, attempting to determine whether there was, in fact, a pre-speech associated with the ancestors of man. Other animal researchers are investigating the social behavior of higher primates—chimpanzees and gorillas in the wild. The results of this research have demonstrated that many prior notions about the behavior of anthropoids were wrong.

Evidently, these investigators hoped that such research could establish a base for a type of communication system from which human language may have developed. Such attempts to relate the "linguistic behavior" of higher primates to man and his ability to learn language appear unpromising. In 1951, two researchers, Dr. and Mrs. Keith J. Hayes, raised a chimpanzee baby (Viki) in their home and attempted to teach her language. They found, even after intensive instruction, that Viki could *say* only a few words, and only after the appropriate stimulus. She never learned the spoken language.

Research and experimentation with chimpanzees continue, however. Drs. R. Allen and Beatrice Gardner also raised a chimp, whom they named Washoe, in their home. Unlike the Hayeses, who attempted to teach Viki to speak, the Gardners taught Washoe a portion of the American Sign Language, the language of the deaf. They found that, through instrumental conditioning (tickling was one of her rewards), Washoe could be taught a number of signs. At the end of two years, Washoe had learned approximately 35 signs that she could use individually or in combinations to communicate her feelings and desires. She could manipulate about 30 different two-sign combinations and four three-sign combinations. Whether there is a relationship here between what Washoe learned and the early development of language in a child will have to wait for further research.

Roger Brown, who has been researching the similarities, poses the question, "Why should anyone care?" He answers, "For the same reason, perhaps, that we care about space travel. It is lonely being the only language-using species in the universe. We want a chimp to talk so that we can say: 'Hello, out there! What's it like, being a chimpanzee?' "

A more promising approach involves looking more closely at the fundamental characteristics of *human* language. In the past we often took for granted that we knew what they were, but research, especially since 1960, has shown that we did not really understand too much about the intricate and complex skills of the language user. One thing we do know, from studies in psycholinguistics and in the biological foundations of language, is that language appears to be a human trait and that it is also species-uniform, that is, no normal person fails to learn a language.

Perhaps the essential property of language, according to Professor Noam Chomsky, is that it provides the means for "expressing indefinitely many thoughts and for reacting appropriately in an indefinite range of new situations."

ASPECTS AND CHARACTERISTICS OF LANGUAGE

To some language theorists, a language is an unbounded set of sentences; each sentence is limited in length and each is constructed out of a limited number of elements or *constituents*. To be technical for the moment, a theory of a specific language like English, for example, defines the sentences of that language. By examining the theories of a number of languages, linguists hope that they can extrapolate a number of linguistic generalizations that are common to and shared by all languages in the world; to determine, in other words, characteristics of languages that are universal to *all* languages. Emmon Bach and Robert Harms, in their book, *Universals in Linguistic Theory*, point to the basic goals and methods of this kind of linguistic investigation. "What is linguistic theory itself," they submit, "if not the attempt to discover what is common to all languages, what is essential in the notion 'natural language,' what are the limits within which languages vary, what are the (universal!) terms by means of which this variation can be described?"

To Charles F. Hockett (*Course in Modern Linguistics*), an essential feature of language is *displacement*, or the ability to talk about objects that are not present. Other features of importance are *productivity*, or the ability to formulate new messages; *duality*, or the capacity to attach symbolic meaning to linguistic units; and *cultural transmission*, or the ability to pass language from one generation to another.

Above all, Hockett points out, normal language behavior is stimulus-free. Noam Chomsky reminds us, in *Language and Mind*, that the proper study of language may lead us closer to an understanding of human nature. But honesty forces him to admit "that we are as far today as Descartes was three centuries ago from understanding just what enables a human to speak in a way that is innovative, free from stimulus control, and also appropriate and coherent."

II. QUESTIONS AND ACTIVITIES

1. Read several accounts of attempts to teach language to chimps, and then decide whether these chimps had actually learned "language." Why or why not?

2. What are some common, everyday definitions of language?

3. If language is partially defined as communication, can we call the noises that dogs make language? Why or why not?

4. If they are not language noises, what are the noises that animals make?

5. What kind of teaching/learning is involved in training an animal, say a dog, to respond to verbal stimuli? How much can an animal learn in this way?

6. What seems to be the difference between the kind of learning that goes on when a child is learning his/her native language and the kind when a dog is taught how to "speak"?

7. What are some other traits or skills that seem to be species-specific—unique to the human race?

8. Linguists point out that we know far more about our language than we can actually explain. What are some activities/skills that we know but would find it difficult to explain without diagrams, pictures, and gestures? For instance, try explaining to someone (perhaps a young child) how to tie shoe laces.

II. FOR FURTHER REFERENCE

Bach, Emmon and Robert Harms, eds. 1968. *Universals in Linguistic Theory*. New York: Holt, Rinehart and Winston.

Bellugi, Ursula. 1970. "Learning the Language." *Psychology Today* 7:32-35, 66.

Bender, M. Lionel. 1973. "Linguistic Indeterminacy: Why You Cannot Reconstruct 'Proto-Human.' " *Language Sciences* 26:7-12.

Brown, Roger. 1973. *A First Language: The Early Stages*. Cambridge, Mass.: Harvard University Press.

———. 1970. "The First Sentences of Child and Chimpanzee," in *Psycholinguistics*. New York: Free Press.

Chomsky, Noam A. 1972. *Language and Mind*. New York: Harcourt Brace Jovanovich.

Diamond, A. S. 1962. *The History and Origin of Language*. New York: Philosophical Library.

Edmonds, Marilyn H. 1976. "New Directions in Theories of Language Acquisition." *Harvard Educational Review* May, 179-97.

Gardner, R. Allen and Beatrice T. Gardner. 1969. "Teaching Sign Language to a Chimpanzee." *Science* 165:664-72.

Grabbe, Lester. 1970. "Origin of Languages." *The Plain Truth* August-September, 00-00.

Gray, Louis H. 1939. *Foundations of Language*. New York: MacMillan.

Hayes, Catherine. 1951. *The Ape in Our House*. New York: Harper.

Hayes, K. J. and C. Hayes. 1952. "A Home-Raised Chimpanzee," in R. G. Kuhlen and G. G. Thompson, eds.: *Psychological Studies of Human Development*. New York: Appleton-Century-Crofts.

Herder, J. G. 1969. "Essay on the Origin of Language," in Peter H. Salus, ed.: *On Language*. New York: Holt, Rinehart and Winston.

Hewes, Gordon W., William Stokoe, and Roger W. Wescott, eds. 1975. *Language Origins*. Silver Spring, Md.: Linstok Press.

Hockett, Charles F. 1958. *A Course in Modern Linguistics*. New York: MacMillan.

Jespersen, Otto. 1922. *Language: Its Nature, Development and Origin*. London: Allen and Unwin.

Kolata, Gina B. 1974. "The Demise of the Neanderthals: Was Language a Factor?" *Science* 186:618-19.

Lenneberg, Eric H. 1967. *Biological Foundations of Language*. New York: John Wiley.

Liberman, Philip and Edmund S. Crelin. 1971. "On the Speech of Neanderthal Man." *Linguistic Inquiry* Spring, 203-222.

Linden, Eugene. 1975. *Apes, Men, and Language*. New York: Saturday Review Press.

Mack, Maynard. 1971. "To See It Feelingly." *Publications of the Modern Language Association* May, 363-73.

Menyuk, Paula. 1970. *Sentences Children Use*. Cambridge, Mass.: M.I.T. Press.

Newman, Edwin H. 1974. *Strictly Speaking: Will America Be the Death of English?* New York: Bobbs-Merrill.

Premack, David. 1970. "The Education of Sarah: A Chimp Learns the Language." *Psychology Today* September, 54-58.

Revész, G. 1956. *The Origins and Prehistory of Language*. New York: Philosophical Library.

Salus, Peter H., ed. 1969. *On Language: Plato to von Humboldt*. New York: Holt, Rinehart and Winston.

Swadesh, Morris. 1971. *The Origin and Diversification of Language*. Chicago: Aldine-Atherton.

Thorndike, E. L. 1900. "The Origin of Language." *Science* 77:173-75.

III. Languages and More Languages: A Tour

MAPPING LANGUAGES

If we could project a language map of the world upon this page, four to five thousand languages would be included, and probably many more, the exact number depending upon our definition of *language*. Africa south of the Sahara has no less than 800 separate languages, a number that does not even come close to approximating the number of dialects spoken in that region.

The terms *dialect* and *language* are often confusing and misleading. Distinctions made in the past between *dialect* and *language* have not always been clear, consistent, or accurate. The speech of Florence and Palermo are every bit as different as the speech of Lisbon and Madrid, but it is common to be told that Florentines and people from Palermo speak the same language, while, at the same time, it is maintained that Spanish and Portuguese are two separate languages. From this we may infer that the distinction between *dialect* and *language* appears to be based more upon political than linguistic considerations. The school child of Palermo does not learn to write the dialect he speaks; he learns a standard Italian based on the dialect of Florence, just because the central government of his country has decreed an arbitrary standard and has directed that every child adhere to it. Portugal, of course, has been politically separate from Spain since the Middle Ages. The people of each country learn to read and write the dialect of their respective capitals or of cities of cultural prestige; the Portuguese learn a standard dialect based on the form of the language spoken in Coimbra, the Spanish a form of the dialect of Madrid.

An even more curious and perplexing situation exists in the geographical area where the northern Germanic languages—Swedish, Norwegian, and Danish—are spoken. Before standardization occurred in Norway, the Norwegians—when Norway was part of Denmark—were believed to be speaking a dialect of Danish. Nobody "wrote" Norwegian any more than anybody today writes Texan, Nebraskan, or Canadian. When Norwegians wrote their own language, they wrote standard Danish, just as today Texans, Nebraskans, and Canadians write English. After the separation from Denmark, a new Norwegian written language was developed, based on the western Scandinavian dialect spoken in Norway.

Even though these northern Germanic languages are labeled separate, "They have continued to influence each other," says Winfred P. Lehmann in his book *Historical Linguistics*, "so that to this day Norwegian and Swedish are mutually intelligible; Danes can readily understand Norwegian and Swedish, though their own speech may cause Norwegians and Swedes difficulties. Technically such mutually intelligible forms of speech are known as dialects. For national forms of speech the term is apparently undignified. The Scandinavian languages are therefore excellent examples of the nonlinguistic designation 'language' for forms of speech used by a nation rather than for forms of speech which are unintelligible to native speakers of other languages."

Our imaginary linguistic map is defined more in shades of color than in patches. The dialects of Spain and Portugal blend into each other in some areas with few pronounced differences along the political boundary. Certainly, centuries of writing the languages differently has had an effect, but the Spanish and Portuguese spoken on either side of the border are more similar than many realize. Seas and uninhabitable mountains make natural breaks in the color gradation, and even more pronounced differences occur where languages of different groups border on each other. The colors on either side of the linguistic boundary between French and the Germanic languages tend to be quite different, yet the boundary itself is extremely complex, with areas like Belgium and Alsace, where both languages exist side by side.

Our imaginary language map shows a few isolated areas of highly contrasting colors. The Basque language of the western Pyrenees bears no relation to its nearest neighbors, or apparently to any other language. Another such area of isolated color appears in the Caucasus region, where Georgia and the other Caucasian languages form another linguistic island.

Soviet and other linguists (such as the late Norwegian Alf Sommerfelt) claim a connection between these two groups, placing Basque and the Caucasian languages together into an Ibero-Caucasian unit, although some linguists feel that the evidence is inadequate. It is nonetheless theoretically impossible to make a categorical statement that one language is totally unrelated to another language. After millennia of separate development, all evidence of relationship may disappear. With evidence to the contrary, there are those who still claim that all languages derive from one single source (*monogenesis*). Those who favor a multiple beginning (*polygenesis*) have no way to prove their hypothesis either. "It is perfectly conceivable," Ronald Langacker submits, "that all human languages are in fact related but that proof of this universal genetic relationship will never be forthcoming. It is equally conceivable that human languages are not all related; in this event, proof is ruled out in principle."

A language map such as the one we have proposed is practically an impossibility. For one thing, finer and finer distinctions in dialects can be drawn until we arrive at small differences even among members of a single family. For this reason linguists have had to recognize the concept of *idiolect*, the speech of an individual.

On another scale, the map is impossible because of *bilingualism*, the use of two (or more) languages by the same people, a fairly common phenomenon in various parts of the world. A good example is Paraguay, where a major part of the population speaks both Spanish and the American Indian language Guaraní. Another is Texas and parts of the Southwest, where a major ethnic group speaks both English and Spanish, most of them employing the Southwest Spanish dialect, a variant of Mexican Spanish heavily influenced by English.

A further complicating situation is a kind of "bidialectism," which linguists refer to as *diglossia*. In diglossia two different forms of what can be recognized easily as the same language are used by the same people for different purposes. Switzerland serves as an excellent illustration of diglossia. A form of standard German is taught in the schools and generally used for most cultural and intellectual purposes, but the Swiss dialects are maintained as the means for ordinary, everyday communication.

COMPARATIVE LINGUISTICS

Methods employed by historical linguists of the 19th century serve to point up the similarities that exist between and among apparently different languages. Most of the languages of Europe belong to the Indo-European family. English, for instance, is a Low German dialect that belongs to Western Germanic; Western Germanic belongs to Germanic; and Germanic belongs to Indo-European. The basis for statements linking two or more languages lies in similarities that each of the many languages share. Three languages as geographically disparate as Polish, Spanish, and English resemble each other to such a degree that we are forced to posit their relatedness:

English: His mother is old.
Spanish: Su madre es vieja.
Polish: Jego matka jest stara.

Upon first glance these three sentences show more differences than similarities, and it is certain that speakers of each language could not understand the spoken sentences of the others. Yet there remain some underlying similarities, not apparent upon superficial examination. First, the word order is the same. Second, the words for *mother* show some correspondence, and words for *is* in Spanish and Polish share *es*. *Vieja* and *stara* appear completely different, and they do come from different roots. But both must be in the feminine singular form (to agree with the feminine singular *mother*) and in both cases the feminine singular sign is the *-a* suffix.

Historical linguists have in the past compared the records of languages in terms of their structures, and from these records have reconstructed earlier stages of languages, in some cases reconstructing a proto-, or earlier, stage of the *one* language from which all the other dialects have ensued.

Word histories, for instance, have been employed to trace the relationship among languages which may be now far apart in geographical distance. Let us examine the words for *mother* and *three* in the languages that follow:

GREEK	LATIN	GERMAN	ENGLISH	NORWEGIAN	GAELIC
mater	*mater*	*Mutter*	*mother*	*mor (moder)*	*mathair*
treis	*tres*	*drei*	*three*	*tre*	*Tri*

RUSSIAN	LITHUANIAN	ALBANIAN	ARMENIAN	SANSKRIT	PERSIAN
mat	*motina*	*(noma)*	*mair*	*matr*	*mader*
tri	*tris*	*tre*	*(erek)*	*tri*	*(se)*

The Albanian word for *mother* does not belong in the same group as the rest, and the Armenian and Persian words for *three*, though related to the others, reveal no obvious correspondences; yet, the observed similarities are much more impressive than the differences. There are thousands of other words as well which reveal further similarities among the languages that we commonly assign to the Indo-European group.

These correspondences can be traced to the fact that the above twelve languages (and we have not presented an exhaustive list) are all related, emanating from a common source, called *Proto-Indo-European*, the parent language. Linguists have followed two lines of inquiry into P.I.E. From studies of the recorded Indo-European languages, by a process known as *reconstruction*, they deduce what the forms of the source may have been like. In a few cases the answer is obvious—for instance, since the apprently related words for *mother* all begin with an *m*, an *m* is reconstructed as having stood at the beginning of this word in Proto-Indo-European. More often than not, some reconstructions involve considerably more ingenuity to produce simple, consistent, and sensible forms from which development could have taken place in the recorded forms of the various members of Indo-European.

The ancient Indian Sanskrit, preserved as a religious language (we have a grammar dating from the 4th century B.C.), is a dialect of Proto-Indo-European. Of living languages, Lithuanian in many respects may be nearest to the parent, since it still preserves word pitch, which has been lost in Sanskrit. Lithuanian is geographically near to the probable location of Proto-Indo-European, and it has developed in the relative isolation of the primeval Baltic forests.

There have been many attempts to approximate the original home of the Indo-European speech community. Since we have no attested records from this community, our conjectures are little more than highly educated guesses. Scholars, moreover, do not agree entirely as to what pieces of evidence give most weight to attempts to locate the original home. The general picture that is obtained from the words we can verify by reconstruction as having existed in the original language would lead us to conclude the existence of a community near, but not on, the open steppe country of eastern Europe. Nearness to open country is suggested by the reconstruction of words for *horse*, *wheel*, and *spoke*, implying the use of carts, if not chariots. The number of tree names, which reasonably solid evidence would ascribe to the vocabulary of the speakers of P.I.E., inclines us toward assigning these people to a forested region. The most significant tree for locating the community is the *beech*. We can confidently associate the meaning of *beech* with a Proto-Indo-European word whose derivation from a verb meaning *eat* indicates that gathering beechnuts provided this community with at least some part of its diet. Knowing this, we can eliminate from consideration as the original home all of Europe north and east of the Königsberg-Odessa (now Kaliningrad) line.

An additional item, the word for *salmon*, gives another indication of the approximate location of this speech community. Here, there is not such general agreement about the evidence. This reconstructed word is the one which was borrowed into English as *lox*. If the original word in P.I.E. referred to the Atlantic salmon, we could then tie the community down to the valleys of the Vistula, the Oder, the Elbe, and conceivably the Weser (any place farther west can be eliminated on other grounds, including rather clear archeological evidence). One of the languages that has preserved the word, however, is Ossetic, an Iranian language from the region of the Caucasus. Some proponents who favor a homeland in that region can therefore argue that the Caspian species of salmon was originally designated by the word. The suggestion of a sojourn in the area of transition from the steppe to the forested northern Caucasus may be considered as a possible alternative hypothesis; however, the more popular theory posits a journey from the steppe to a forested northern zone.

From this tentative location, the members of the Indo-European community spread until the language stretched from Iceland in the west to its eastern limit, where the Brahmaputra River pushes up between Burma and Tibet. In more recent times, the various members of the Indo-European language group have scattered even farther, until today they cover the Americas and a large part of Africa, as well as Australia and the Pacific Islands. Only in the last decade has it started to ebb as new nations, once dependent upon the West, have asserted their independence.

The remainder of this chapter will be devoted to a discussion of the languages and groups within the Indo-European family and a sketch of the other language families and the areas they cover; in other words, a "tour of Babel." The Appendix includes a listing of those languages which we will discuss.

THE INDO-EUROPEAN LANGUAGES

Indo-European is divided into eastern and western groups. The eastern group includes the languages of India and Persia, the Baltic and Slavic languages, and two groups now found only in one isolated language each: Armenian and Albanian.

Western Indo-European includes the Hellenic group, whose only modern representative is Greek. It also includes the Italic languages (represented by the Romance group and several dead languages of Italy), the Germanic group, and the Celtic. An extinct language called Tocharian once spoken in central Asia, belonged—strangely enough—to the western group. The Hittites, a people mentioned in the Bible, once ruled an empire centered in what is now eastern Turkey. The inscriptions they left give us only an imperfect picture of their language but it was obviously related to Indo-European. Some scholars feel it may have become separated from the parent Indo-European stock before divisions within the stock, such as into the eastern and western groups, were relevant.

An accurate chart of all these languages is shown under "Indo-European" in Webster's Third International Dictionary and goes into far more detail than is practical here. A few points are worth mentioning. The largest language in the Indic or Indo-Aryan branch of Indo-European is Hindustani, which in two somewhat different standard forms is the principal official language of two of the heavily populated countries of the world—India and Pakistan. Pakistan uses a form of this language which is called Urdu and has a great many more words borrowed from Persian and Arabic than does the Hindi used in India. Two other Indo-Aryan tongues of the subcontinent are spoken by large numbers of people and embody long established and flourishing literary traditions; these two are Marathi, with more than 30 million speakers in the Bombay region, and Bengali, the language of Bangladesh and the Calcutta area in India. The latter, with probably 75 million speakers, is ninth largest in number of speakers among the languages of the world. Singhalese, the major language of Sri Lanka (formerly Ceylon), is another important Indic language. Besides the large number of languages spoken throughout India, the Indic group includes the language of the gypsies (Romany) and Sanskrit. The latter is the Hindu classical language. As we said before, it is probably the closest we can come to *Proto-Indo-European* in a recorded language. A grammar of Sanskrit, written more than 2,000 years ago by a man named Panini, gives surprisingly modern insights into the structure of the language.

The Iranian language group includes Persian, Pashto of Afghanistan, and Kurdish, a language whose speakers are divided among Iran, Iraq, Turkey, and the USSR. Minor members of the family include the Ossetic language spoken in the northern Caucasus—which we have already had cause to mention—and the languages of various tribes of the Pamir plateau, which Soviet linguists have only recently begun to study.

The Slavic (Russian, Polish, Czech, etc.) and Baltic (Lettish and Lithuanian) languages also belong to the eastern division of Indo-European. These languages use either of two different alphabets. The difference traces back to the time the Slavic peoples were Christianized. The missionaries from Rome brought with them the Latin alphabet—the same one that came to England. The modifications in each case were slight, so Polish, Czech, and the other languages that use the Roman letters look fairly familiar to us. The use of this alphabet still characterizes the countries whose people are principally Roman Catholic or Protestant. There were other missionaries in the area from the earliest times—those from the Byzantine church. One of these, St. Cyril from Macedonia, gave his name to the Cyrillic alphabet. He is said to have been the first to adapt the Greek alphabet to the writing of Slavic languages. Like the Roman alphabet in this area, the Cyrillic alphabet is associated with a church, in this case the Eastern Orthodox Church. Russian and Bulgarian use the Cyrillic alphabet and in these countries the influence of the Eastern Orthodox Church is strongest. Serbian and Croatian are just dialects of a single language. The principal reason for listing them separately is that Croatian is written in Roman letters and Serbian in Cyrillic. Again the difference in alphabets reflects the difference between the Catholic Croatians and the Eastern Orthodox Serbs.

Turning to the western group, we have the Romance languages, which are all descendants of Latin. As the Latin-speaking Roman Empire disintegrated, the speech of the various areas became differentiated. The major modern descendants of Latin are French, Spanish, Portuguese, Italian, Rumanian, and Catalan (Catalonian). There are half a dozen or so less prominent Romance languages including Romansch, which is the fourth official language of Switzerland even though it is spoken by less than a hundred thousand Swiss.

The Celtic group is struggling to hold its own. The whole Celtic-speaking world was overrun by speakers of Germanic and Romance tongues and the Celtic languages began to fade away. Now that Ireland is self-governing, great efforts are being made to promote the use of Irish Gaelic, but in the other Celtic areas the speakers are fewer every year. Cornish has died out, and improved communications are spreading the use of English and French where Scots Gaelic, Welsh, Manx, and Breton once flourished. Welsh is the best preserved, having taken a new lease on life during the religious movements of the late eighteenth century. Recent decades have seen the official recognition of the language and the safeguarding of its position in the schools. Perhaps the current phase of Welsh nationalism will avert any further erosion of the language.

Finally, we have the Germanic languages. These include the Scandinavian, extinct Gothic, and the Germanic-Dutch group. Both English and Yiddish belong in the latter group. The relationship is disguised in both cases. Yiddish has a great many Slavic and other loan words and is written in the Hebrew alphabet. It is, however, basically a Germanic language.

English has several distinguishing characteristics. It has "simplified" itself more than most other Indo-European languages by dropping many of the word endings (*inflection*) that characterized P.I.E. Its vocabulary is unusually complex as a result of the Norman Conquest of 1066. Sir Walter Scott in *Ivahoe* has the jester point out that domestic animals use their Anglo-Saxon names when in the field (cow, calf, pig, sheep) but are served up to the Norman overlord as beef, veal, pork, and mutton—words borrowed from Norman French. This double vocabulary goes much further than most of us may realize. Usually the Germanic word is considered direct, or even vulgar, and the word of Romance derivation is considered refined. This starts with the well-known "four-letter," Anglo-Saxon words with their acceptable, Romance-derived alternates and goes through such other pairs as sweat—perspire, brave—valorous, think—cogitate, and literally myriads of others. Its final claim to fame is that English is second to none as a second language. More than any other language in the world, people learn English in addition to their native language.

THE OTHER LANGUAGE FAMILIES

Leaving the Indo-European, only one other language family covers anything like the same land area. This is the Altaic group, which includes Turkish and extends past the Altai mountains of Central Asia. Just how far it goes is still under investigation, though it is clear it goes far enough to include the Yakut of northern Siberia. Almost all experts include the Mongol and Manchu dialects, but the status of Korean and Japanese is not clear. Some include both the latter languages in the Altaic group; some include only Korean; others group them separately as an unrelated family; and still others put both outside the Altaic family and furthermore separate them from each other, leaving three distinct divisions. Many, but by no means all, linguists see a connection between the Finno-Ugric group (Finnish, Hungarian, and Estonian) and the Altaic group. It is probably best to wait for further investigations before taking a definite position on these questions. The connection between all these languages would be based on their spread from a central Asian source with the expansion of the nomadic tribes.

In the Middle East the principal language family is the Semitic. The largest group included is Arabic, spreading from Arabia northward into Iraq, Jordan, Syria, and west across the upper portion of Africa. In addition, it is the liturgical language of Islam and, as such, reaches far south into Africa and east and north into Asia and nearby Europe. Other Semitic languages are Hebrew and Amharic. The latter is the official language of Ethiopia, spoken by Coptic Christians claiming descent from one of the ten lost tribes of Israel. Hebrew is basically the language of the Old Testament. It has more recently been modernized by the linguistic architects of Israel and is now the official language of the modern Israeli state.

Semitic languages take their name from Shem, the second son of Noah. Shem's brother Ham gave his name to the Hamitic languages, which seem to be distantly related to the Semitic. Hamitic languages border the great deserts of Africa. They are spoken by the Berbers and Tuaregs of northwest Africa and the Sahara. Hausa, Galla, and Somali in Ethiopia and Somalia continue the spread of this family to Africa's opposite coast. Semitic and Hamitic are grouped together by linguists in one larger family called Afro-Asiatic.

If we were to draw a line east and slanting a bit down on the map all the way across Africa from the point where the western coast makes its right-angle bend to the south, we would have approximately demarcated the northern limit of the vast Bantu family of languages. Most of the languages of western Africa south of the Sahara are now believed to be related, and Bantu is grouped among them in the Niger-Congo family, which is among the more extensive language families of the world. Sandwiched between the Niger-Congo and the Afro-Asiatic languages are many others. In a belt from the eastern Sahara stretching south and east as far as Tanganyika are found several families, such as the Nilotic languages, whose possible relationships are not yet thoroughly explored.

A peculiar feature of certain south African languages is their use of *click consonants*. We hear some of these clicks in the sound of a kiss, the deprecating sound usually spelled *tsk-tsk*, and the sound used to start a horse or a mule moving. The very fact that we cannot spell these sounds shows how foreign they are to Indo-European speech. Clicks are found in some of the southern Bantu languages, the best known of which is Zulu, but historical study has shown that these sounds did not originally exist in any Bantu languages but were imported from another family—the Bushman or Khoisan group of languages spoken by the earlier inhabitants of the region.

Afrikaans is a dialect of Dutch derived from the immigrants who helped settle South Africa. This makes it a transplanted Indo-European language. Its use is being furthered by the present government of the Republic of South Africa.

Starting at Madagascar, a language family of the Islanders, the Austronesian family, spreads through Indonesia, the Philippines, Maori of New Zealand, all the islands of Micronesia, and on east to Hawaii, Easter Island, and Tahiti. Javanese, with more than 40 million speakers, is the largest member of the family. This language group reaches the mainland only in Malayan and scattered hill tribes of southeast Asia. There are still some hundred thousand aboriginal Formosans in the eastern half of the island of Taiwan whose languages belong to this group.

The last major language family of the non-Western world is the Sino-Tibetan. This includes the Chinese language family. It is customary to speak of the several dialects of the Chinese language, probably because there is a common writing system that speakers of any dialect of Chinese can use. However, it would be more accurate to speak of separate Chinese languages, since the speaker from Peking can understand a speaker from Canton no better than a Frenchman can understand an Italian.

The Northern Chinese or Mandarin language is spoken by two-thirds of China, which gives it the greatest number of native speakers of any language in the world. The most closely related language to Mandarin is the Wu language of Shanghai, Wenchow, and the surrounding region. Cantonese is the major south-China language, spoken throughout the densely populated Canton region, including the British-controlled island of Hong Kong. Its use extends west as far as the island of Hainan. Also, it is a major language among the overseas Chinese—including most of the Chinese in the continental United States. The coastal languages between Cantonese and Wu in Fukien and eastern Kuangtung provinces are referred to as Min. It is linguistically most reasonable to regard these as belonging to two languages. The more prominent is spoken in the region of the cities of Amoy and Swatow and by most of the native Chinese of the island of Taiwan. Together with Cantonese, it is spoken in the cities of all the countries around the South China Sea. The other Min language is spoken in the districts about the city of Foochow. The two inland Chinese languages are called Hakka and Hsiang and are found principally in Kiangsi and Hunan provinces respectively. Hakka is also the language of the earliest Chinese settlers of Taiwan, mostly now confined to rural districts, and is the major Chinese language spoken in the Hawaiian Islands. How speakers of such different languages can communicate in writing is a secret we will share with you in the chapter on writing. (Japanese, a language as far removed from Chinese as either of them is from English, also uses an adaptation of this same system of characters of writing).

Besides the Chinese language group, the Sino-Tibetan family includes the languages of Tibet and southeast Asia. Burmese is possibly the most prominent. These are generally tone languages like Chinese. What sounds to us like the same word said four different ways—with high, low, rising, or falling tones—can have meanings as different as "to meow like a kitten," "secret," "uncooked rice," and "honey." All four of these words in Mandarin Chinese sound to an English speaker like our pronoun "me."

The Dravidian language family was in India before the invasion of Indo-Europeans and many Dravidian languages are still spoken in south India. Four of these—Tamil, Telugu, Kannada, and Malayalam—have speakers numbering in the millions. There are more isolated families in Asia, too. Cambodian is the only widely spoken language in the Mon-Khmer family. Vietnamese is thought by some scholars to be a remote relative even though it is a tone language while Cambodian and languages closely related to it are not. This question, like so many others, must still be considered unsettled.

The Australian aborigines and the Papuans of New Guinea all live in the general area of Austronesian languages; however, none of their languages are Austronesian. Some linguists classify the Hyperborean languages of northern Siberia with the Eskimo languages of North America. Others feel that these, the Eskimo, and even some American Indian languages should be grouped with the Ural-Altaic.

The languages of the Americas are divided into hundreds of families and even more individual tongues usually classed as Amerindian. Some of these were widespread; more than half the area of North and South America was covered by only sixteen of the groups. Even today the Quechua language of Peru, which was one of the principal languages of the vast Inca empire, is still spoken by a few million people. Other South American Indian languages which continue to be important are Aymará, used in parts of Peru and Bolivia, and Guaraní, spoken together with Spanish by most Paraguayans. At least a hundred thousand Araucanians in Chile still maintain their language, and Goajiro (Wahiro) in Colombia and Venezuela may have even more speakers. The Mayan languages of Yucatan and Guatemala and the Nahuatl or Aztec languages of Mexico also continue to be used by sizable groups.

In the United States and Canada there are not native American languages spoken by groups anywhere as large as those we have mentioned farther south. At least three, though, show a considerable measure of vitality. The largest of these is Navajo, spoken by more than 50,000 people. At least 40,000 Cree are the principal human population of the vast stretches of muskeg extending both east and west from the southern portion of Hudson Bay. South of them, and likewise covering a belt stretching half the distance across the continent, there are probably as many speakers of Ojibway. Other Amerindian groups are represented by the isolated languages of single, small tribes. The relationships between the groups are tentative. This multiplicity of languages made problems for the Indians themselves. If a man traveled out of his own tribal area, he was likely to find that the local inhabitants could not understand a word he said. The nomadic Indians of the great plains of North America had a solution for this problem. They developed a gesture language with a sign of the hands standing for each word.

This tour of the world's languages has been necessarily very sketchy. The subject is just too great for proper presentation in a few pages. More detailed treatment can be carried out and has been completed in several areas. Linguistic atlases of parts of Europe and the United States have been prepared. These are immense projects tracing hundreds and thousands of dialect variations. Thus, each study must decide just how deep to push its differences and distinctions, and a quick sketch like ours pays for its speed with many rough and indistinct edges.

A LIST OF LANGUAGES

We will conclude our brief survey by including in the Appendix a list of the 300 languages that were considered of sufficient importance or interest to Americans for files of information about them to be kept at the Center for Applied Linguistics in Arlington, Virginia. Many of the languages also have other names. Decisions as to whether we are dealing in some cases with two separate languages or two variants of one and the same language are often difficult, as we have warned earlier in this chapter. The figures are intended to represent the number of persons for whom the language is the main medium of communication; the paucity of accurate surveys makes these educated guesses subject to constant revision.

III. QUESTIONS AND ACTIVITIES

1. Is there a regional dialect in the United States that has more status than the other regional dialects?

2. Which do you suppose has more status, British English or American English?

3. On the national news networks, the various correspondents are from different geographical regions of the country. Can we tell from listening to them which region they are from? For example, Roger Mudd, Dan Rather, Walter Cronkite, and Harry Reasoner are from different regions. Harry Reasoner grew up in Iowa. Can you tell where the others are from?

4. During the 1976 presidential campaign, a Georgia state official was hoping that Governor Carter would be the next president, saying that it would be nice to have a president who did not have an accent. What do you think the state official meant by his remark?

5. The Spanish spoken in the Southwest is often called a dialect, while the Spanish spoken in Madrid or Mexico City is called a language, and in Mexico, the Indian languages are referred to as dialects. Why would one spoken form be called a "dialect" while the other form is called a "language?"

III. FOR FURTHER REFERENCE

Allen, Harold B. and Gary Underwood, eds. 1971. *Readings in American Dialectology*. New York: Appleton-Century-Crofts.

Bloomfield, Morton W. and Leonard Newmark. 1963. *A Linguistic Introduction to the History of English*. New York: Alfred A. Knopf.

Haugen, Einar. 1970. "The Ecology of Language." *Linguistic Reporter* Winter, Supplement 25.

_____. 1969. *The Norwegian Language in America: A Study in Bilingual Behavior*. 2nd ed. Bloomington: Indiana University Press.

Langacker, Ronald W. 1968. *Language and Its Structure*. New York: Harcourt, Brace and World.

Lehmann, Winfred P., ed. 1975. *Language and Linguistics in the People's Republic of China*. Austin: University of Texas Press.

_____. 1973. *Historical Linguistics: An Introduction*. 2nd ed. New York: Holt, Rinehart and Winston.

Mackey, William F. 1968. *Bilingualism as a World Problem*. Montreal: Harvest House.

Marckwardt, Albert H. 1958. *American English*. New York: Oxford University Press.

McDavid, Raven I., Jr. 1958. "The Dialects of American English," in W. Nelson Francis: *The Structure of American English*. New York: Ronald Press.

Muller, Siegfried H. 1964. *The World's Living Languages*. New York: Unger.

Ornstein, Jacob. 1960. "Passport from Babel." *Texas Quarterly 3:150-55.*

Pederson, Holger. 1962. *The Discovery of Language.* Bloomington: Indiana University Press.

Weinreich, Uriel. 1953. *Languages in Contact.* New York: Linguistic Circle of New York.

Williamson, Juanita V. and Virginia Burke. 1971. *A Various Language: Perspectives on American Dialects.* New York: Holt, Rinehart and Winston.

IV. Winds of Change: The New Linguistics

LINGUISTIC REVOLUTIONS

In 1954, W. Nelson Francis wrote, "A long overdue revolution is at present taking place in the study of English grammar—a revolution as sweeping in its consequences as the Darwinian revolution in biology. It is the result of the application to English of methods of descriptive analysis originally developed for use with languages of primitive people." And approximately twenty years later, in a text entitled *A New English Grammar*, N. R. Cattell writes, "In the last twenty or thirty years, a revolution has taken place in the academic approach to grammar. Grammar, instead of being a dead subject, with all its facts compiled for all time, has become part of the lively young social science of linguistics, in which what we know is dwarfed by what we do not know but are fascinated to find out."

Both men wrote of revolution; and today it remains common to find such an epithet as "revolution" assigned to each advance in linguistic science. Perhaps "revolution" is too strong a label to describe the changes that have swept through the linguistic world since the early 1950s—changes whose roots can be traced back as far as the beginning of this century and even earlier.

In a discipline that has been characterized as "revolutionary," differing views may occasionally lead to schism. A few years ago two young instructors at a western university resigned over ideological differences—in language theory. To an outsider it may seem incongruous that matters pertaining to the theory of language could attract such loyalty and arouse such wrath. We might hope that if linguistics purports to be a science, its practitioners would assume a more dispassionate stance toward their subject. But such has not been, and is not now, the case.

Linguists Paul Garvin ("Moderation in Linguistic Theory") and Victor Yngve ("On Achieving Agreement in Linguistics") observe that this kind of extremism still exists within the discipline of language study. Garvin, an explicator and interpreter of theoretical linguistics, argues for moderation because he believes that "only a moderate theoretical position can assure the continuity and further development of one's discipline," while Yngve pleads for an ecumenical spirit and observes that a "kind of generation gap in the discipline exists: The younger generation is not content to accept the values of their parents."

Before we examine the effects of the linguistic revolution, a caveat is in order for our reader. "Revolution," we feel, has a way of implying that truth resides with the rebel and that there is something peculiar and even pernicious about those "unenlightened" who choose to maintain the faith. Discovery can lead to violent disagreements, as we have seen, and yet disagreements within a discipline are healthy signs that research is on-going and that questions are being asked and answers sought. To disparage the research of previous generations of scholars as somehow vacuous and trivial and its progenitors as the advocates of falsehoods is quite another matter, however. We must always remind ourselves that for a science to be viable it must be incremental; dogma in any form tends to be stifling and unproductive.

While it is true that great and revolutionary changes have occurred and will continue to occur in linguistic science, much to the consternation of teachers, textbook writers, publishers, and students, it is fascinating, nevertheless, to observe what in the short space of twenty years has occurred to cause Francis and Cattell to call such changes "revolutionary." Francis, in his bold statements, refers to the then revolutionary kind of language study called *structural* or *descriptive*; structural linguistics was designed to replace the older and more traditional study of language, designated pre- or unscientific by himself and other structuralists. Cattell not only acknowledges the revolutionary fervor of structural linguistics but also presents the outlines of a current "new" grammar, called *generative-transformational* by its most famous advocate, Noam A. Chomsky of the Massachusetts Institute of Technology.

Generative-transformational grammar is revolutionary, according to Cattell, since it marks a distinct step forward in the study of language. Not surprisingly, some of the early papers explicating generative-transformational theory argue against the principles of language study associated with structural linguistics. Since the publication of *Syntactic Structures*, Chomsky's initial monograph which served to give impetus to this theory, generative-transformational theory has undergone major modifications, one made by Chomsky himself, as contained in his *Aspects of the Theory of Syntax,* the others by his students and colleagues. We shall examine the revision proposed by Charles Fillmore, which he has labeled *Case Grammar,* in our chapter on Semantics.

We must not, however, in our résumé, give the impression that these two "revolutions" comprise the linguistic world as it exists today. On the contrary, there are various "schools" of language study, each claiming its place in the dynamic discipline of linguistics and each with its own advocates and critics. In reading through the linguistic literature we may come upon references to Leonard Bloomfield's *Neo-structuralism,* Kenneth L. Pike's *Tagmemics,* Sydney Lamb's *Stratificational Analysis,* M. A. K. Halliday's *Scale and Category Grammar,* and André Martinet's *Functional Theory.*

While structural and generative-transformational grammars are perhaps the most current in the United States, perhaps in the world, we do not wish to suggest that these other theories hold less promise or contain less truth than those we will examine. Perhaps any one of the theories we have mentioned will rise to prominence in the years ahead. In the sciences, as well as linguistics, theories are constantly being revised, or even replaced, by those which hold more insight.

These theories—and we have listed only a few—with their unfamiliar and esoteric titles reflect a much changed attitude toward the study of language. Just a few short years ago, Cattell reminds us, grammarians thought they knew most of what there was to know about language and the theories employed to explain and describe it. As a beginning point of our survey, we shall first examine a few of the characteristics of traditional (18th-19th century) grammar, as newer theories stand either in refutation (structural grammar) or in partial agreement (generative-transformational grammar) with the aims of this tradition. Traditional grammar is also perhaps the best known of all current English grammars—at least to many generations of school children. Its study still is associated in many parts of the country with the learning of definitions and of certain rules for speaking and writing "correct" English, and with an emphasis on writing. These attributes were the very ones later criticized and attacked by the structural grammarians.

Our purpose here and in the chapters that follow will not be to present detailed technical introductions or even to survey all current schools of modern linguistic theory. Rather, we aim to examine in outline in these chapters what we believe to be the major thrust of modern linguistic study, beginning with traditional grammar, followed by structural and generative-transformational grammars. Current from the early part of this century and still viable today, structural grammar was a reaction to the concepts held by traditional grammarians. Generative-transformational grammar, in turn, is in part a reaction to the concepts held by structural grammarians.

PARTS OF SPEECH: SOME TRADITIONAL DEFINITIONS

The definitions of the parts of speech do provide us with a convenient point of departure. Most traditional grammars list and define eight parts of speech, commonly called noun, verb, pronoun, adjective, adverb, conjunction, preposition, and interjection. The parts of speech are classified on the basis of two criteria: *notional* (meaning) and *functional* (relation). *Notion* refers to the qualities of a word. For instance, a noun in this grammar is the "name of a person, place, or thing." We must *know* the meaning of the word before we can classify it. *Function* refers to what a word does in a sentence. An adjective in traditional grammar is any word that "modifies a noun."

There is, of course, the obvious difficulty of defining a category without first defining the terms *word* and *modify*. What is most striking about traditional grammar, however, is that the classification system—meaning and function—is mixed. It would be as difficult, for instance, to separate black rough beans from white smooth beans if we happened occasionally to discover that we had a black smooth bean or a white rough bean. A noun, traditional grammar tells us, is the "name of something," yet we have difficulty in categorizing a word such as "effect." Obviously it is neither a "person," nor a "place," nor is it a "thing." Most of the definitions run into the same sort of difficulty. For example, a pronoun is described as any word that "takes the place of a noun"; but while *nobody* is an indefinite pronoun, we would be hard put to determine what *nobody* stands for.

Another example is the definition for a preposition. A preposition is a word that "relates a noun or pronoun in a sentence with another word." This definition is functional. Yet in the sentence *I am a student*, *am* relates *I* to another word in the sentence, *student*. The conclusion that follows is that *am* is a preposition, which is an obviously wrong conclusion. And finally the definition of a sentence states that it contains a "complete thought." Yet, when we query, what is a "complete thought," we may hear, "a sentence is." The traditional definitions, structural grammarians concluded, are either circular or too vague to be of much value. As we shall see, it was just this particular defect that the structuralists attempted to correct by suggesting a set of explicit guidelines for determining the parts of speech of any language.

How then, we ask, could a student or a grammarian correctly label the parts of speech in English using these traditional definitions? May we suggest that it is because he already knows, by virtue of his being a native speaker, what the sentences and the word classes of his language are. He relies upon his *own* intelligence (he knows how to *apply* the traditional definitions), and his *own* intuition, to judge whether he has labeled correctly. Since the definitions are vague, he could not rely upon the substance of the definitions.

TO BE OR NOT TO BE—CORRECT

The 19th century "Doctrine of Correctness," which aims for a standard of writing and speaking to be observed by every educated person, reflects, in part, attempts of the schools in the United States to teach a "common" dialect to immigrants and the children of immigrants. In England, on the other hand, the "Doctrine" was applied largely to the lower socio-economic classes who wished to shed their linguistic identity—a liability, they felt, that stood in their way to social mobility. George Bernard Shaw's *Pygmalion*, his "Fair Lady," is an account of one attempt of a teacher to purge the dialect of a lower-class girl of certain "linguistic impurities" which had socially stigmatized her.

In the United States it was not surprising to encounter various communities in which English was not the first language of the populace. Children of these communities spoke the language of their parents: various Slavic dialects, German, Norwegian, Swedish, Danish, and some non-Indo-European languages, including Finnish and Chinese. The function of the school superintendent in these linguistically diverse areas included the supervision of the language of instruction, to make certain that instruction was being carried on in English. Today, the language of instruction, except in some foreign language classes, remains English. We might add that the practice of teaching a "standard" variety of English during a time of heavy immigration made sense, for if the children of immigrants were to be acculturated, then the "proper" English dialect could act as one catalyst. Yet in the 1970's the practice of teaching a "standard" or "correct" form of English still persists in most English classes.

ACCORDING TO THE RULE

Since Latin was considered by some grammarians to be the perfect language, it was logical to force Latinate structure onto a language as different as English. Especially significant in the transference of the categories of Latin grammar to English was the listing of rules, called *prescriptive rules* today, which decreed how English must be spoken or written, and not how it actually was spoken or written. Traditional grammar, then, was an attempt to bend the children to the grammar rather than to bend the grammar to reflect the language habits of the children, or even of adults: to teach students how they must write and talk rather than to describe how they actually talked and wrote. Such prescriptive rules as, "Don't end a sentence with a preposition" (which was sometimes put, "Don't use a preposition to end a sentence with"); "Don't split infinitives"; "Use *I shall* rather than *I will*"; and similar rules, had as much weight in the language class as the Biblical Commandments, and were taught to the student through exercises: he was taught what was "right" by having him correct sentences that were "wrong."

WRITING

Traditional grammar tended to emphasize the written language, ignoring, for the most part, the spoken; we suspect this was primarily because the sacred documents and literature were written. But it is speech rather than writing, that is primary, countered the structuralists. Writing, a late innovation of the human race, is a way of recording speech. Traditionalists pointed to the written language as preserving the "correct" or "pure" way of using language. And even here, we may recognize, they may have missed an important distinction between writing and speech: although writing is a way of recording the spoken language, we do not always talk as we write, nor do we often write as we talk. Examples of the difference between writing and speech can be found in all languages that have a writing system. The long and complex sentence structures that are often found in written German discourses, for example, can very seldom be heard in actual speech; in English, extemporaneous, daily speech and report writing often bear no similarity.

The above criticisms, which serve to point up the various shortcomings of traditional grammar, were stated by those revolutionaries who were to call themselves structuralists. We do not wish, however, in this review to lump all traditional grammars together. We have been reviewing the tradition of the 18th century, a tradition that has been called "prescientific," a tradition that gave little attention to the spoken language, that placed emphasis on the way people should be using the language, and a tradition that employed two different criteria to classify the words of the English language. We have yet to mention other important traditional grammars, those associated with the work of Otto Jespersen, G. O. Curme, E. Kruisinga, Henry Sweet (the professor who inspired *Pygmalion*), and other scholars who wrote important grammars of the English language, grammars that have been called "pre-descriptive" because they anticipated the advent of structuralism.

While it is sometimes useful to disparage one's adversary, in this case traditional grammar, we must not be so hasty in our condemnation that we overlook the fact that traditional grammar established high goals for itself. For one, by the traditional grammarian's attempts to transfer the categories of Latin to a superficially different language such as English, he may have been seeking attributes common not only to Latin and English but attributes common to all languages. While structuralists tended to emphasize the differences to be found among languages, later linguists—for example, the generative-transformational grammarians—have returned to the goals of traditional grammar and are investigating the possibility that all languages, in a deep abstract sense, are alike.

WINDS OF CHANGE

At the end of the 19th century, language study, we have seen, was oriented toward the written word and documents, and tended to look backward, being more concerned with the history of languages than with how they were then spoken and written. In universities and colleges, departments of language and literature flourished, with literature dominating. The department devoted exclusively to the study of language had not yet appeared. The principal product of these language and literature departments, the public school teacher, sallied forth to classroom assignments armed with a modicum of language skill and knowledge, more knowledge of literature than of language, and less knowledge of "how to teach." However, during this time the seeds of revolution were being strewn.

The Swiss scholar, Ferdinand de Saussure, is often considered to be the father of modern structural linguistics. His lectures were gathered by his students and published in 1916 under the title *Cours de Linguistique Générale*. Nevertheless, it was Leonard Bloomfield who later gave impetus to the distinct brand of American linguistics called structural or descriptive. All linguists have been profoundly affected by Bloomfield and his insights into language, and owe a great debt to the research of this significant scholar. He was for many years at the University of Chicago, and later at Yale University, where he enjoyed the prominence he so richly deserved.

Early in his career, Bloomfield became dissatisfied with the traditionalism of the existing professional organizations and, discouraged with them as a forum for new ideas in language study, helped found the Linguistic Society of America in 1924. The LSA, as it is called, continues to meet twice a year to hear and discuss papers on language. Together with his followers, Bloomfield attacked what he felt to be the subjective, vague, and unsubstantiated claims of traditional grammar and hammered away against the centuries-old confusion between writing and speech—for it was, above all, speech that intrigued Leonard Bloomfield and his colleagues. However, as structuralism progressed, Bloomfield and other American structuralists came to pay increasing amounts of attention to reading and writing.

The *Bloomfieldians*, as they are now called, submitted that language consisted of levels, each level hierarchically linked to the one above and below it. In 1914, discussing the goals of the linguist, Bloomfield said, "The first task of the linguistic investigator is the analysis of a language into distinctive sounds, their variations, and the like. When he has completed this, he turns to the analysis of the semantic structure,—to what we call the morphology and syntax of the language, its grammatical system." These early views have been refined, systematized, and codified and may be found in his monumental book, *Language*, which was published in 1933.

Bloomfield knew traditional grammar well and also had access to the works of many gifted predecessors and contemporaries. The earliest of these was the Hindu grammarian we know by the name of Panini, who, as early as the 4th century B.C., had written an amazingly perceptive description of the sounds and structure of Sanskrit, the ancient religious language of India. Nevertheless, not until the 19th century, when manuscripts became more available, did western scholars learn of the descriptive methods of Panini.

Of importance also in the development of American structuralism was the work of the German-trained anthropologist Franz Boas, who emigrated to American in 1886 and began to work with American Indian languages. His writings on the Indians of British Columbia set a new standard in the description of American Indian languages, and his Introduction to the

Handbook of American Indian Languages, reprinted by Georgetown University Press, still remains a benchmark in the history of linguistic description.

American-educated Edward Sapir followed the course charted by his teacher, Boas, contributing his own analyses of the American Indian languages. The most extensive of these was his description of the Southern Paiute language. Sapir is also noted for his general theoretical works on linguistic subjects. One of these prepared specifically for the general reader, his book titled *Language*, still enjoys wide popularity, although written in 1921. In it, he relates what he conceives language to be, "what is its variability in place and time, and what are its relations to other fundamental human interests—the problem of thought, the nature of historical process, race, culture, art."

The structuralists spent a great deal of effort analyzing the "exotic" languages of the world. Bloomfield himself did a structural analysis of Tagalog, now one of the official languages of the Philippines, and fairly recently his important linguistic study, *The Menomini Language*, a grammar of an American Indian language of the Algonquin family, made its appearance. Other structuralists interested themselves in such widely divergent languages as Melanesian Pidgin, Hungarian, Japanese, and the various dialects of Chinese.

An emphasis in these studies was upon the level of language called *phonological*. An extremely significant role in the development of the phonological level was played by another linguistic tradition, the Prague Linguistic Circle, founded in Czechslovakia in 1927 by Vilem Mathesius and Josef Mukarovsky, who headed a group of scholars that developed the concept of the *phoneme*—Bloomfield's "distinctive sounds and their variations." The concept of the phoneme was proposed first about 1812 by Baudouin de Courtenay, a Russo-Polish scholar. Although the concept of the phoneme that these scholars introduced, and other new formulations, may at first appear difficult and even confusing to individuals accustomed only to traditional grammar, abstractions such as the phoneme are necessary to linguistic science and serve to give order to disorder.

The phoneme is an important concept in linguistics—just how important we will see in the following chapter. Boas and Bloomfield, we must remember, both believed that an analysis of a language must begin with the study of its "distinctive sounds, their variations, and the like"—its *phonemes*, in other words. Only when the phonemes were determined could analysis begin on the next level of language, the "morphology and syntax of the language, its grammatical system." And once the phonemes were determined for a language, analysis could begin on the next unit of language, the *morpheme* (minimal unit of meaning). *Syntax* (the arrangement of words in a sentence) would depend upon a previous determination of the morphemic level of that language.

In the chapters immediately following, we will introduce our readers to some perhaps mystifying concepts, drawing from a number of schools of linguistic thought. No particular linguistic theory is advocated; we draw from several, concentrating upon structural, generative-transformational, and case grammars, in the belief that our readers need the breadth that such an approach entails.

IV. QUESTIONS AND ACTIVITIES

1. Examine some pre-1950 English grammars that have been used in the public schools. Do the definitions of the parts of speech differ?

2. What do grammars say about usage (the "correct" way to speak and write)? Are there any rules of language use that seem to be contradictory or arbitrary?

3. The use of two negatives in one sentence ("I *don't* have *none*") is used to categorize speakers of the English language. Supposedly speakers who use double negatives are less educated (and may be from a different socioeconomic class) than those who do not. Can you think of any situation in which an educated speaker could utter two negatives?

4. Is there a "standard" or "correct" English? Who establishes the "standard"? What role does the English teacher play or assume in matters of "correct" usage?

5. Look at a transcript (or record one of your own) of an extemporaneous speech. What do we do in speech that we cannot do in writing? How do we know that someone is reading from (or has memorized) a carefully prepared speech?

6. Is it possible to be ironical in speech? For instance, can we call someone a name and not mean it? How do we do this?

7. What is contained in a school grammar? Is the grammar solely confined to a description of language? In order to respond to this query, compare pre-1950 with current grammars. Why would publishers include within school grammars information other than language information?

IV. FOR FURTHER REFERENCE

Algeo, John. 1970. "Tagmemics: A Brief Overview." *Journal of English Linguistics* 4:1-6.

Bloomfield, Leonard. 1933. *Language.* New York: Holt.

_____. 1944. "Secondary and Tertiary Responses to Language." *Language* 20:45-55.

Cattell, N. R. 1969. *The New English Grammar.* Cambridge, Mass.: M.I.T. Press.

Chomsky, Noam A. 1966. *Cartesian Linguistics.* New York: Harper and Row.

_____. 1966. "The Current Scene in Linguistics: Present Directions." *College English* 27:587-95.

Davis, Philip W. 1973. *Modern Theories of Language.* Englewood Cliffs, N.J.: Prentice-Hall.

Francis, W. Nelson. 1954. "Revolution in Grammar." *Quarterly Journal of Speech* 40:299-312.

Garvin, Paul. 1970. "Moderation in Linguistic Theory." *Language Sciences* February, 1-3.

Gray, Bennison. 1974. "Toward a Semi-Revolution in Grammar." *Language Sciences* 29:1-12.

Griffin, Peg. 1974. "Linguistic Terminology." *Linguistic Reporter* 16(9):2.

Halliday, M. A. K. 1961. "Categories of the Theory of Grammar." *Word* 17:241-292.

Hill, Archibald A. 1958. *An Introduction to Linguistic Structures*. New York: Harcourt, Brace, and World.

Lamb, Sydney. 1966. *Outline of Stratificational Grammar*. Washington, D.C.: Georgetown University Press.

Lehmann, Winfred P. 1975. "Linguistics—What Are They?" *Journal of the Linguistic Association of the Southwest* 1(2).

Martinet, André. 1962. *A Functional View of Language*. Cambridge: Oxford University Press.

O'Neil, Wayne. 1970. "Comes the Revolution." *Harvard Graduate School of Education Bulletin* 14:2-3.

Pike, Kenneth L. 1967. *Language in Relation to a Unified Theory of the Structure of Human Behavior*. 2nd ed, rev. The Hague: Mouton.

Robins, R. H. 1970. "General Linguistics in Great Britain, 1930-1960," in *Diversions of Bloomsbury: Selected Writings on Linguistics*. Amsterdam: North-Holland Publishing.

Saussure, Ferdinand de. 1916. *Cours de Linguistique Générale*. Paris: Payot.

Sapir, Edward. 1921. *Language*. New York: Harcourt, Brace and World.

Smart, Walter Kay. 1957. *English Review Grammar*. 4th ed. New York: Appleton-Century-Crofts.

Trager, George L. and Henry Lee Smith, Jr. 1957. *An Outline of English Structure*. Washington, D.C.: American Council of Learned Societies.

Yngve, Victor. 1969. "On Achieving Agreement in Linguistics," in *Papers from the Fifth Regional Meeting of the Chicago Linguistic Society, Department of Linguistics*. Chicago: University of Chicago.

V. Phonology: A Sign of Structure

MAKING SOUNDS

Phonology, or the study of language sounds and their distribution, is the subject of this chapter. A description of the distinctive sounds and their variations (the *phonemes*) of any language is dependent upon the science of *phonetics*, especially articulatory phonetics. Articulatory phonetics provides a means of describing each and every language sound made. Phoneticians employ a special alphabet, the *International Phonetic Alphabet*, which features many more symbols than the conventional western alphabet to characterize and describe the sounds of language. These phoneticians believe that the study of speech sounds is that aspect of linguistic science nearest to the physical sciences, since a description of sounds involves not only a description of the actual physiological organs employed in the production of speech but also a description of the acoustic effects that sounds make on the ear.

It has been proposed that the concept of the phoneme has been to language science what the discovery of the atom has been to the natural sciences, particularly physics. Although it is true that certain contemporary schools of linguistics are less concerned today with the phoneme than the Bloomfieldian structuralists were, the concept still remains of fundamental significance for a large number of linguists. Any theory of language, moreover, must take phonology into account; and in this chapter we shall be discussing two accounts, or theories, of phonological structure. We shall begin our examination of the phonological facts of language with an analysis and description of some of the principles and descriptive techniques associated with the structural school of linguistics, to be followed by a description of some of the principles and descriptive techniques of generative-transformational grammar.

STRUCTURAL PHONOLOGY

Structural (descriptive) linguists, following Leonard Bloomfield and his European predecessors, remind us that language sounds are "organized" noises, which is another way of stating that language consists of units, classes, or families of sounds that we call *phonemes*. The very term phoneme reflects an abstract entity, one that is not perceivable to the average speaker of a language; and the terms that are used to describe the variations of the phoneme, the *phone* and *allophone*, describe concrete phonetic facts about a language. We have slipped in here, quite on purpose, a number of terms that we will need to define further. But let us not get ahead of our story. We must first discuss what we mean by "speech sound."

There are a number of speech sounds that human beings can make and a number of organs that are involved. To make a speech sound in English, breath is expelled from the lungs through the larynx (the "voice box") into the oral cavity or mouth and the breath is emitted either from the mouth or from the mouth and nose. The manner in which it is expelled or released determines what sort of sound will be heard. There may be a point of constriction in the

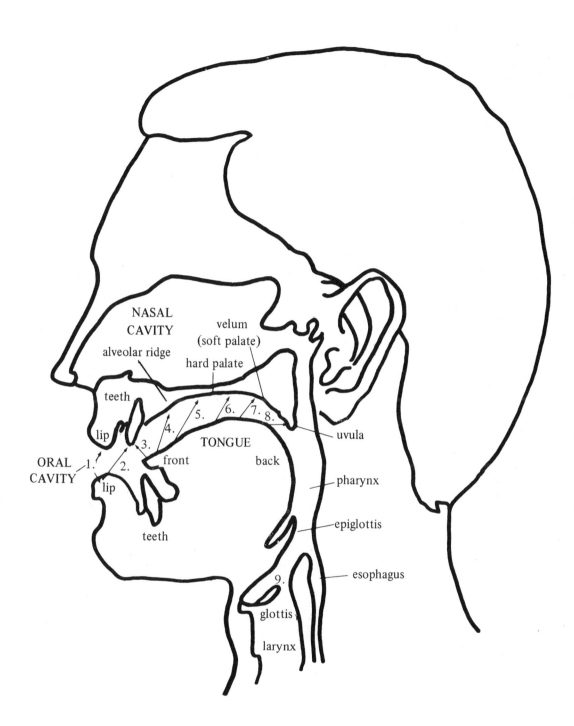

The Vocal Tract. *Places of Articulation*: 1. bilabial; 2. labiodental; 3. dental or interdental; 4. alveolar; 5. palatoalveolar; 6. palatal; 7. velar; 8. uvular; 9. glottal

mouth; and what takes place at the point of constriction, such as the interruption of air, either partially or completely, aids in determining the kind of sound that is made.

Although there are certain organs of the oral tract that are important in the production of sounds, these organs have other functions besides the production of language noises, such as aiding in breathing, eating, drinking, and coughing. These organs are the *lungs*, the *bronchial tubes*, and the *throat*, including the *larynx*, which contains the *vocal bands* and *glottis*. In the back of the throat is the *uvula* (Latin for "little grape"), which is the soft, pointed organ at the rear of the *palate*. The palate or roof of the mouth is divided into the back portion known as the *velum* or "soft palate," and the front portion, which has bone underneath and is known as the "hard palate." Finally, there are the *tongue, alveolar ridge, teeth*, and *lips*. The most mobile of all of these components of production is the tongue, which plays an important role in determining the kind of sound that will be produced by the speaker. We have provided a chart of the mouth and throat with the appropriate organs of speech labeled.

These components, which we have briefly described, act in concert to produce the sounds of language. A speaker may want, for instance, to say the word "too." He pushes air into the mouth, and as he slightly opens his lips, his tongue touches the ridge of gum behind the upper teeth. When the tongue retracts to release the air, *t* is heard. A split second afterward, in fact merged with the sound *t*, comes the sound symbolized in writing by *oo*, during which time the lips are kept slightly parted and are, at the same time, rounded. As the air is pushed out, the tongue is raised and glides toward the soft palate.

What we have described, albeit impressionistically, is a brief and simple illustration of what is involved in making the sounds for the word "too." It has been found convenient to devise special alphabets to aid in the representation of not only these sounds but all language sounds; the best known of these is the revised and widely used alphabet of the *International Phonetic Association* (commonly referred to as the *I.P.A.*). We present here, in a chart organized according to articulatory phenomena (which we explain below), the major types of sounds (the *phones*) which a phonetician might observe in many, if not most, varieties of American English. Our reader will notice that our chart contains a number of symbols, some with *diacritics*, that may be unfamiliar. These symbols are employed to signify what is *heard*. We have listed beside each symbol a word indicating the pronunciation of that symbol in context. Pronunciations can, and do, differ, however. The reader, therefore, must be certain that the sound actually occurs in his dialect. For instance, if the speaker pronounces "which" and "witch" differently, then he possibly pronounces "which" with initial [ʍ] and "witch" with initial [w]. If there is no difference in pronunciation between these words for the speaker, then both are pronounced with [w].

Even though there is an I.P.A., phonetic symbols employed by phoneticians and linguists may differ from those advocated by the I.P.A. The symbols which we employ in our text may well differ from those employed in others. We offer these symbols as a representative set. Let us now look at a sentence reduced to these phonetic symbols:

[ʍɪč bʊk ar yu kipɪŋ ɪn ðə barəm əv ðæt trʌŋk]
("Which book are you keeping at the bottom of that trunk?")

For clarity, we have put spaces between the words in the sample sentence; in actual speech, of course, there would be no spaces. We will return to this alphabet when we discuss the *phoneme*.

*   *   *

As the Phonetic Alphabet illustrates, there are two basic kinds of language sounds, quite commonly called *vowels* and *consonants*. A third set is neither totally consonant nor totally vowel, but shares characteristics of both; these sounds are sometimes called *semivowels*. In the production of vowels the tongue and the lips are of greatest importance. As the tongue is raised or lowered, pulled back or pushed upward, and as the lips are rounded or kept neutral, different vowels are formed. We can feel these organs at work if we pronounce the vowels of the English

PHONETIC ALPHABET

(Partial Listing of Symbols: Consonants and Vowels)

Consonants

STOPS			
[p] *s*py	[t] *s*ty	[k] *s*ky
[pʰ] *p*ie	[tʰ] *t*ie	[kʰ] *k*ind
[b] *b*uy	[d] *d*ie	[g] *g*irl
	[ɾ] a*t*om*	

AFFRICATES

[č] *ch*ump
[ǰ] *j*ump

FRICATIVES

[f] *f*ree   [θ] *th*ing   [s] *s*igh   [š] *sh*y   [h] *h*igh
[v] *v*ise   [ð] *th*e   [z] *z*oo   [ž] A*s*ia

NASALS

[m] *m*y   [n] *n*igh   [ŋ] you*ng*

LIQUIDS

[l] *l*ip   [ɫ] hu*ll*
[r] th*r*ee
[j] *r*ye

Semivowels

[w] *w*itch   [y] *y*et
[ʍ] *wh*ich*

Vowels

[i] m*ee*t		[u] b*oo*t
[ɪ] m*i*t		[ʊ] f*oo*t
[e] m*a*te	[ʌ] m*u*tt	[o] p*o*rk*
[ɛ] m*e*t	[ə] sof*a*	[ou] b*oa*t*
[æ] m*a*t	[a] p*o*t	[ɔ] c*au*ght*
	[aɪ] m*i*ght*	[ɔɪ] b*o*y
	[dʊ] h*ou*se	

*reader's pronunciation may differ

alphabet: *a, e, i, o, u*. Vowels are also characterized by the free and unimpeded flow of air through the mouth. Consonants, by way of contrast, are characterized by total or partial closure of the vocal tract. We will point to these distinctions as we describe the sounds of English. We begin our structural description of the phonological system of English with the consonants.

ENGLISH SOUNDS: CONSONANTS

In producing consonants, we must remind ourselves that the air coming from the lungs through the mouth (the vocal tract) is totally or partially impeded so.newhere along its path. Consonants may be classified into sets or classes on the basis of three phonetic criteria or features:

1. *Manner of articulation* (the *kind* of sound being produced in the mouth or the kind of impedance which the air undergoes). Air may be completely or partially stopped.

2. *The point or place of articulation* (the important parts of the vocal tract which are used in making the sound). These include the lips, various parts of the tongue, the teeth, the alveolar ridge (the ridge of gum behind the upper teeth), the soft and hard palates, the vocal cords, and the glottis. The glottis is like the hole in the donut; it is the space between the vocal bands.

3. *The presence or absence of voicing.* The larynx contains two cords, or bands, which may close off air completely, or may be kept open, permitting them to vibrate while allowing air to pass through. In English, certain consonant sounds are *voiced* (vibration of vocal bands) while others are *voiceless* (no vibration of vocal bands).

We will explore each of these three features as we describe the various kinds of consonants that the English language has.

Voicing

Perhaps the easiest characteristic to define is *voicing*. English consonants may be voiced or voiceless. For instance, if we make the sound *s* as in "sip," and then make the sound for *z* as in "zip," we notice that *z* is characterized by a "buzzing" noise while *s* is not. The difference between *z* and *s* is a difference in voicing, the *s* being voiceless and the *z* voiced. Phonetically, the vocal cords vibrate when making *z*; they do not when making *s*. We will see that English has sets of consonants which are distinguished on the basis of voicing.

Manner of Articulation

The *manner of articulation* (the kind of sound being formed) may be a bit more difficult to perceive. There are various kinds of consonantal sounds in English. One kind is the *stop* (or *plosive*). When we make the initial consonant sound in the word "top," and hold it, we notice that the air is completely stopped by the tongue, which is placed on the upper ridge of gum behind the teeth, the alveolar ridge. Thus, the *t* consonant is called a stop. English has six consonants that are stops. These are the *p* and *b*; the *t* and *d*; and the *k* and *g*. What distinguishes the stop consonant *p* from *b*, *t* from *d* and *k* from *g*, is the feature of voice: *b, d,* and *g* are voiced, and *p, t,* and *k* are usually voiceless.

Another kind of consonant in English is characterized by the sound that occurs first in the word "sap." As we make the *s*, which is voiceless, we notice that the air is not stopped completely but moved gradually and continually from the lungs past the tongue and out through the lips. This sound, symbolized by *s*, is called a *fricative* or *spirant*. English has four sets of fricative consonants; four are voiced and four are voiceless. We are already familiar with the distinction between voiceless *s* and voiced *z*. The feature of voice serves to distinguish, also, the *v* from the *f*: "vat" versus "fat."

There are two sets of fricatives that we must describe with symbols which are not in the English alphabet. One set is commonly referred to as the *th* sound, or sounds, and occurs in the words "thin" and "then." We observe that we do not have merely one *th* sound but two *th* sounds, which are distinguished by the feature of voice. The *th* sound in "thin," similar to the *th* sounds that we have in "think," "thatch," and "ether," is voiceless. The symbol which is employed to describe this voiceless fricative is θ (a Greek symbol), called the *theta*, as the *th* sound in "theta" is voiceless. The other *th* sound, as found in "then," "they," "than," and "either," is voiced. The symbol employed to describe this *th* sound is ð, called, mnemonically, the "eth," as "eth" contains the voiced *th* fricative.

The remaining set of fricatives can be symbolized by symbols found in the I.P.A. or by modified symbols of the English alphabet. One fricative is symbolized in the English alphabet by the diagraph (two letters) *sh*, as in the *sh* sounds of "shoot," "shone," and "shame." Phonetically, this *sh* sound is indicated by š. It is voiceless. If we voice the *sh*, we hear the first sound in "Zhivago" and the middle sound (represented by the *s*) that we have in "allusion." This fricative is indicated by ž. We have, then, eight fricatives in English or four sets of two each, the members of each set distinguished by voice. *f*, *s*, θ, and š are voiceless while *v*, *z*, ð, and ž are voiced. One additional fricative remains in the sound pattern of English—the *h* sound, as found in the words "hot," "ham," and "hit." We will have more to say about the fricative consonant class below.

The next kind of sound may also be difficult to conceptualize as it consists of a stop followed by a fricative. If we slowly make the sound that occurs first in the word "chop," we notice that as we make the *ch* we first make the *t* (the air is completely stopped) while at the same time we slowly move our tongue down from the alveolar ridge, causing air to be released. This sound of a stop followed by the slow release of the tongue into a fricative is called an *affricate*. English has two affricates, one of which can be symbolized by the written *ch* as in "chip." *Ch* is voiceless. The other affricate is voiced and is occasionally symbolized by ǰ, as in "judge." In structural phonology, we employ the symbol č for the written *ch* and ǰ for *j* (in the I.P.A., two symbols are used—tʃ for č and dȝ for ǰ).

English also has *nasal* consonants. If we make the sound which occurs first in the word "mop," we have articulated a nasal consonant. Nasal consonants are characterized by the dropping of the *velum* (the soft palate), which allows air to go up through the nasal passages and out through the nose. What makes the articulation of nasals possible is the flexibility of the velum, which can stop air from going up through the nasal passages or can allow air to be emitted from the nose. English has three nasal consonants, symbolized in writing by *m*, *n*, and *ng* (as in "sing"). The *m* is a bilabial nasal, the *n* an alveolar, and the *ng* a velar. The *ng* is used in the writing system since there is no one symbol that can accurately symbolize it. In phonology, the *ng* is symbolized by ŋ.

English has one *lateral* and one *retroflex* consonant, commonly called *liquids*. The *lateral* is symbolized in English orthography (the writing system) by *l*, as in the initial sound of "lip." We should notice that the *l* involves raising the tongue, as in "lip," and allowing, at the same time, air to escape from one or both sides of the tongue. The variety of the *l* sound that occurs in the word "pool," however, is different. This *l* [ɫ] involves raising the *back* of the tongue, while the *l* in "lip" involves raising the *front* of the tongue. The *l* in "lip" is occasionally called a *front l*, while the *l* in "pool" is oftentimes called a *back l*.

The *retroflex*, the *r*, is made by curling the tongue back toward the hard palate, as in the initial sound of "rap." *Retro* (back) and *flex* (curl) characterize the movement of the tongue. While all English speakers pronounce the *r* when it occurs initially, as in "rap" (or after an initial consonant, as in "spray"), some speakers in areas of the United States do not pronounce the *r* when it occurs in final word position, as in words like "car," or in positions before consonants which appear in the middle or at the end of words, such as "park." Parts of New England are famous for "r-dropping," pronouncing "car" as "cah." There are other variants of *r* which occur, too—the *r* which occurs in "rye" [ɹ] or "three," for example.

Point of Articulation

The third characteristic that linguists employ to classify consonants is the *point of articulation*: the significant parts of the mouth (oral tract) that come into play in the production of sounds. The two lips come together in the articulation of the sounds *b, p,* and *m.* We therefore call these sounds *bilabial.* The lower lip may touch the upper teeth, for instance in the pronunciation of *v.* The *v* is *labial* (lip) and *dental* (teeth), or *labio-dental.*

The tip of the tongue is an important instrument in the articulation of sounds. The tongue may, for certain consonants, touch the bottom portion of the upper teeth or even slightly protrude between the teeth, as in the initial sound of "then." The fricative sound in "then" is *dental* or *interdental.* The *th* sound that occurs in the word "thin" is also dental or interdental.

The tip of the tongue may touch the alveolar ridge, as in the *t* of "tar" or the *d* of "din." The middle of the tongue, the blade, is also important in the production of English consonants, for instance in the articulation of the *s* and *z* sounds in "sap" and "zap." The tongue does not touch the ridge (these are *fricatives*) but air is directed from the lungs into the groove of the tongue toward the alveolar ridge. The *sh* sound, as in "shoot," is articulated just behind the alveolar ridge where the hard palate begins, and is the reason for describing it as an *alveo-palatal fricative.*

The back of the tongue also functions in the production of English consonants. For *k,* as in the word "kit," the back of the tongue touches the velum, closing off the air passage. The back of the tongue as a major articulation device is also apparent in the pronunciation of the word "kosher."

If we review the entire range of consonants in English, we find that there are six sets: *stops* (also called *plosives*); *fricatives* (*spirants*); *affricates* (*stop* plus *fricative*); *semivowels*; *nasals*; and *liquids* (*lateral* and *retroflex*). Occasionally, the nasal, lateral, and retroflex consonants are grouped together into one set, since they share the feature, or quality, of *resonance*: the nasals, lateral, and retroflex sounds can be held indefinitely, and all are voiced. Resonance is thus a kind of acoustic effect that these sounds have in common.

THE PHONEME

In our discussion of the consonants in English we have been referring to "sound" as though each consonant consists of the identical sound wherever it might appear in a word. Most, especially those who have had no training in phonetics, believe that the *t* sound is just that: a *t* sound. However, linguists have found that language sounds can be classified into larger abstract units, and these units are the *phonemes* of a language. However, we are usually not aware of this language fact until it is pointed out to us, perhaps in a beginning class on the nature of language.

The abstract unit called the *phoneme* actually consists of a "family" of sounds, all of which are phonetically similar. Native speakers "hear" in phonemes and are usually unaware that each phoneme consists of a variety of slightly different sounds, depending upon where the sound occurs in a word. To make the concept of the phoneme clearer, we only have to listen carefully to the various pronunciations of the *t.* Linguists do not talk about the varieties of the *t* sound, but refer to the *allophones* that are members of the phoneme /t/. An individual allophone is enclosed in phonetic brackets, for example [tʰ]. Phonemes, on the other hand, are enclosed within slant lines, for example /t/. The I.P.A. chart indicates some but not all of the sounds that may be heard in English, and we will be referring to this chart as we discuss some of the phonemes of the English language.

One pronunciation of the phoneme /t/ is that which occurs in the initial position of a word when it is accompanied by a strong puff of air, as in the word "tin." You can feel the puff of air if you hold your hand in front of your lips while pronouncing "tin." The I.P.A. symbol used to indicate this fact is [tʰ]. The [ʰ] mark accompanying the [tʰ] means that it occurs with a strong puff of air. When the phoneme /t/ follows *s,* as in "stake," almost no air follows. This phonetic fact is indicated in the I.P.A. by the symbol [t], with no mark following the [t]. Or when /t/ occurs between vowels, as in "butter," "letter," "sitter," the sound (allophone) that is heard is not distinct (at least in most American dialects) from /d/ as in "ladder." The I.P.A. symbol employed to record this manifestation of the /t/ phoneme is [ɾ]. In spite of these variations, and others we have not mentioned, all variations belong to one class that we call the phoneme /t/. We hear the abstract unit /t/ but usually ignore (or are not aware of) these allophonic variations.

The phoneme /k/ also consists of a family of related sounds. In initial position, /k/ is pronounced like /t/, with a strong puff of air (technically called *aspiration*), as in "kit." There is little or no aspiration if /k/ follows *s*, as in "skin." Both [kʰ] and [k] belong to the same phoneme, however, and native speakers do not pay attention to the actual variants in pronunciation. We could perform a similar analysis with all the consonant phonemes of English, as well as with the vowels, but we shall leave any further analysis to the reader. We have included at the end of this chapter some exercises designed to sharpen our reader's ear.

By way of summarizing, we have three columns: the first column contains a word with the phoneme; the second column a physical description of the sound; and the third the phoneme to which the sound belongs.

word	allophone	phoneme
top	[tʰ]	/t/
stop	[t]	/t/
letter	[ɾ]	/t/

Now we are ready to describe the entire set of phonemes of the English language, and we begin with the consonants. We shall commence with the *stops*, one of the six classes of consonants we referred to earlier. We will employ our three criteria, or features (*voicing, point of articulation, and manner of articulation*), to classify the consonant phonemes of English.

CONSONANT PHONEMES

The *stops* are made when the air is completely impeded at some point in the oral cavity. The stop consonants can be arrayed on a chart in the following manner:

Point of Articulation	Manner of Articulation	Voicing		Sample Word
bilabial	stop	/b/	+	bob
		/p/	-	pop
alveolar	stop	/d/	+	dad
		/t/	-	tap
velar	stop	/g/	+	gag
		/k/	-	kick

We can now say, using these three criteria, that /b/ is a *voiced bilabial stop*, and that /p/ is a *voiceless bilabial stop*. All consonants, not only stops, may now be classified in a similar fashion.

The sounds classifed as *spirants* or *fricatives* result if the air passage is not completely sealed. Again, the point at which the narrowing is made determines the kind of fricative that we hear. The fricatives of English are the following:

labio-dental	fricative	/v/	+	vat
		/f/	-	fat
interdental	fricative	/ð/	+	then
		/θ/	-	thin

alveolar	fricative	/z/	+	zen
		/s/	-	sin
alveo-palatal	fricative	/ž/	+	vision
		/š/	-	shin
glottal	fricative	/h/	-	hot

The *affricates*, which we have described previously, consist of a stop plus a following fricative, described in phonetics as /č/. /č/ is the *ch* sound we have in "check." The voiced counterpart of /č/ is described as /ǰ/ in phonemics, and is the initial consonant sound we have in "Jane."

| palatal | affricate | /ǰ/ | + | jerk |
| | affricate | /č/ | — | chief |

There is one *lateral* phoneme in English, the /l/. For classification purposes we list it as alveolar, recognizing, however, that there are variants (allophones) of this phoneme which occur in the velar region, and elsewhere. We described one variant in the section in which we discussed point of articulation. There is one *retroflex* consonant, /r/, which occurs initially as in "ring" and in final position in most American dialects, as in "fur." There are also other positions in which /r/ can occur.

Nasals in English are usually voiced, with the nasal passage open. The point of articulation determines which type of nasal is heard.

bilabial	nasal	/m/	man
alveolar	nasal	/n/	nan
velar	nasal	/ŋ/	sing

/ŋ/, sometimes called a "hooked" *n*, does not occur in word-initial position in English; it occurs in medial position ("singer") or in final position ("sing") only.

One last category remains, the *semivowels*, /w/ and /y/, which function both as consonants, as in "wet" and "yet," and as vowels. (We will discuss their vocalic nature below.) /w/ is a bilabial semivowel, as in "water," and /y/ is an alveolar semivowel, as in "young." Occasionally /h/, for reasons that need not detain us here, is classified as a semivowel.

This concludes our discussion of the consonants of English. We have included an exercise in transcription at the end of this chapter so that our readers may have the opportunity of becoming proficient in transcribing the sounds of English.

The consonants may be placed on a chart in such a way as to show their relationship and position in respect to each other:

	Bilabial	Labio-dental	Inter-dental	Alveolar	(Alveo-)palatal	Velar	Glottal
Stops	p b			t d		k g	
Fricatives		f v	θ ð	s z	š ž		h
Affricates					č ǰ		
Nasals	m			n		ŋ	
Lateral				l			
Retroflex				r			
Semivowels	w			y			

A number of excellent texts have been added recently to those already in existence on articulatory and acoustic phonetics. We cannot here hope to cover the subject except briefly, but for those who might develop an interest in phonology we recommend they pursue the subject using the texts in our bibliography.

"STRANGE" CONSONANT SOUNDS IN OTHER LANGUAGES

It is patently parochial but rather understandable to believe that the sounds of one's own language constitute a basic set and the sounds of other languages are derivatives of this set. Many languages, of course, use rather un-English sounds, but we also must remember that some English sounds impress the speakers of many other languages in much the same way. It is merely a question of what the speakers of languages are accustomed to hearing. The *th*/θ/ sound of "thin"—to use an example from English—can strike the uninitiated (for example, the native German speaker) as suitable for nothing except imitating a leak in an inner tube; the *wh* sound in "which" /hw/, used by those English speakers who make a distinction between "which" /hw/ and "witch" /w/ may seem to some naturally designed only for blowing out candles.

Consonant sounds produced by simultaneous blocking at two points in the vocal tract also may seem unusual to some speakers, not only to English speakers. An example is the single sound at the beginning of the name of *Kp*elle, a name of a language spoken in Liberia and Guinea. At the beginning of this word the back of the tongue is closed against the soft palate as for English /k/ while at the same time the lips are closed as for English /p/. When the glottis closes simultaneously with another blockage of air and the air trapped above the glottis is forced out, we have the ejective or emphatic consonants [p!], [t!], and [k!], found in some American Indian languages.

The so-called implosive stops [ɓ] and [ɗ], of many African languages similarly involve double blockage. For these speakers the glottis (the space between the vocal bands) is not so tightly closed and a little air passes up through it so that the bands vibrate, making these sounds voiced. At the same time, the larynx moves down and the throat is expanded so that when the upper blockage by the lips [ɓ] or tongue [ɗ] is opened, air moves slightly inward at the front of the mouth. Implosive [g], a sound children sometimes use to imitate frogs, is formed in the same way.

Often considered to be some of the more unusual sounds are the sounds called *clicks* found. in the Bushman languages of South Africa and also in two neighboring Bantu languages, Zulu and Xhosa. Clicks make use of the air space between two points of articulation, one of which is at the back of the mouth. Air is sucked in past a point of articulation made by the front of the tongue. The name "Xhosa" begins with one of these sounds. American English speakers use clicks, although not as speech sounds. A lateral click is used to start horses and a dental tongue-tip click to express disapproval—a sound often symbolized in the orthograph by "tsk-tsk." The sound made by a kiss is a bilabial click.

The glottis itself is the place of formation of a voiceless plosive produced by the vocal cords exactly as./p/ is formed by the lips. The glottis is closed and when released suddenly the effect resembles a weak cough. Heard before initial vowels when the speaker hesitates or says "uh-uh" for "no," it is a sound that can be distinctive (phonemic), as in the contrast in Danish between /hun/"her" and /hunʔ/"dog." The glottal sound in English is the fricative /h/, which occurs in "how."

ENGLISH SOUNDS: VOWELS

Vowels differ from consonants in the gross and obvious sense that the air passage is not impeded. Consonants are characterized by partial or complete interruption of the air from the lungs. A vowel may be defined as a sound produced by the passage of air through the oral cavity without appreciable stoppage or obstruction. Vowels in English differ from consonants in other ways, too. Vowels are voiced; some consonants are voiceless. Even though we here make the distinction between vowels and consonants, some linguists prefer to emphasize the similarities between the two categories, stating in effect that vowels are merely *minus* consonantal and that consonants are merely *minus* vocalic (see below). Structuralists, however, prefer to emphasize the distinction.

Vowels are more difficult to categorize than consonants, we believe, partly because English dialects differ more in the quality of vowels (the actual variation of the vowel heard) than in the quality of consonants. A warning here is perhaps appropriate: we are describing the most general dialect of English that is available to the authors, the dialect of the upper Midwest. Vowels in the New England region, the South, and other regions will differ in quality, some appreciably.

Vowel Quality

The *quality* of the vowel is chiefly determined by whether the tongue (an important organ in the production of vowels) is high in the mouth, at midpoint in the mouth, or low. The tongue, in the articulation of vowels, may be in the front of the mouth, the central region of the mouth, or in the back. Thus, there are two essential criteria, or features, that linguists employ in the description of vowels, one *vertical* (high, mid, low) and the other *horizontal* (front, central, back). We shall begin our description with the vowels articulated in the front region of the mouth, and also describe their height—*high, mid,* or *low.*

The *front vowel*—so named because they are articulated in the front position of the mouth—are symbolized as /I/, /i/, /ɛ/, /e/, and /æ/. We have provided a list of words that may be useful in "hearing" these vowels; but we must remember that these words and their vowels approximate upper Midwest pronunciation. Our reader, therefore, should not be confused or concerned if he finds that he pronounces these words differently. The examples:

/I/	(high-*front*):	the vowel of "sit."
/i/	(high-*front*):	the vowel of "seat."
/ɛ/	(mid-*front*):	the vowel of "set."
/e/	(mid-*front*):	the vowel of "say."
/æ/	(low-*front*):	the vowel of "sat."

The *back vowels* are the following:

/ʊ/	(high-*back*):	the vowel of "look."
/u/	(high-*back*):	the vowel of "boot."
/o/	(mid-*back*):	the vowel of "pork," in some dialects, or of "coat."
/ɔ/	(low-*back*):	the vowel in some pronunciations of "caught."

The symbol /ɔ/ is occasionally called "open o." Some American dialects do not contain the /ɔ/. The authors have differentiated the vowel in the word "caught," which has /ɔ/, from that in the word "cot," which contains /a/ (see below). Speakers of other dialects may pronounce the words identically and thus may have only the vowel /a/ (see below).

The *central vowels* occur in the following words:

/a/	(low-*central*):	the vowel of "psalm" or "father," or "cot" (see above).
/ə/	(mid-*central*):	the vowel of "cut" or "but."

This vowel occurs in words whose vowels may not be stressed. The vowel is also called *schwa.*

Each vowel may be placed on a chart which shows its height and position in relationship to the others. The vowel chart is an attempt to chart the position of the tongue when it is articulating the vowel sound, and it may help to think of the chart as a side-view of the mouth.

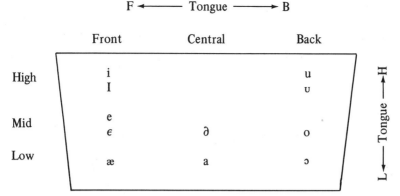

The Diphthong

Single vowels may combine with the semivowels (/w/ and /y/) to form a *diphthong*, a glide of the tongue from one vowel position or region in the mouth to another. In the dialect of the upper Midwest which we are describing we have the following diphthongs:

/oy/ (mid-back):   the vowel of "boy." Some dialects pronounce "boy" with /ɔy/, however.

/ay/ (low-central):   the vowel of "bite." Some dialects, especially in the South and Southwest, do not have this glide.

/aw/ (low-central):   the vowel of "bout."

/w/ and /y/ indicate the direction of the glide. /w/ is a back glide, with the tongue rising and moving back. /y/ is a front glide, also with the tongue rising but moving toward the front of the mouth. In some dialects of American English, speakers also glide the mid- and high-front and the high-back vowels, as in "seed," "paid," "food," and "boat." These *vowels plus glides* are often described, especially in spelling books, as *long vowels*. The long vowels, so called, are distinguished from the *short vowels* by three phonetic qualities: the vowels plus glide take longer to say; they are higher in the mouth; and the vowels end in an up-glide. Whether we record these phonological facts with a single vowel symbol or with a vowel plus glide is a matter of choice of symbol. Structuralists have preferred to record "seed" as /siyd/ while generative-transformational grammarians have preferred the single symbol: /sid/. Whichever symbol is chosen (and symbols based on all three qualities have been employed) some qualities are then regarded as redundant. The chart below shows the direction of these glides.

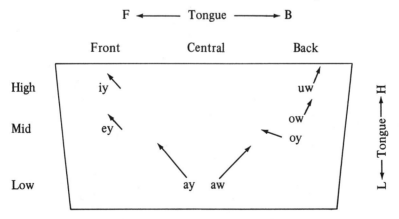

We must remember, finally, that the words and their pronunciations cited here only approximate the sounds that are heard. We have not indicated the allophones of these phonemes and their distribution. In addition, many speakers do not have all the distinctions we have indicated.

There remains one additional feature about English vowels that we should point out: in English the high back vowels are automatically pronounced with lips rounded and the front vowels are pronounced with lips flat, or in neutral position. Such may not be the case in other languages. In German and French, for instance, some front vowels are round and some unround. Whether a vowel is rounded or unrounded is not automatically determined in these languages as it is in English. In German, the umlaut sign (¨) is placed over front vowels that are rounded: *ü* is actually a high-front round vowel. In early Old English (about the 8th century), a vowel symbolized as *y* in the written documents was a round high-front vowel. While French and German have round high-front vowels, it is also possible for languages to have unrounded vowels pronounced in the back of the mouth, for example, Vietnamese *ú* and *ó*.

This brings us to the conclusion of our structural discussion of English consonants and vowels. We are ready now to rewrite the sentence in phonemic symbols which we wrote previously in phonetic symbols:

/hwɪč bʊk ər yuw kipiŋ in ðə batəm əv ðæt trəŋk/

THE UNIVERSAL PHONEME

As we have learned, the *phoneme* was, and still is, an extremely important discovery in linguistics. All languages have a set of phonemes, and all native speakers of these languages are intuitively, but not consciously, aware of the various differences in the sounds that constitute one phoneme. All languages, it was determined, have a limited number of distinctive units; the number may be different for any one language, each language having between 25 and 50. English, again depending upon the dialect analyzed, has approximately 45 phonemes.

Charles A. Ferguson, former Director of the Center for Applied Linguistics, has this to say about the phonemic principle: "The fundamental discovery of structural linguistics in the realm of speech sounds is that in any given language certain distinctions between sounds matter, and others do not, while the differences that matter for one language are not necessarily those that matter for another." He points out that the *s* sound in the word "seat" and the *s* sound in the word "salt" are not phonemic differences in English, and in fact it is difficult to persuade the speaker of English that there is any difference at all between the two pronunciations of *s*. Yet the two *s* sounds are quite different and a speaker of Arabic would note that the *s* sound of "seat" is like his Arabic *sin* س , while the *s* of English "salt" is like Arabic *sad* ص . The two *s*'s in Arabic constitute phonemic differences while the two *s*'s in English are merely phonetic differences. English speakers do not hear the differences in *s* sounds. By way of contrast, we find in Arabic the sounds of English /ɛ/ in "bet" and /ə/ in "but," but they do not matter in Arabic, that is, they do not differentiate one word from another and hence they are not phonemic. These differences in Arabic are nondistinctive, or noncontrastive, and, similarly, Arabic speakers do not actually hear the difference between /ɛ/ and /ə/.

There is much more to a description of organized speech sounds than a mere description of the type or quality of sounds. For one, there is the quantity or length of sound—the duration required to produce the sound or the length of time that the air stream is emitted. Even in English, in environments in which there is no phonemic distinction, there are very real phonetic differences in length. Vowels followed by voiced consonants are usually longer than vowels followed by voiceless ones; or to follow Samuel Morse's formulation (*Historical Outlines of English Phonology and Morphology*):

1. Unstressed vowels are always short (pean*u*t)
2. Diphthongs are always long (m*ee*t) (sh*oo*t)
3. Stressed vowels are always long or half-long
   a. Long if before a voiced sound or voiced combination (b*i*d)
   b. Half-long before voiceless sounds or voiceless combinations (b*i*t)

For one last example we can compare the duration of the vowel *o* in "rope" and "robe," or the *a* in "bat" and "bad." We find that in most American dialects the vowel followed by the voiced consonant is perceptibly longer in duration. In the I.P.A. the difference in vowels between "rope" and "robe" would be signaled as follows: [o]—[o:]. We should notice, too, that the difference between short and long vowels in English does not appear to be phonemic. Length of vowel is predictable, for example, in the words "bat" and "bad;" however, some linguists believe that length is phonemic in certain dialects of English. In these dialects, the words "Polly" and "Pali," and "bomb" and "balm" exhibit a difference in quantity of vowel: "Polly" is pronounced with a short vowel [a] and "Pali" with a long vowel [a:]; "bomb" is pronounced with a short vowel [a] and "balm" with a long vowel [a:]. In these dialects we would have a distinction between /pali/ and /pa:li/ and a distinction between /bam/ and /ba:m/.

In languages such as Czech and German, which have short and long vowels in which length is phonemic, length is marked by diacritics. Thus, in the Czech word *vidíte* ("you see") the second *i* has the accent sign to indicate its length and that it is longer than the first *i*. In Russian, however, a language related to Czech, length is not phonemic and most vowels are of "medium" length.

Consonants may be long or short, also. In effect, double consonants are long consonants. In English length of consonants is not phonemic, but in Italian and Japanese long consonants are frequent and phonemic. In Japanese, *kite* means "stamp," *kitte* (with long *t*) means "come."

We still have not said anything about the *suprasegmental phonemes*: stress, pitch, juncture, and tone, so termed because they are written over the segmentals, the consonants and vowels, and because they spread in time (except for juncture) over more than one segmental phoneme. Although we can only briefly mention them here, it is no less true that the suprasegmentals are not mere garnishes but are part and parcel of the grammar of any language. *Stress* is a difficult notion to define, but we usually mean by it *prominence of syllable*. In English, for example, heavy stress usually falls on the first syllable if the word is Germanic in origin—Swéden, Nórway, óxen—but moves, according to predictable rules, if the word is derived from Greek, Latin, French—psýcho, psychólogy, psychológical. In French, word stress is also predictable, and one of the characteristics of a French accent, as so many successful comedians have learned, is that stress placement falls on the last syllable. Stress varies greatly in languages, and in some languages it is phonemic. In Japanese, having the stress fall on the last or first syllable in the word *hana* determines whether "nose" or "flower" is said.

Another type of suprasegmental is the *pitch* or tonal accent. While all languages have pitch, in some languages it assumes a much more important status. Mandarin Chinese has four tones, as follows:

| high level | *yī* | "1" | low falling-rising | *wŭ* | "5" |
| mid, rising to high | *shŕ* | "10" | falling | *lyòu* | "6" |

Serbo-Croatian, one of the languages of Yugoslavia, has the same number of tones but its tones occur *only* on the stressed syllable of a word, and length is involved with tone. Swedish and Norwegian also make tonal distinctions associated with a stress accent. In Swedish, for instance, /bǿner/, with stress and tonal contour on the first syllable, indicates the word "peasants," while when it is pronounced with stress but with a different tonal contour, it means "beans." Mandarin Chinese has a system both of the tonal and of the stress type. Mandarin /iantzin/ with stress on the first syllable means "eye;" with stress and falling tone on the second syllable it means "glass."

Pitch is also important in English. If we say, "I am going downtown," and we hear from one of our colleagues, "Where?" with rising pitch, we know that he did not hear us the first time and wants the statement repeated. But if our colleague says, "Where?" with falling pitch, we know that he has heard but wants us to tell him which specific department store we intend to visit.

GENERATIVE-TRANSFORMATIONAL PHONOLOGY

Within the linguistic tradition that we term *structural*, we have described the consonant phonemes in terms of three criteria, and the vowel phonemes in terms of two. For the consonants, structuralists employ three features: voice, manner of articulation, and point of articulation. For the vowels, structuralists employ the criteria of tongue height and tongue depth. Within structural phonology the phoneme is regarded as an autonomous, independent unit—and these are the labels which structuralists employ to describe this concept. Contrast is employed to isolate and identify the phonemes of a language. The contrast between "fuss"/fəs/ and "fuzz"/fəz/ is the contrast between /s/ and /z/. These words, which constitute a minimal pair, are pronounced identically except for this difference or contrast of one phoneme.

Generative-transformational linguists argue that the "autonomous," independent phoneme obscures a number of general phonological facts, facts that all language speakers are intuitively, but perhaps not consciously aware of. They also argue that the concept of the phoneme advocated by the structuralists tends to obscure generalizations that can be revealed at a more abstract level of analysis. Their own research leads them away from the articulatory features that structuralists use to describe segments (consonants and vowels) to a limited set of features that can theoretically characterize any segment in the language—past, present, and future.

Specifically, generative phonologists wish to reveal and emphasize the following:

1. There are similarities among consonants and vowels. In descriptions prepared by structural grammarians, the consonants and vowels are defined with two different and unrelated sets of features. Consonants and vowels are even displayed, as we have indicated, on two separate charts. Here the structuralists tend to emphasize the *differences* in phonological representations while the generative grammarians emphasize the *similarities*. Morris Halle and Noam Chomsky in their work *The Sound Pattern of English* submit that between 15 and 25 features, a relatively small set, can be combined in ways to define the segmental phonemes of any language.

2. The distinctive features advocated by Halle and Chomsky would constitute a universal set and would account for all the possible sound types in language. Here then is an attempt to relate the sound segments of all languages—to emphasize their similarities and to describe how their sound segments interrelate. Each speaker would use these features in different ways, depending upon the language(s) that he speaks. Generative grammarians are interested, too, in defining "possible sound" for language in general.

3. Structural grammarians fail to define a natural class of sounds and how these classes relate to other classes of sounds. There are, as pointed out by generative grammarians, a number of classes of sound types in any language. We shall explore this concept below.

4. The phoneme in the view of the generative grammarian is a *systematic phoneme*; this concept is useful to explain how sound segments behave in morphemes, words and even higher units, such as phrases, clauses, and sentences. They are, in other words, interested in the dependent relationships between and among segments at more abstract levels.

All of the above attempts at explanation may, at first glance, seem rather obtuse, vague, academic, and recondite to our reader; but we wish to point out that what the generative grammarians have contributed through their new way of looking at the world of phonology is an attempt at explaining the knowledge that is available to the fluent speaker of any language. This knowledge, a great deal of which is tacit, is the linguistic knowledge that the speaker brings to bear when actually using language. A theory is basically explanatory: it forces us to look at data in a certain way, occasionally ignoring data that do not fit into the theory (the exceptions). We have good evidence that structural theorists (of autonomous phonemics) view language in one way. Their theory obscured facts and relations that later generative-transformational theorists (of systematic phonemics) would find crucial for an understanding of the principles of language. However, to be cautious for the moment, it might well be that as time goes on, generative-transformational grammar will be shown to have missed some of the insights of structural grammar, just as time has shown that structuralism obscured some of the insights of traditional neogrammarian study.

We will simplify to a degree the feature classification system employed by generative phonologists. The features that we shall incorporate into our sketch are the following:

Vocalic: no obstruction in the oral passage
Consonantal: major obstruction in the oral passage
Continuant: air is continuous in the air passage
Nasal: air is emitted from the nasal passage—the velum is lowered
Abrupt release: a feature to characterize *stops*
Lateral: the tongue is raised and air escapes from one or both sides of the tongue
Voice: the vocal chords vibrate
Tense: the vocal organs are tense; the opposite of tense is *lax*
Strident: sounds have friction or "noisiness"
Coronal: the blade of the tongue is raised and sound is articulated in the middle region of mouth. This feature includes palatal articulation but excludes velars and labials.
Anterior: sound is made in the front of the mouth, from the alveolar ridge forward; excludes palatals and velars
Front: the tongue is in front region of the mouth
High: the tongue is high in the mouth
Low: the tongue is low in the mouth
Back: the tongue is in the back region of the mouth

These 15 features will enable us to characterize groups of sound segments into classes or sets and to describe each member of a set. Before we begin to illustrate this particular system we need to advise our reader that:

1. This is not the only set of features available. Revisions in the system are constantly taking place as new languages are analyzed and new features are found.

2. Each feature is indicated by its presence (a plus sign) or its absence (a minus sign). The choice is binary: a segment is either +*vocalic* or -*vocalic*. To use an analogy, we can say that a person is either +*thin* or -*thin*. He cannot be both *thin* and *not thin*. -*thin*, however, does not mean that the person is *fat*. He could be *medium*. We could employ additional features to characterize a person as *tall* or *short*, as *adult* or *child*, and so on. This convention we will have to keep in mind as we proceed.

3. Following a distinctive feature analysis is similar to following or playing a game according to its rules, for instance, the game of duplicate bridge. In bridge we must keep track of the number of points in our own and our partner's hand, the bidding, the order in which trump is drawn, and so on. Bridge is a very complicated game. Following an explication of, or attempting to read, a distinctive feature analysis of a language is also complicated.

We will also have to follow an order in determining distinctive features. Features are listed according to their generality. A more general classification contains more segments in the set; a less general classification contains fewer segments in its set. For instance, a decision as to whether a segment is *vocalic* is made before we enquire whether a segment is *strident*. We will have more segments in the set distinguished by *vocalic* than we will have in the set distinguished by *strident*.

We are prepared now to commence with our explanation of the feature system. We will be using a new convention to illustrate the use of distinctive features; and this convention is an upside down branching-tree (also important for the explication of syntactic relationships). Each plus or minus (the presence or absence of a feature) is indicated by two branches, the *plus branch* and the *minus branch*. For a simple example, let us look to electricity: electricity may be either on (+) or off (-). It cannot be both. We can display such knowledge on a branching-tree diagram:

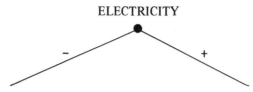

The point at which the branches separate (or are joined) may be called "point of reference" or the "node." We have indicated, in this example, the "node" with a large point.

DISTINCTIVE FEATURE ANALYSIS: ENGLISH VOWELS AND CONSONANTS

Vocalic

Beginning with the distinctive feature analysis of the segmentals of English, we first determine whether a segment is *vocalic*:

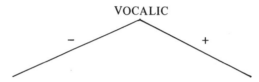

On the left side (under the left branch, the - side) we have all consonants, including *h*, *w*, and *y*; and on the right side of the tree (the + side) we have all the vowels, including *l* and *r*. We thus have two natural classes or sets: those segments which are +*vocalic* and those which are not.

Consonantal

We next determine whether a segment is *consonantal* (merely designating a segment as plus or minus *vocalic* does not determine the "true" consonants and "true" vowels, as we shall see). We now have six branches in our tree:

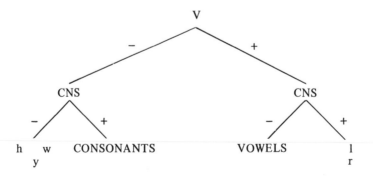

Let us look at the right side of the tree diagram first. A segment that has been initially identified as +*vocalic* may be further categorized as either + or -*consonantal*. If it is -*consonantal* we have the class of segments called vowels. If it is +*consonantal* we have the set *l* and *r*, which have, according to this classification, attributes of both vowels and consonants (*l* and *r* are commonly referred to as "liquids"). Thus, on the right side of the diagram we have characterized two sets: the vowels and the liquids. On the left side of the diagram, the class of segments that are -*vocalic* and +*consonantal* are the consonants, and the segments that are -*vocalic* and -*consonantal* are the semivowels (which includes *h*). With the use of two features, *vocalic* and *consonantal*, we have characterized four classes of segments:

Vowels	Liquids	Consonants	Semivowels
+V	+V	-V	-V
-CNS	+CNS	+CNS	-CNS

Continuant

The next feature in our list is *continuant*. This feature distinguishes the fricatives as a class from the stops, affricates, and nasals. The fricatives are all continuants, and the feature characterizes the natural class of fricatives. We also need to notice that

1. all vowels, by definition, are continuants,
2. stops, nasals, and affricates form a class separate from the fricatives, and
3. as we make finer and finer distinctions the classes of segments become smaller.

[f] would be described at this level (as would all fricatives) as:

[f]

$$\begin{bmatrix} -V \\ +CNS \\ +CT \end{bmatrix}$$

Nasal

The feature *nasal* distinguishes the class of nasals from the class that includes stops and affricates. The nasals ([m], [n], and [ŋ]) all have the features

$$\begin{bmatrix} -V \\ +CNS \\ -CT \\ +NS \end{bmatrix}$$

Let us recapitulate for the moment what our four features (*vocalic, consonantal, continuant,* and *nasal*) have defined. We have characterized a number of different but related classes of segments: we have identified the classes of nasals, stops-fricatives, liquids, and semivowels, and the large class of vowels. On a diagram the classification would yield the following:

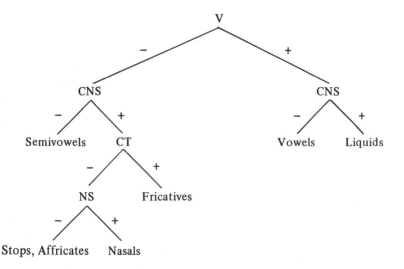

[m] (like all nasals) has the following feature classification:

[m]

$$\begin{bmatrix} -V \\ +CNS \\ -CT \\ +NS \end{bmatrix}$$

and [p] (and the rest of the stops and affricates) has the classification:

[p]

$$\begin{bmatrix} -V \\ +CNS \\ -CT \\ -NS \end{bmatrix}$$

Lateral

The feature *lateral* pertains to the set that we have identified as liquids: [l] and [r]. Both are *+vocalic* and *+consonantal*. Laterality distinguishes [l] from [r]. [l] is *+lateral* and [r] is *-lateral*. In some languages, Japanese happens to be one of them, laterality is not a distinctive feature of the sound system; the Japanese do not distinguish the sound [l] from the sound [r]. To the Japanese, the English sound [l] and [r] sound like the same sound; thus, we have the anecdotal "flied lice." The feature system has faithfully captured their relatedness, and helps to explain why some language groups find it difficult to distinguish these two sounds.

Abrupt Release
(see Julia Falk, *Linguistics and Language*)

The feature *abrupt release* serves to distinguish the affricate class [č] and [ǰ]—which are combinations of *stop* and a following *fricative*—from the class of stops [p b t d k g]. Our diagram, after the addition of the features *lateral* and *abrupt release*, has the following configuration:

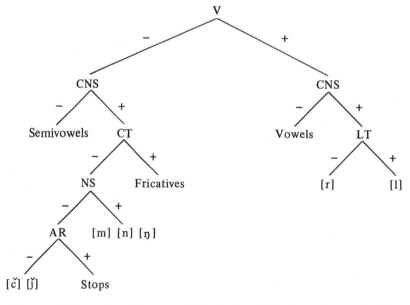

We need to remind ourselves that as we "climb down" the branches, each additional feature specifies a class of segments, but with each feature that we specify the classes become smaller. Our ultimate goal is to reach the specification for each individual segment.

Anterior

The feature *anterior* can aid us in characterizing and identifying a further class of segments. This feature is employed to distinguish consonants articulated from the alveolar region forward from those made from the alveolar region backward. With the addition of this feature our tree has the following design (we are working with the *-vocalic* side of the diagram):

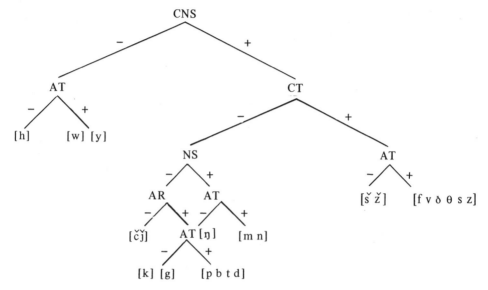

We should also notice that the feature *anterior* identifies and isolates a class of consonants that are articulated from the alveolar region forward [w y p b t d m n f v θ ð s z].

Our tree diagram begins to articulate greater degrees of abstractness as we add more and more distinctive features, and at the same time the diagram becomes more and more specific in the classification of the segments of English. As we distinguish the presence or absence of a feature we identify and characterize the notion of a class or set of segments. We have found that classes of segments may share one or more features (indeed, that is a defining characteristic). Classes "act" in the same manner in phonology. For instance, the class identified with these features

$$\begin{bmatrix} -V \\ +CNS \\ -CT \\ -NS \\ +AR \end{bmatrix}$$

may appear in similar phonological environments, say before [r], as in the following words: pray, brag, treat, drag, grey, and Kremlin. If we change one feature, the NS to a plus (+), then we change the class of segments. We do not have words with the following phonological shape: mrag, nrik, and ŋrep. We should add a reference here to the unacceptable words, "as every native speaker of English knows," for this statement is precisely what the feature system attempts to capture: the phonological knowledge of the fluent speaker of English. Every fluent speaker knows that there are no words in English in which we have an initial nasal followed immediately by [r].

Coronal

The feature *coronal* refers to the position of the tongue. The blade of the tongue is raised when articulating coronal sounds. The feature *coronal* serves to distinguish [p b] from [t d]; [w] from [y]; [m] from [n]; and [f v] from [s z θ ð]. With the addition of this feature we have the following classification (∅ indicates an empty set):

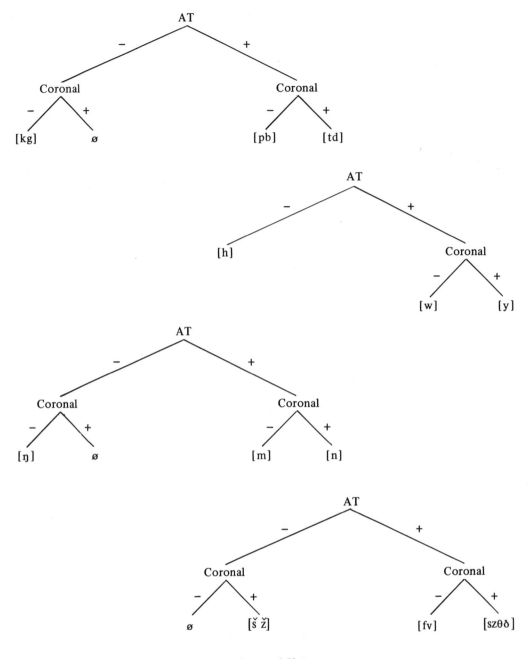

Strident and Voice

Two additional features are important for the classification of the consonants. These are the features ± (plus or minus) *strident* and the feature ± *voice*. Stridency serves to distinguish [θ] and [ð] which are *-strident* from those fricatives which are *+strident* [f v s z š ž]. The two affricates are also *+strident*.

Voicing serves to differentiate voiced consonants from those which are not: [b] from [p]; [d] from [t]; [g] from [k]; [č] from [ǰ]; [v] from [f]; [θ] from [ð]; [s] from [z]; and [š] from [ž]. With the addition of these two features, the classification of the consonants (those which we initially identified as *-vocalic*) has been completed (we have already specified those segments belonging to the nasal and semivowel subsets). Various stages of our tree diagram would indicate the following information (stops, affricates, and fricatives):

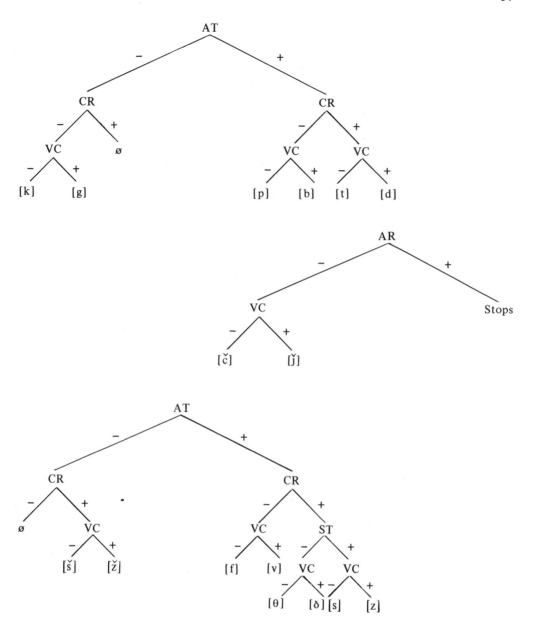

Each segment that we initially listed as *-vocalic* can now be given a unique set of features which identify and characterize only it. When we return to the various stages of our tree diagram, we find that we can "trace" the features associated with any *-vocalic* segment, say [f]. [f], beginning with the first and most general feature we identified, is

$$
\begin{bmatrix}
\text{-V} \\
\text{+CNS} \\
\text{+CT} \\
\text{+AT} \\
\text{-CR} \\
\text{-VC}
\end{bmatrix}
$$

[f] differs from [v] by one feature—*voice*; from [s] by two; and from [š] by three. (The class we identified as [f] and [v] also shares with [s z š ž č ǰ] the feature *strident.*)

Back to Vocalic

The vowels are the $\begin{bmatrix} +V \\ -CNS \end{bmatrix}$ class.

Vowels can also be specified by a set of features. We have already specified the general class of vowel and now we need to distinguish subsets within the class of vowel (as we did for the consonants). The feature *back* will distinguish those vowels which are articulated in the back region of the mouth from those which are not:

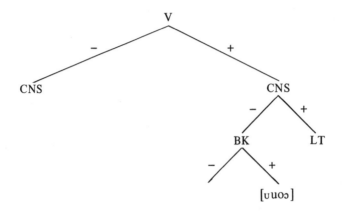

We know from the previous section on articulatory phonetics that the back vowels of English are [ʊ u o ɔ]. Vowels that are -*back* are either + or - *front:*

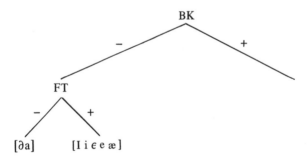

Vowels that are +*front* are [I i E e æ]. Those that are -*front* and -*back* are [ə] and [a].

With two features (*back* and *front*) we have identified three general sets of vowels: front vowels, back vowels, and those which are neither. If vowels are -*back* and -*front*, they are *central*. We do not have to employ the feature *central* since any vowel which is -*back* and -*front* is by definition *central*.

Vowels are also characterized as ±*high* and ±*low*. Vowels may be either +*high* and -*low* or -*high* and +*low*. They cannot be both +*high* and +*low*. If vowels are neither +*high* nor +*low* (that is, they are -*high* and -*low*) then they are *mid*. Our diagram, with the features of *front*, *back*, *high*, and *low* specified, will give us the following set of vowels:

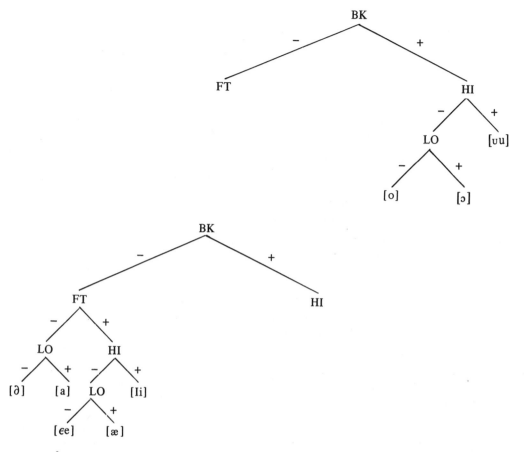

We still have not distinguished [e] from [ɛ]; [u] from [ʊ]; and [i] from [I]. The first member of each pair is designated as *+tense*; and the second number is *-tense* (or lax). Tense vowels (including [o]) are those which are glided in American English (and these may impressionistically be called "long" vowels):

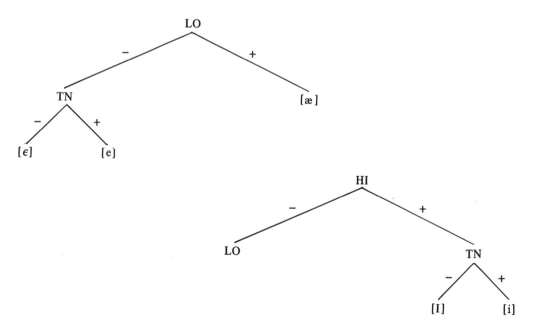

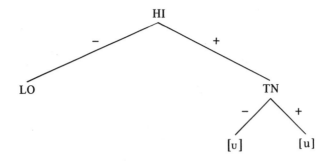

IMPLICATIONS

Now that we have taken our reader through a set of features similar to those advocated by generative phonologists, the obvious question which remains is, "What are the implications for this way of looking at language noises?"

1. One obvious implication, and one that we continue to emphasize, is that distinctive feature analysis reflects the linguistic competence of the native speaker; the native speaker is aware of and operates within the set of generalizations that generative phonologists term "distinctive features." For example, the speaker of English is aware that for the words "cat" and "dog" there is a plural: "cats," "dogs." Yet even though the native speaker is aware that the *s* denotes the plural, he may not be aware of the fact that he pronounces the written *s* differently. He pronounces the plural of "cat" as [s] and the plural of "dog" as [z]. The [s] and [z] are related; and they differ by one distinctive feature—*voice*. At this level, the word level, the [s] and [z] are related and the native speaker, even though not consciously aware of how he pronounces the plural, must intuitively be aware of this phonological rule or principle of pronunciation.

Another example of a phonological rule is seen in the past tense of a category of English verbs. The verb "walk" has a past tense which is symbolized as *-ed* in the writing system. "Walk" becomes "walked." "Appeal" has the identical *-ed* in the past tense—"appealed." However, the past tense of "walk" is pronounced as [t] while the past tense of "appeal" is pronounced [d]. The distinction of *voice*, which is important for the correct pronunciation of the plural, is also important for the correct pronunciation of the past tense. What is important, and what we wish to emphasize, is that there is a close and systematic relationship between [s] and [z] and between [t] and [d] at a higher and more abstract level of analysis—*the word*.

2. We have already indicated an implication for the teaching of foreign or second languages. The [l] and [r] distinction causes many pronunciation and hearing problems for the Japanese and other East Asians.

Speakers of Spanish tend to confuse the [b] with the [v]. The distinction in this case is between +*continuant* and -*continuant*. Spanish speakers do not "hear" the distinction between [b] and [v] because they learned to disregard the distinction between -*continuant* [b] and +*continuant* [v].

English speakers learning a foreign language often encounter the same sorts of difficulties experienced by the Japanese and the Spanish speaker. English speakers hearing *ich* (the German word for "I") will pronounce the *ch* (a velar fricative or a -*anterior*, -*coronal*, +*continuant* segment) as [k]. Here we have a -*continuant* [k] substituting for a +*continuant* in German. In sum, an account of a "foreign accent" may partially be characterized by reference to a set of distinctive features.

3. In regional and social dialects of American English we have instances of features employed differently and in different combinations. In one dialect spoken by lower socio-economic groups in the inner city (a dialect that we may call Black English) a difference in pronunciation

may be explained if we look to a distinctive feature analysis. The word "brother," which is pronounced with a -*strident* fricative (continuant) [ð] in Standard English is pronounced with a +*strident* [v] in Black English. [brəðər] is pronounced as [brəvə] (also with the deletion of final [r]).

4. There is evidence from the discipline of speech disorders (speech pathology) that a person having difficulty with pronouncing a particular class or subset of sounds has only to learn to pronounce one member of the set in order to pronounce all members of the set correctly. A person, for instance, who has difficulty in voicing [p t k] has only to learn to voice one member of the set, say [p], in order to learn to pronounce all members of the set correctly. This gives evidence that speakers are intuitively aware of general sets of sounds.

5. In the area of language acquisition (studies in psycholinguistics) we find that babies gradually refine their phonological system by adding distinctive features according to a maturational timetable. All children, it appears, acquire the distinction between *vocalic* and *consonantal* very early, which accounts, partially, for the widespread "ma" as a first utterance in many languages. Further research reveals that features are learned in an order, from most general to most specific.

This concludes our discussion of the level of language that we have called phonological. From this discussion we can see that an adequate understanding of the phonological system of even one language is a matter of enormous significance and complexity.

V. QUESTIONS AND ACTIVITIES

1. Record in writing the following phonemic notation:
   twɪŋkəltwɪŋkəllɪtəlstarhawaywɔndərwətyuarəpəbəvðəwɔrldsowhay

2. Write in phonemic notation:

   like a diamond in the sky
   twinkle, twinkle little star
   how I wonder what you are.

3. What is the phonological rule that serves to capture the difference in pronunciation in the following set of words?

loaf	loaves
house (noun)	house (verb)
tithe (noun)	tithe (verb)

4. What is the systematic relationship in the above set of words? Are there other pairs of words in English that demonstrate the existence of the same relationship?

5. "Rinso" was the name of a popular soap product a number of years ago. Why is this "made up" term a good choice for the name of a soap? Examine other names used for detergents. If you were to select a name for a new soap, would you suggest "puz?" Why or why not?

6. Imagine that you have the responsibility for selecting, from three names submitted, the name for a new candy bar. The three names are "tak," "dink," and "firch." Which one do you think is most appropriate? Perhaps you might want to propose a different name. What one would you suggest? Why?

7. Consider the following two columns of words:

deduce	deduction
ration	rational
divine	divinity
sign	signature
convene	convention
phone	phonic
nation	national

   The first column contains words with *tense* vowels. The second column contains words with *lax* vowels. After we transcribe these words, we may ask: Does each pair represent instances of different words or of related words? What is the nature of the phonological distinction between column one and column two? Is there a generalization to be drawn? Why doesn't the spelling system indicate the change in vowel quality? How regular, then, is the spelling system in the cases above?

8. Record these words in phonemics:

cat	cad
right	ride
sit	Syd
beat	bead

   What is the phonemic difference between the last consonant in column one and the last consonant in column two? Listen to the vowels of column one and those of column two. Is there a difference in length (duration) of the vowel in column two? What can account for this difference?

9. The /r/ appears to be a difficult sound for children to learn. In the phonological system of many young children the /w/ substitutes for initial /r/. Can you think of a reason for this substitution? Are /r/ and /w/ similar in articulation?

10. Consider the following list of words:

astónish	maintáin	collápse
édit	caroúse	exhaúst
consíder	appéar	eléct
imágine	cajóle	usúrp
cáncel	careén	lamént

Can we predict where stress will fall in each word? that is, is stress predictable? First record each word in phonemic notation. Then attempt to construct a rule of stress placement in these words. (In column two, each word is stressed on the last syllable: what kinds of vowels appear in the last syllable? How does the syllabic structure of column three differ from one and two?)

V. FOR FURTHER REFERENCE

Chomsky, Noam A. and Morris Halle. 1968. *The Sound Pattern of English*. New York: Harper and Row.

Falk Julia S. 1973. "Phonetic Features" and "Phonemics," in *Linguistics and Language*. Lexington, Mass.: Xerox.

Gleason, Henry A. 1955. *Workbook in Descriptive Linguistics*. New York: Holt, Rinehart and Winston.

Lehmann, Winfred P. 1971. "Articulatory Phonetics," "Acoustic Phonetics," "Autonomous Phonemics," and "Distinctive Features Analysis of Sounds," in *Descriptive Linguistics: An Introduction*. New York: Random House.

Makkai, Valerie Becker. 1972. *Phonological Theory*. New York: Holt, Rinehart and Winston.

Wang, William S-Y. 1973. "Approaches to Phonology," in Thomas A. Sebeok, ed.: *Current Trends in Linguistics: Linguistics in North America*. The Hague: Mouton.

VI. Morphology and Syntax: More Signs

ANALYZING A GRAMMAR

In the next two chapters we shall examine the structural systems termed *morphology*, *syntax*, and *semantics*. In the study of language, morphology and syntax are sometimes grouped together and studied as a system, and we shall follow that tradition. Like phonology, morphology and syntax both comprise a system or level of language, and both also fit into what linguists call a *grammar*, which we have learned is a theory of one or more languages.

MORPHOLOGY

We have previously described the abstract unit called the *phoneme*. Like the phoneme, the *morpheme* is an abstract unit, but on a higher level of abstraction; it might be said, generally, to consist of a sequence of classes of phonemes that have meaning. The *-eme* is part of both terms and refers to a classification of units. Just as the phoneme consisted of a family of similar sound types, the morpheme consists, also, of a family of units. As the phoneme is the minimal unit in the sound system, the morpheme (from *morphe*, a Greek word meaning "shape" or "form") is the minimum unit of meaning. Words, sentences, and even entire paragraphs can all be regarded as being built ultimately out of morphemes.

"Minimal" means that an utterance cannot be divided into other, smaller meaningful units. By way of contrast, phonemes do not have meaning: there is no meaning attached to any one phoneme of /kæt/. If we examine the entire sequence, however, we have a meaningful item. Moreover, we have three phonemes—/k/, /æ/, and /t/—which, placed together into this particular order, have meaning as a unit. There is a morpheme { æ t }(morphemes are denoted by braces) but this would leave the single phoneme /k/, which has no meaning. Therefore, /kæt/ is a *minimal* unit of meaning and is thus a morpheme.

Still another definition of morpheme is that it is a sequence of sounds that has *function* in a word. "Distrustfulness" has four functional parts: *dis*, *trust*, *ful*, and *ness*. All four parts of this word function in other words of the language: *dis*prove, *trust*y, beauti*ful*, and happi*ness*. We should notice, too, that these parts cannot be broken into smaller meaningful units.

All languages have morphemes, just as all languages have phonemes. Phonemes consist of a set or family of variant but phonetically similar sounds; for example, the phoneme /t/ has a set of variants called *allophones*. Morphemes also have variants and these variants are called *allomorphs*. While allophones must be phonetically similar, allomorphs must be similar in meaning. For instance, the most widely used form of the plural in English has three variants. (We have already discussed two of these variants in the chapter on phonology.) If we say that the plural is denoted by the symbol { s }, then we can establish that the plural has three alternate pronunciations: /s/, /əz/, and /z/. The pronunciation /əz/ occurs if the noun ends in any one of these consonants /č ǰ s z š ž/. Two are affricates /č ǰ/ and four are fricatives /s z š ž/. The following nouns illustrate the pronunciation of the /əz/ allomorph of the plural morpheme:

64

the horse	the horses
the buzz	the buzzes
the brush	the brushes
the garage	the garages

(some may pronounce "garage" with /ž/ and some with /ǰ/. In any case, however, the word is pronounced according to the rule)

the catch	the catches
the judge	the judges

The pronunciation of the plural as /s/ occurs after nouns ending in voiceless consonants, other than the voiceless consonants listed above. We notice that voicing is important since the voiceless alternate (allomorph) of the plural occurs after nouns whose last consonant is voiceless, as in the following set of nouns:

the cat	the cats
the book	the books
the desk	the desks
the mat	the mats
the chunk	the chunks

The /z/ allomorph of the plural occurs after nouns whose last phoneme is voiced—either consonants other than fricatives and affricates or vowels. We have the following set of words with this variant:

the dog	the dogs
the pencil	the pencils
the table	the tables
the chair	the chairs
the pen	the pens
the play	the plays

The /s/, /z/, and /əz/ are allomorphs of the plural morpheme that we can symbolize as { s }. Native speakers, we must assume, are aware only of the abstraction that we call plural and not of the various ways to pronounce the plural morpheme. Occasionally speakers will even deny that they pronounce the plural differently. Children, however, will learn these rules of pronunciation and will attempt to force exceptions into the "regular" rules of pronunciation. Children can be heard to pronounce the plural of "ox" as "oxes," the plural of "child" as "childs," and the plural of "foot" as "foots," until told differently.

Morphological analysis is not without its complications, however. Let us consider the following set of English words:

rejection	reversion	reception
conjecture	conversion	conception
injection	inversion	inception

We may not feel that the forms *ject, vers,* and *cept,* or *re, con,* and *in* share in each case a visible meaning-similarity to go with the similarity in sound. Indeed, we do have identical sounds in language which have completely different meanings. Words that have the same spelling and sound, such as "bear," but that have different meanings are termed homonyms: "She could not bear the pain," and "She killed the bear." Some morphemes are spelled differently but sound identical in speech: "She killed the bear with her bare hands." Punsters have always made use of this characteristic of English. The technical term that we employ to describe words or morphemes that sound the same is *homophonous morpheme* (or, less accurately, *homophonous word*): *homo* means "the same" and *phonous* means "sound."

From an analysis of the Latinate morphemes, we can see that it is often difficult to categorize morphemes. In the above set of words derived from Latin, we might have difficulty in assigning a meaning to the various morphemes that occur in the words. Even so, we can and do create new words from Latin morphemes. The anthropological terms "uxorilocal" and "virilocal," employed to distinguish whether a newly married couple establishes housekeeping in the wife's former place of residence or in the husband's, are "made up" or created by the anthropologist to describe these two situations.

A word may consist of one or more *morphemes*—which is one definition for *word*. Some morphemes, notably *prefixes* and *suffixes*, must be attached to other morphemes—they cannot stand alone—while other morphemes may stand alone. If a morpheme cannot stand alone, it is called *bound*, and if it can stand alone, it is called *free*. All prefixes and suffixes in English are *bound morphemes*. The morphemes in { k æ ts } consist of the bound plural morpheme { s } and the morpheme { kæt }, which is a *free base*. A *base* is a unit to which other morphemes may be added. Not all base morphemes are free, however; some are bound, as in our Latin examples: *ject*, *vers*, and *cept*. These Latin bases are bound and must therefore have other morphemes attached to them before they can be said.

In English there are both bound and free bases, as we have described. All prefixes and suffixes are bound. Linguists also subcategorize suffixes and prefixes into *inflectional* and *derivational*. While all prefixes in English are derivational, suffixes may be either inflectional or derivational. There is a distinction between derivation and inflection: *inflectional suffixes* do not change the basic meaning of the word or its grammatical class, while *derivational morphemes* may involve a change in meaning and/or grammatical class.

An example of a derivational suffix is *ment*. *Ment* is derivational, since it changes a word from one grammatical class to another, in this case from verb to noun. "Govern," a verb ("The president's job is to govern the nation"), becomes a noun when *ment* is added: "government." There is a rather rich set of derivational prefixes and suffixes that have come to English from Latin, French, and Greek. In the word "distrustfulness" we had four functioning parts. Now we are able to analyze this word using our morphological criteria. "Distrustfulness" contains the free base *trust*, the prefix *dis*, and the suffixes *ful* and *ness*. We notice, too, that the prefix and suffixes are derivational: "trust" with the addition of *dis* becomes "distrust" (still a verb but the meaning has changed); "distrust" becomes "distrustful," an adjective, as in the phrase, "The distrustful man"; "distrustful" becomes "distrustfulness," a noun, as in "He hated the man's distrustfulness."

In contrast to the derivational suffix { ment }, the plural morpheme { s } is inflectional. If we add the plural to "cat" the basic meaning of the word remains unchanged and "cat" also remains a noun. We will employ the set of inflectional suffixes in English to define some of the parts of speech. The inflections in English are the following:

1. *Plural* (attaches to most nouns): We have already isolated the allomorph of the regular plural morpheme.

2. *Possessive*: The possessive is attached to a noun and has the following characteristics:
   Sarah's coat (an apostrophe plus *s*)
   The boys' coats (here, an *s* plus apostrophe to denote that there is more than one boy)

3. *Third-person singular*: The third-person singular is the morpheme which is attached to the verb.

	Singular	*Plural*
First	I play the game	We play the game
Second	You play the game	You play the game
Third	He/she/it plays the game	They play the game

The only change to the verb "play" is the third-person singular ("He/she/it plays the game"), to which the third-person singular morpheme { s } is added.

4. *Past Tense*: The past tense morpheme can be symbolized as { -ed }, and is attached to most verbs. Although more verbs add { -ed } to indicate past time—"He played ball"—there remains a set of verbs that indicate past tense by changing the vowel of the base—"He drove downtown yesterday"; "He sang in the choir two years ago."

5. *Present Participle*: The present participle is signaled by the *-ing* which is attached to a verb: "She is playing ball."

6. *Past Participle*: The past participle (-ed or -en) also attaches to the verb: "He had driven to Dallas before" or "He has walked to school before."

7. *Comparative and Superlative*: The comparative and superlative attach to adjectives: "hard," "harder," and "hardest."

We could be accused, quite rightly, of putting the cart before the horse by saying certain inflections attach themselves to certain parts of speech, before we define *part of speech*. Before going on, let us now examine the parts of speech in English.

PARTS OF SPEECH

Unlike traditional grammarians, who relied upon notional and relational criteria to define the parts of speech, linguists have categorized and defined parts of speech both through the use of inflectional morphemes and through positions that inflectional parts of speech occupy in sentences.

The inflections which we will employ to define a set of speech parts are the following:

1. plural { s }
2. possessive { *'s* } or { *s'* }
3. third-person singular { s }
4. past tense { *-ed* } or change of vowel
5. present participle { *-ing* }
6. past participle { *-ed* } or { *-en* }
7. comparative { *-er* } and superlative { *-est* }

NOUN: any word which can take a plural and/or possessive morpheme. Both the plural and the possessive are inflectional morphemes. "Cat" is a noun by this definition.

VERB: a word which takes the inflectional morpheme third-person singular and which fits into the following pattern:

Base
1. walk
2. sing

Third-person singular
1. (He) walks
2. (She) sings

Past tense
1. (He) walked
2. (She) sang

Present participle
1. (He is) walking
2. (She is) singing

Past participle
1. (He has) walk*ed*
2. (She has) su*ng*

Verbs which follow pattern 1 (most verbs do) have historically been called *weak* or *regular*, and verbs which follow pattern 2 have been called *strong* or *irregular*.

ADJECTIVE: a word which takes the inflection *-er* and *-est*, as in the words "pretty," "prettier," "prettiest." "Pretty" is categorized then as an adjective.

PRONOUN: may be partially defined as any word which fits into the following pattern:

Nominative (subject)
I (I like ice cream)

Accusative (object)
me (She loves me)

Possessive
a. my (book)
b. mine (That book is mine)

ADVERBS: cannot be categorized morphologically. Though it was possible to read in some traditional grammars that adverbs take *-ly*, this was not sufficient to categorize adverbs such as "fast." In the sentence "Don't drive fast," the adverb does not take *-ly*. And in the phrase "the lonely man," "lone" takes *-ly* but is not an adverb. "Lonely" in this phrase is an adjective (lonely, lonelier, loneliest).

For the categories of *preposition* (in, on, to, by, . . .), *conjunction* (and, but, or, . . .), *article* (the, a), and *interjection* (oh, well, hey, . . .), we find no morphological criteria, and in order to define these classes we must list the members of the entire class. Morphological identification has other difficulties as well. When we attempt to determine the status of words such as "hit" (is "hit" a noun or verb?), and the status of words such as "beautiful" (which is intuitively an adjective but which cannot be inflected with the *-er* and *-est*) and compare them with words such as "poor" (morphologically an adjective) which may appear in positions in sentences which are "normally" noun positions (for instance, "The *poor* are always at a disadvantage"), we see that "poor," an adjective, functions as a noun in this sentence and not as an adjective. We must use an additional criterion to categorize this word in terms of a part of speech. Inflectional criteria are just not sufficient.

Linguists (following Charles C. Fries and his colleagues) posited a set of position slots wherein the various parts of speech (those morphologically defined) may occur. One of the more innovative contributions of Professor Fries has been to point out that languages operate with grammatical *indicators*, as he called them, and these indicators are useful in determining the positions in which inflectional parts of speech occur. Linguists have pointed to the various indicators of English sentences as seen in the following sentence: "The vencular lobemities may have been molently perfluced."

Here, in spite of the nonsensical nature of some of the words, there is every indication that "vencular" is an *adjective*, "lobemities" a *noun* in the plural, "molently" an *adverb* derived from an *adjective* (molent), and "perfluced" the past participle of a *verb*; "vencular," "molently," "lobemities," and "perfluced" could all very well be technical terms in English. What, in part, provides the sentence with its plausibility are its morphological signals. The suffixes *-s*, *-ly*, and *-ed* are a few of the strongest; there are also *-ar* and *-ent*, which are common suffixes of *adjectives*, the suffix *-ity* which is attached to the *noun*, and the familiar *verb* prefix *per*. Also, familiar words like "the" and "may have been" are as important for their signals as for the information which they provide to the reader about the class of words in the sentence.

For instance, we notice the clear meaning of the word "ship" in the sentence, "The ship sails today," whereas the sentence without "the" would be ambiguous: "Ship sails today."

The label "function word" has been given to a fairly small closed set of words that serve as grammatical *indicators*; this list includes *prepositions, conjunctions, articles, pronouns,* and *auxiliary* (helping) *verbs*. These sets are closed, since it seems extremely unlikely that they will ever add new members. The open sets include *nouns, adjectives (adverbs),* and *verbs*. New words are constantly being added to these classes every day.

Word order serves to mark function in the above nonsense sentence. The position of *vencular* before *lobemities,* a noun, leads to the assumption that *vencular* is an adjective. Lewis Carroll's Looking-Glass poem "Jabberwocky" begins with such a skeleton of indicators accompanied by unfamiliar words where we would anticipate the nouns, verbs and adjectives (adverbs) would occur:

> 'Twas _____ and the _____y _____s
> Did _____ and _____ in the _____
> All _____y were the _____ s,
> And the _____ _____s out_____.

The mood of the full poem is captured beautifully in Alice's reaction: "Somehow it seems to fill my head with ideas—only I don't exactly know what they are!"

Linguists have used the grammatical indicators to posit test frames to determine the part of speech status for any word. We will not list here all the frames available (for a more complete set see James Sledd's book, *A Short Introduction to English Grammar*); one test frame for the noun will be sufficient to give an illustration of this method:

> The _____ seemed good.
> _____ seemed good.

Any form which fits into one or both of the above frames will be a noun. We can say *the beer seemed good* and *Dallas seemed good*; *beer* and *Dallas* would then be nouns. We can also say that *the poor seemed good. Poor,* a morphological adjective, functions as a noun if it occurs in this position.

The three grammatical characteristics we have mentioned—prefixes and suffixes, function words, and word order—are fairly universal in language. The extent to which they are employed and/or important for particular languages is, of course, subject to variation. Latin, for instance, relies more heavily on inflectional suffixes than English, while in Vietnamese, inflection and derivation do not play a role. Each language has its own patterns for creating words, word groups, clauses, sentences, and connected units of discourse.

IMMEDIATE CONSTITUENT ANALYSIS

It should be apparent now that morphemes combine to make larger units of discourse. In order to examine the structure of words and sentences, including clauses and phrases, linguists employ a method they have labeled *Immediate Constituent analysis*. Expressed simply, IC analysis employs a scheme whereby chunks of language are examined to determine structural relationship. For one example, let us examine *ungentlemanly. Ungentlemanly* consists of the constituents, *un* (a derivational prefix) and *gentlemanly. Gentlemanly* may be divided into *gentleman* and *ly* (a derivational suffix), *gentleman* into *gentle* and *man. Gentle* and *man* are parts of the word that may not be further divided.

The manner in which we have provided an IC analysis of *ungentlemanly* depends, in this and other examples, upon our feeling for word structure. When approaching a language not previously studied, very little about structure may be apparent at first glance. The linguist would be forced to examine, to compare and to contrast, lists of words, or sets of sentences. If, for instance, English happened to be unfamiliar, then to determine the constituents or parts of *ungentlemanly* he would have to encounter words like *unfair* and *unknown,* words which would serve as models for *ungentlemanly*, and words, too, which have no readily conceivable analysis except into *un* and a base.

Immediate Constituent analysis is pursued, as we have indicated, to the point at which there are no more divisible chunks. At this point we have reached the *ultimate* morphemes, the *ultimate* constituents. Just where this point lies is not always an easy question. Leonard Bloomfield once felt that both *fl-* as found in *flash, flicker, flare, flame*, and *gl-* as found in *gleam, glimmer, glitter, glow, glint* represented morphemes. Some linguists feel, however, that they are no longer dealing with recombinable units, and it is difficult to determine whether the pieces remaining, like *eam, immer, itter, ow, int* are morphemes. Instead they have named *fl* and *gl phonesthemes*—sound groups that convey a certain impression about the words of which they are a part. The theory that purports to deal with such word phenomena is not highly developed, but obviously such phenomena will have to be accounted for in any analysis of the English language.

Sentences can also be analyzed using the principle of IC analysis. The sentence, *the old man hit the muddy ball*, can first be segmented into *the old man/hit the muddy ball*; *hit the muddy ball* into *hit/the muddy ball*; *the old man* into *the/old man*; *old man* into *old/man*; *the muddy ball* into *the/muddy ball*; *muddy ball* into *muddy/ball*. The relationship of these constituents, as they are called, can be portrayed using the following Immediate Constituent diagram:

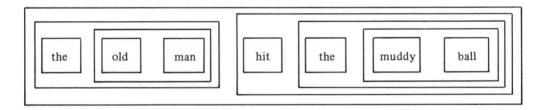

In linguistics, such diagrams are also called "Chinese boxes." One box fits inside another, which fits inside another, and so on. If we look within the diagram, we can see displayed a number of relationships. For example each word has a box around it.

These words, then, are the ultimate constituents of the sentence. Linguists posit that *old* and *man* are more immediately related than *the* is to *old*; hence, they would show this relationship with a box surrounding *old* and *man*.

The words of the phrase *the old man* are more immediately related than they are to the constituents of the rest of the sentence. Therefore, another box would be placed around the words, signifying this relationship.

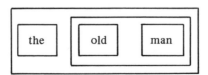

Several relationships are clearly indicated in this diagram: the generalization that *old man* is more immediately related than is the constituent *the* to *old* or *the* to *man*, and that the phrase *the old man* is a unit (constituent) as is *hit the muddy ball*. More relationships can be perceived if we examine the right side of the diagram; however, we will leave further analysis to our reader.

To talk about relationships and order of words within a sentence, as we have been doing, is to talk about *syntax*. And it is in the area of syntax that the linguistic revolution described by Cattell had its initial impact, and perhaps its greatest contribution.

A NEW APPROACH TO SYNTAX

Linguistics is, and continues to be, the study of language. Any approach to a description of language is based upon a set of axioms and postulates, and the more popular school of linguistic thought in the United States during the first half of the present century employed a set of axioms and postulates that were later to be called structural. In 1957, with the publication of *Syntactic Structures* by Noam Chomsky, the linguistic world dramatically changed. A new set of axioms and postulates was presented. No one, least of all linguists, could foresee at that time the wide impact of the theory that Chomsky called generative-transformational and its effect not only on linguistics but on the closely allied disciplines of philosophy, psychology, and sociology.

Syntactic Structures, a formal and technical brief of generative-transformational theory, marshalled a number of criticisms that were leveled at the more entrenched school of linguistics. Although we are, in this text, not concerned with settling or even pursuing these theoretical issues, we do hope to present a reasonably cogent explanation of the general characteristics of generative-transformational theory and to consider in broad outline a few of its major tenets.

If we look upon the history of theoretical thought in linguistics as a continuum, it is not surprising to see therein a struggle between established theory, the conservatives, and the revolutionaries, the radicals. Just as structural theory contained criticisms of traditional grammar, so too we might expect generative-transformational theory to contain criticisms of the older, more established school of linguistic inquiry. And just as structural theory purported to present a more insightful theory of language than that presented in traditional grammar, so too does generative-transformational theory purport to offer a more insightful grammar than structural. A viable science, we must always remind ourselves, never stands still. Like language itself it is always changing.

Since 1957, almost a generation has passed, and generative-transformational theory has undergone such major modification that today there is no one general generative-transformational theory that we can point to as the accurate representative of this school. On the contrary, there are many generative-transformational theories. One is even called "standard" theory, a revision advocated by Professor Chomsky himself in his book *Aspects of the Theory of Syntax* (1965). There are also an "extended standard" theory, and "interpretive" theory, a "generative semantic" theory, and case grammar, a revision. We shall examine case grammar in the following chapter. And we have not exhausted the possibilities. All generative-transformational theories, however, have evolved to a certain extent from the theory explicated in *Syntactic Structures*.

The theory, or theories, associated with generative-transformational grammars continues to be the most influential, not to mention the most controversial, on the linguistic scene today; and whether Chomsky is ultimately more right or wrong, "no linguist," John Lyons sagely points out, "who wishes to keep abreast of current developments in his subject can afford to ignore Chomsky's theoretical pronouncements. Every other 'school' of linguistics at the present time tends to define its position in relation to Chomsky's views on particular issues."

Structural linguistics was criticized on several counts. As a point of departure, let us examine Charles C. Fries' definition of grammar, which, as we shall see, conflicted with Chomsky's. "The grammar of a language," Fries argued, "consists of the devices that signal structural meaning." Robert B. Lees, Chomsky's student, explored this definition of grammar in his article, "Transformational Grammar and the Fries Network." He maintained that the "main contribution of . . . structuralism to our understanding of language has been its replacement of vague notional definitions of parts of speech by very precise so-called 'formal' definitions of word classes. While in certain respects," he continued, "a so-called structural grammar is very precise, it is so just by virtue of the fact that it attempts to accomplish so little of interest."

We can imagine that the above criticism, and others similar to it, created deeply felt animosity within the discipline of linguistics. Yet "turn about is fair play": traditional grammarians were the recipients of some harsh criticism from the structuralists. Chomsky, however, was more charitable in his assessment of the linguistics of the first half of this century. "The major achievement of structural linguistics," Chomsky maintains ("The Current Scene in Linguistics: Present Directions"), "is to have provided a factual and methodological basis that makes it possible to return to the problems that occupied the traditional universal grammarians with some hope of extending and deepening their theory of language structure and language use. Modern descriptive linguistics has enormously enriched the range of factual material available, and has provided entirely new standards of clarity and objectivity. Given this advance in precision and objectivity, it becomes possible to return, with new hope for success, to the problem of constructing the theory of a particular language—its grammar—and to the still more ambitious study of the general theory of language."

The goal of language study has usually been directed toward the preparation of a description of a language. More than a description is needed, Chomsky argues, and a study should not only list and describe the language data of a particular language, but it should reveal what its speakers *know* about the language. (We will discuss this kind of "knowledge" below.) Linguistic study should also be concerned with what Descartes, a 17th century philosopher, termed the *faculté de langage*: the ability, believed by Descartes to reflect the innate properties of mind, of the human being to learn language. Linguistic study should begin where Descartes left off, according to Chomsky, with studying these supposedly innate principles of linguistic behavior. Not only could this kind of language study reveal the properties of a single language, but it could also reveal the properties common to all languages. Languages sound different, and some may be more difficult than others for us to learn. Yet, Chomsky argues, we should not be misled: languages are more alike than they are different. What else would account for the fact that children have little difficulty in learning the language or languages of their environment? This 17th-century notion of language has guided the research of modern-day generative-transformational linguists.

We shall not be discussing the complete theory of language associated with generative-transformational linguists. It would be impossible for us to do so in one section of one chapter of a book. In keeping with the major thrust of our text, we shall explore a few of the major tenets of generative-transformational theory, leaving to our reader, if he chooses, to explore further the axioms and postulates of this major school of linguistic science. We have listed in the bibliography a few appropriate texts with which this study can continue.

We will discuss a few of the tenets of generative theory under two headings—Creativity and Linguistic Engineering.

CREATIVITY

In our first chapter we pointed to the linguistic fact that a speaker of a language has knowledge of an unbounded set of sentences of that language. "Knowledge" is the important word here. In Fries' view, a grammar of a language "consists of the devices that signal structural meaning." In contrast, generative-transformational grammarians argue that since a language consists of an infinite set of sentences, a grammar should go beyond the describing of the "devices that signal structural meaning" and should describe the knowledge of language that every native speaker has.

The notion of "novel" is given much emphasis in generative-transformational grammar. Since, generative-transformational grammarians maintain, a language consists of an unbounded set of sentences, most of these sentences that we hear or that we ourselves speak must be new. When we actively use language, we are therefore creating new sentences, and this ability to create new utterances is unique to the human race. Chomsky and others maintain that language is a species-specific attribute. The implications of this view of language have been influential in education and are particularly important for speech pathologists, psychologists, and language teachers.

Generative grammarians speak about "knowledge of language" in a particular sense, and employ terms that characterize what a native speaker knows about his language, his linguistic *competence*, and what a native speaker actually does when he speaks his language, his linguistic *performance*. Linguistic competence is often equated with subconscious or even tacit knowledge. Linguistic performance characterizes the activities of the speaker while actually using the language: his style, the mistakes that he makes, the hesitation phenomena like "uh," and so on.

Native speakers have a number of capabilities that are illustrative of this kind of language knowledge. Among these are the following; we shall speak of these as "feelings" or "intuitions."

1. A feeling that some sounds or arrays of sounds belong to the English language while others do not. "Nadack" is a possible English word while "Ndcak" is not.

2. A feeling that some words go together while others do not; we can say, for instance, "The dog looks terrifying," but we cannot so easily say, "The dog looks barking."

3. A feeling for the word classes of his language—the parts of speech. This sentence is possible: "He saw a picture of Redford," while this one is not: "He saw a difficult of." Native speakers, especially children, may have difficulty in labeling the parts of speech when called upon to do so. Yet they must know the parts of speech or they will have difficulty speaking their language, putting the words in their proper positions. The inability to label is perhaps more an indictment of the exercise, and the practice of the educational system to promote such an exercise, than it is of the child himself.

4. A feeling that certain sentences are structurally related to others while others are not related. The sentence, "The hot dog was eaten by the boy," is not structurally related to the sentence, "The hot dog was eaten by the river." In the first sentence, "the boy" is the "doer," or agent, while in the second the agent has been deleted: *someone* ate the hot dog by the river. And if we examine the following sentences we see that they appear superficially to be different, but that they really are expressing similar content:

John broke the window.
The window was broken by John.
It was the window that John broke.
What John broke was the window.
What John did to the window was to break it.
The window, John broke it.
John broke it, the window.
This is the window John broke.
This is the window (which was) broken by John.
John's breaking of the window (caused a stir on campus).
The breaking of the window by John (signaled an end to the violence).
For John to break the window (was a mistake).
(It was said) that John broke the window.

5. A feeling for structural differences. Some sentences may appear to have identical structure but when examined more closely they are found to have distinct structures. The two sentences, now classics, that generative grammarians use to illustrate this intuition are the following:

(1) John is easy to please.
(2) John is eager to please.

These sentences appear to have similar structures, to portray similar relationships, and to receive identical immediate constituent analysis. Yet the sentences are different, more different than the two words, "eager" and "easy," would lead us to believe. Even though "John" appears first in each sentence, its roles or functions in the sentences differ. In sentence (1), "John" is the one being pleased (John is easy for someone to please), while in sentence (2) "John" is doing the pleasing (John is eager to please someone).

We have other evidence that these sentences differ structurally. For (1), we can say, "It is easy to please John" and "To please John is easy." Both of these sentences share or have the same meaning as sentence (1). We have no comparable sentences for (2): we cannot say, "It is eager to please John," or "To please John is eager," and retain the same meaning.

6. A feeling that some sentences have more than one meaning. The sentences

(1) Visiting relatives bored me.
(2) The shooting of the hunters surprised no one.

are ambiguous. "Visting relatives," the source of ambiguity in sentence (1), could mean, to paraphrase, "Relatives who visit are boring," or "To visit relatives bores me."

That native speakers have these intuitions is *prima facie* evidence to generative grammarians that language is characterized by "rule-governed behavior." "Rule-governed behavior" is an abstract characterization of the speaker's linguistic competence. Even though a language is an unlimited number of sentences, an infinite set, a native speaker neither (a) memorizes all the sentences that he will ever say in his lifetime, nor (b) hears all the sentences that will be said in his lifetime. Life, obviously, is far too limited for those tasks. *What he does is assimilate a number of rules or principles that will give him access to the set of sentences that he will encounter in his lifetime.*

We were taught and learned rules or principles, other than those of language, in school. In our arithmetic lessons we were instructed in the rules of addition, subtraction, division, and multiplication. And these rules of arithmetic were replaced by more abstract, general rules as we became more adept at mathematics. The rules or principles of algebra are far more complex, abstract, and general than the rules of simple addition.

What is important in our rule learning is that we did not have to memorize all the answers to the arithmetic problems that we encountered or would encounter in our lifetimes. We learned a limited set of rules that would enable us to arrive at an unlimited number of solutions.

If we take the rules of multiplication as examples, we can see that as children we learned a system which would give us all possible products—not just a few, or even one million, but all. We had "knowledge" of an infinite set, an unbounded number of possible products. The rules that we learned were finite and limited in number. We learned the products of multiples from 1 to 9, including 0, but we did not have to learn the products of numbers like 18 times 27, or 43502.34 times 76023.978. If we followed the rules, we could obtain the correct answers.

A similar kind of rule learning is characteristic of language, although there is one crucial and very important difference. We have to be taught arithmetic; we do not have to be taught how to speak our first language. Even for a language-related activity, reading, a great majority of us were formally instructed in its rules. A child, though, in learning his language, assimilates a finite set of rules which guides him in the use of his native language and enables him to understand and speak novel sentences. As we "know" an infinite set of products, we also "know" an infinite set of sentences.

The skills associated with arithmetic provide us with still another analogy that we can associate with "rule-governed behavior." In simple arithmetic we have a hierarchy of skills. We must be able to do one task before we learn another. That is, we must be able to add before we learn to multiply. We cannot be taught how to multiply before we know how to add. The same ordered-task relationship also holds for the skill of division. We must know how to add, subtract, and multiply before we can be instructed in division. One set of principles must be learned first, followed by another set, which is followed by still another. A similar kind of hierarchical relationship occurs in generative-transformational grammar. While the rules are limited in number, like the rules of multiplication, they are carefully ordered. We will explore this relationship in the next section, entitled "Linguistic Engineering."

LINGUISTIC ENGINEERING

There are a number of excellent introductory texts to generative-transformational grammar which instruct the student to write increasingly more complex and general rules of the language or languages which he is studying and analyzing. The bibliography following this chapter lists a number of these texts designed for the student of linguistics. Here, we are limited in our approach, and we list some of the attributes of one kind of generative-transformational grammar in order to provide our reader with an understanding of the form such a grammar might take in texts or articles on the subject. We will be working in this section with a set of rules and a new set of terminology, since every school of linguistics has its own technical language—a language to talk about language. Just as the principles of multiplication are a grammar of multiplication, the rules that we will specify in our short grammar of the syntax of English are a characteristic part of one kind of generative-transformational grammar of English.

Three features peculiar to a generative-transformational grammar are the following:

1. There is a limited number of rules or principles which serve to reflect the language competence or knowledge of a native speaker. Rules must be limited, as we have said, since the brain is finite and is incapable of acquiring an infinite set.

2. These rules are arranged in an order: rule 1 must precede rule 2, which must precede rule 3, and so on. Some rules are not ordered, but these will not concern us here.

3. The rules can be equated with instructions:
   Sentence → Sentence Indicator + Noun Phrase + Auxiliary + Verb Phrase
   This can be abbreviated to: S → SI + NP + Aux + VP

The arrow is a symbol for the instruction "rewrite." This rule instructs us to "rewrite" Sentence as Sentence Indicator *plus* Noun Phrase *plus* Auxiliary *plus* Verb Phrase. A GT grammar consists of a limited number of these rules, with one important addition: the property of "recursiveness" or "repeatability" (which we will discuss below). These rules will specify the sentences of English. (Of course, no complete grammar has ever been written, and all grammars are imperfect.)

Properties of GT Grammar

In this section, we shall be employing the following terminology to describe generative-transformational grammar, which may, perhaps, be new to our reader:

1. *Generate.* The term *generate* is often confusing in discussions of generative-transformational grammar. Its precise meaning is often not even clear among theoretical linguists of this school of linguistics. A GT grammar, it is often put, is designed to generate all and nothing but the sentences of a language, and for each sentence it generates it will provide a structural description ("structural", in this sense, means an explicit description). Similarly, a good zoology will generate all and nothing but animals—even the giraffe, as Robert Lees once said.

Speakers produce sentences; GT grammars generate them. Thus a synonym for *generate* is "specify" or "enumerate."

2. *Phrase Structure Rules* (PSR) and *Transformational Rules* (TR); *surface and deep structure.* Phrase structure rules specify (generate) the deep or abstract structure of a sentence. Or conversely, a deep structure is generated by PSR's. PSR's generate the underlying structure of the sentence (containing the meaning of the sentence), which provides the input structure for various transformations, which, when applied, yield less abstract structures. Ultimately, after transformations have been applied, the surface structure of the sentence (what we actually see, hear, or speak) is reached. For instance, the two sentences, "John is easy to please" and "John is eager to please" have identical surface structures but different deep structures (John is, after all, doing something in one sentence and in the other having something done to him).

We have mentioned that speakers have certain linguistic sensitivities, and one of these is a sensitivity that allows them to discern ambiguities. Ambiguous sentences, we can now say, are sentences that have two (or more) surface meanings; and since they are ambiguous they must have two (or more) deep structures, with each deep structure characterizing one of the meanings. The sentence, "She loves exciting men," must have two deep structures. In the language of the linguist, the surface structure is derived from two deep structures.

It is important that a grammar have a deep structure component since surface structures tend to obscure relationships that can only be perceived by positing a set of PSR's that generate deep, abstract structures, for example, the "eager" and "easy" sentences. All of this terminology is "heady" material to digest at one sitting; but if our reader is still with us, let's proceed.

3. *Recursion* or *repeatability* (the property that allows a set of finite rules to be used over, and over, and over, and over ... again). Since GT grammars consist of a finite set of rules, there must be a way to apply these rules more than once; otherwise there would be no way that a grammar could reflect the ability of a native speaker to understand and speak, theoretically, an infinite number of new sentences. The property that is added is one of recursion.

Generative grammarians often employ alphabetic symbols to explain principles of grammar; and we shall follow that tradition briefly. Suppose we wish to add to our grammar the property of recursiveness. We need that property to generate an infinite set of results from our finite set of rules. And suppose we have one rule in our alphabetic grammar that reads:

$$X \rightarrow A + B$$

This rule instructs us to rewrite X as $A + B$ (wherever we find X we replace it with $A + B$). We can portray the result of this instruction on a tree-diagram:

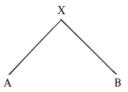

$A + B$ is the result of following the rule that says rewrite X as $A + B$. The rule can only give one $A + B$, however. There is no set of instructions to get us back to X. In other words, there is no language that says, "Go back and go through the rule as many times as you want." In generative grammars we must have explicit rules: we do not do anything unless there is a rule. In order for a grammar to yield an infinite number of outputs we need to add the property of recursiveness, which will allow us to use the rule as many times as we want. We can add recursiveness to our grammar by placing *X*, which is on the left side of the arrow, on the right side of the arrow as well. Our revised rule now reads:

$$X \rightarrow A + B + (X)$$

On a tree diagram we could have this result:

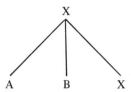

The addition of the *X* to the right side of the arrow enables us to employ the rule again, and again, to yield an infinite number of *A + B's*. Having the identical symbol to the left and to the right of the arrow provides us with the option (denoted by the parentheses) of going back to the rule and rewriting *X* as many times as we want. Our use of the rule three times would give us the following diagram:

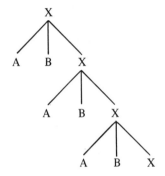

For every *X* that we choose to the right, we are able to employ the rule again. We can specify in this way in infinite number of *A + B's* (*AB, ABAB, ABABAB, ABABABAB*, and so on).

Our explanation above may seem to our reader a difficult and arduous, and perhaps unnecessary, trip around Dobbins's barn; but we wish to point out, and argue at the same time, that language works in the same way. We need the kind of rule described above to reflect an important characteristic of language and to explain the language competence of the native speaker—namely, his ability to create a large number of sentences that he has never heard, never spoken, never read, and never written before. The native speaker does not memorize all the sentences that he will need in his lifetime; instead he acquires a system that will enable him to create just those sentences which he will need. We, therefore, must build into our grammar the property of sentence recursiveness.

Since our first rule reads

1. S → SI + NP + Aux + VP

we know that for it to be adequate there must be a way to return to the rule in order to specify more than one sentence. How this is accomplished we shall see in our explication of *sentence embedding*.

To sum up: the rules that we list are indicative of those which we might expect to find in some formal presentations of generative-transformational theory. Let us now consider the following set of phrase structure and transformational rules.

PHRASE STRUCTURE RULES

1. Sentence → Sentence Indicator + Noun Phrase + Auxiliary + Verb Phrase

2. SI → $\left\{\begin{array}{l} \text{Positive} \\ \text{Command (Imperative)} \\ \text{Negative} \\ \text{Passive} \\ \text{Question} \end{array}\right\}$

(Brackets indicate that a choice is to be made from the constituents listed.)

SI is the constituent that indicates in the deep structure the kind of sentence that is to be generated:

        Positive: John shot the mongoose
        Negative: John didn't shoot the mongoose
        Command: Shoot the mongoose
        Passive: The mongoose was shot by John
        Question: Did John shoot the mongoose?
                    Who shot the mongoose?

Rule #2 actually says that SI may be replaced by one of the above constituents; but we know that the constituents may occur in the same sentence: for example, Question + Negative = Didn't John shoot the mongoose? Yet there are certain restrictions: there is no Passive + Command sentence.

3. Verb Phrase → Verb + $\left\{\begin{array}{l} \text{Noun Phrase} \\ \text{Prepositional Phrase} \\ \text{Adjective} \\ \emptyset \end{array}\right\}$

Rule #3 is an instruction to replace Verb Phrase with a Verb and one of the following constituents: Noun Phrase, Prepositional Phrase, Adjective, or Nothing (∅). We may choose either a Verb plus a Noun Phrase, a Verb plus a Prepositional Phrase, a Verb plus an Adjective, or a Verb plus Nothing (∅). We cannot choose all four possibilities at the same time.

So far, we have listed three rules. By following the first three rules, we can generate at least four different results:

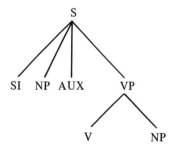   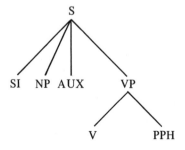

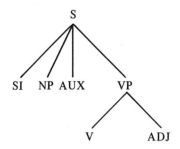 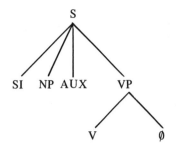

4. Prepositional Phrase → Preposition + NP

5. NP → (Article) + Noun + (Sentence)

A Noun Phrase consists of an optional Article, a Noun, and an optional Sentence. Here is where we can add the property of recursiveness in the form of an optional *S* to the right of the arrow. One possible result of the first five phrase structure rules is displayed in the following diagram:

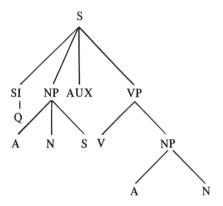

6. Auxiliary → Tense Marker + (Modal)

Tense is either the third-person singular morpheme or the past tense morpheme.

7. Modal → can, may, shall, will

Modal may be any of the above words (there are additional modals in English but for our purposes the above will be sufficient).

The next five rules will give us additional lexicon (words).

8. Noun → boy, dog, animal, woman, park, dog, year, mongoose, brother

9. Adjective → red, blue, dilapidated, cool, beautiful, handsome, old

10. Verb → eat, elapse, shoot, please, laugh, be

11. Article → the, a(n)

12. Preposition → to, on, at

For expediency and simplicity, we have left the categories incomplete. There are many more Prepositions, Modals, Nouns, Verbs, and Adjectives than we have indicated here.

PSR's: A Summary

   A summary of the rules is in order. We have twelve rules, and if we follow the rules until we reach Rule # 12 a number of possible sentences will be generated. Among the deep structures that the above phrase structure rules can generate are the following set:

1.

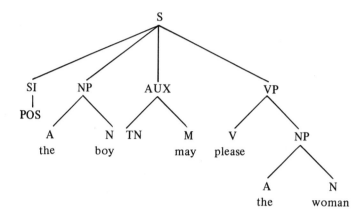

2.

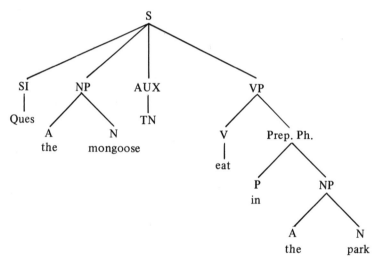

3.

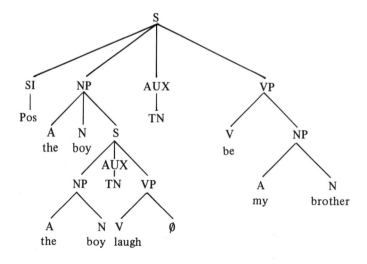

These simplified rules have explicated some important notions about English syntax. There are four major abstract units, which are called *Sentence Indicator, Noun Phrase, Auxiliary*, and *Verb Phrase*. Within the major units there are a number of optional subunits. We have sentences that are *+Question, +Negative*, and so on. The *NP* constituent must have a noun, but the other constituents (*Article* and *Sentence*) are optional. The *Auxiliary* constituent must have a *Tense Marker* but a *Modal* is optional. The *VP* must have a *Verb* but, as we have seen, the constituents that can follow the *Verb* are optional.

Our rules are not complete, of course; and there are a number of additional sentences that may be generated by following the rules, not all of which are sentences that are well formed. Our rules would therefore not "generate all and nothing but the sentences of the English language." On the contrary, there are a number of unwanted consequences (an infinite number, in theory). To restrict our grammar, or any grammar to generate only those sentences which are possible English sentences is impossible at the present time; and it is incumbent on us to recognize that the Phrase Structure component of generative grammars is inadequate. For instance, the verb "elapse" in our grammar can only occur after a noun that is associated with time. Sentences such as "The year elapsed," "The month elapsed," and "The day elapsed" are sentences that could occur in English; but sentences such as "The boy elapsed" or "The dog elapsed the woman" are sentences that lie outside the possible sentences of English, and we would therefore not want our grammar to generate them. If we were to make our rules more restrictive, we would have to make them sensitive to what words and constituents can come before and after such verbs as "elapse."

We have been rather redundant in the above paragraph for the purpose of pointing to a fact of life in language research. Because one grammar, or a set of grammars, may be imperfect is not a reason for abandoning research into the problems that beset such grammars. As linguistic research progresses, we shall have more insightful grammars replacing those which are less so; and perhaps in time generative theory itself will prove to be invalid and another theory will be substituted in its place. As we work within the discipline of language research and as we learn more about language competence and linguistic knowledge, we learn more about the intricacies of the human brain. So if "grammar" has become to our reader an esoteric subject pursued only by those whom we call linguists, and if he wishes to return to the "good old days," we hope that he will reconsider—give it a second thought—and bear with us as we continue into the subject that is for us, and that we hope will become for our reader, a most rewarding study.

TRANSFORMATIONAL RULES

We have as yet not said much about the transformational component of a generative-transformational grammar. The transformational part of the grammar operates on the deep, abstract structures as specified by the PSR's of the grammar. Transformational rules operate on bits and pieces of the deep structure: these rules may *delete* constituents (see the Command Transformation), *add* constituents (see the Reflexive Transformation), or *change* constituents around (see the Question Transformation). We will follow, as much as possible, the transformational rules as specified in *Aspects of the Theory of Syntax*, but modified for our purposes.

For illustrative purposes, let us take two sentences generated by our PSR's: "The boy shot the mongoose" and "The boy could shoot the mongoose." Transformations that could apply to these sentences (if the correct deep structure is specified) are the following:

Question transform:	Did the boy shoot the mongoose?
	Could the boy shoot the mongoose?
Negative transform:	The boy didn't shoot the mongoose
	The boy couldn't shoot the mongoose

Passive transform: The mongoose was shot by the boy
                                           The mongoose could be shot by the boy

Command transform: Shoot the mongoose!

In order for these sentences to appear in their correct surface structure forms, the transformational rules would need to be applied to their deep structures. The modified deep structures, as specified by our PSR's, are represented by the following trees:

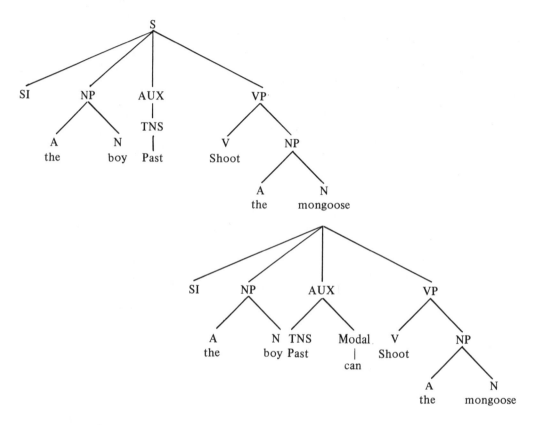

We need to notice that the above sentences, as generated by PSR's, are in non-sayable forms. The PSR's generate an abstract deep structure, within which the meaning of the sentence is specified.

The *Aux* constituent generates a tense marker in sentence #1 (obligatory) and a tense marker plus a modal in sentence #2.

Let us work with sentence #1 first and compare it with sentence #2 as we do. In sentence #1 we have a tense marker (the past tense morpheme) that needs to be attached to another constituent (all tense markers are bound morphemes). We cannot, in other words, leave it hanging. If we have a positive declarative sentence (one without negative, questions, or passive transformations), the tense morpheme is attached to *shoot* (whose past tense has a change in vowel) and the surface sentence reads

The boy shot the mongoose

If there is a modal in the sentence, the tense marker is attached to the modal: *can* becomes *could* (*could* has other meanings than the past of *can*).

The abstract structure provided by the PSR's becomes increasingly important as we examine the *yes/no question* (a question that can be answered by "yes" or "no"). In sentence #2, the *yes/no question* is:

Could the boy shoot the mongoose?

We need to be aware of the fact that the constituents *tense marker* and *modal* move to sentence initial position. The verb remains. In the case of the sentence with no *modal*, the *yes/no question* is

Did the boy shoot the mongoose?

Our reader's own question might well be: "Where did the 'did' come from?" If we look upon both surface manifestations of the *yes/no question* as exhibiting the same process (instead of two different processes) we have the answer. In *yes/no questions* the *tense marker* always moves to sentence initial position, and just in case there is a *modal* it also moves. In general terms, the constituents which fall under the *Aux* in our PSR's moves to the beginning of the sentence. For the *yes/no* transformation to apply to deep structure we need to have indicated by the *sentence indicator* that the deep structure contains a *question*. In formal terminology, we can describe the process as follows (double arrows are a convention to indicate transformations):

$$Q + NP + Aux + VP \Rightarrow Aux + NP + VP$$

There is no problem if there is a *modal*, since the *tense marker* attaches itself to the *modal* ("Could the boy shoot the mongoose?"). But there appears to be a problem if we have no *modal*. We cannot say the sentence, "Tense marker the boy shoot the mongoose?" And since all tense markers are bound morphemes they must be attached to another constituent: for that purpose, English provides a form of "do." Tense markers attach themselves to "do." In the sentence that we have, the tense marker is past; past attaches itself to "do"; the past tense of "do" is "did"; and the surface sentence then reads, "Did the boy shoot the mongoose?" Let us rehearse for the moment:

1. We first generate a deep structure that contains a question (specified by the sentence indicator). The surface form of the sentence is a *yes/no question*.

2. We are reminded that deep structures reveal relationships that are occasionally absent in the surface structures. How could we relate, for example, the two sentences, "Could the boy shoot the mongoose" and "Did the boy shoot the mongoose" without having an abstract structure? In terms of language acquisition, what we have said is important. Instead of the child learning two rules, one for sentences containing modals and the other for sentences that do not, the child learns one rule that applies to the deep structure of the kind we have described.

Command (Imperative) and Reflexive Transformations

A typical command sentence is, "Shoot the mongoose" and a typical reflexive sentence is, "He shot himself." In traditional grammar, the sentence "Shoot the mongoose" was said to have an "understood you" as its subject. This intuition was correct, but traditional grammar did not offer an explanation for the supposition.

Generative-transformational grammarians agree with the "you understood" intuition but wish to offer explicit proof that the "you" is really there. Here is an instance of where grammars with deep underlying structures have the capacity to prove what heretofore could only be accepted on faith. As we have said, there are transformations that delete deep structure constituents. The command transformation is one such transformation that deletes deep structure constituents. Let us begin our explanation of the "you understood" with an analysis of the *reflexive* (which we have not talked about before) followed by an examination of the *command sentence*. Our purpose for ordering our explanations will become clear as we proceed.

We can encounter English sentences similar to those of the following set:

$$\left\{ \begin{array}{l} \text{He shot himself} \\ \text{She shot herself} \\ \text{We shot ourselves} \\ \text{They shot themselves} \\ \text{You shot yourself} \end{array} \right\}$$

From an examination of these sentences it is rather clear that for the reflexive transformation to apply (which involves the attachment of a form of the morpheme *self*) there must be two Noun Phrases in the deep structure, and these Noun Phrases must be identical. A tree diagram demonstrating this relationship follows:

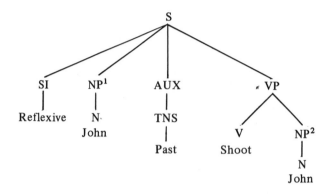

NP^1 must equal NP^2. If there are two identical NP's in the deep structure, where one NP appears directly under S and the other NP directly under the VP in the same sentence, the second NP must be replaced by a reflexive pronoun. We have no sentence in English like "John shot John," except where we are talking about two different persons. And, furthermore, we have no reflexive sentences of the following type:

John shot myself

John shot yourself

John shot ourselves

We can only have "John shot himself." Continuing this line of reasoning, let us now examine the sentence "You shot yourself." The deep structure for this sentence must be an abstract structure with each NP specifying "you."

The above analysis will aid us in determining the deep structure analysis of the *command sentence*. Command sentences have the following surface form:

$$\left\{ \begin{array}{l} \text{Shut the door} \\ \text{Go to the board} \\ \text{Don't throw erasers} \\ \text{Stand back} \\ \text{Wash yourself} \end{array} \right\}$$

With the last sentence, our reader may say, "aha!" He knows what the explanation is. If reflexives must have two identical NP's, then it is clear that the deep structure for a sentence such as, "Wash yourself," must be the following:

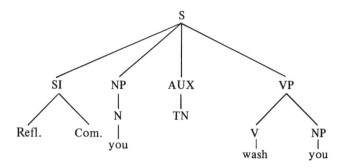

We first apply the reflexive transformation: "You wash yourself." Then the command transformation deletes the "you" and we have in the surface form, "Wash yourself." Arguments similar to the one above have led generative-transformational grammarians to posit that language consists of two structures: *deep* and *surface*. Deep structures, once again, reveal the linguistic knowledge that is available to the speaker. A speaker "knows" that for the reflexive sentence there must be two identical NP's, and he knows, also, that the command transformation deletes a "you," a constituent that appears in the deep structure.

Embedding and Adding (the recursive S)

There are also sentences that are a product of *subordination* (to use the traditional term—*embedding* is the modern term) and *addition*. A favorite story of children, for example, is the one about the house that Jack built. This story is made longer and more complicated by *embedding* a number of sentences into the main sentence, "This is the house." Beginning with this sentence, the story becomes increasingly more complicated, as illustrated by the following set of sentences:

1. This is the house that Jack built.
2. This is the malt that lay in the house that Jack built.
3. This is the rat that ate the malt, that lay in the house that Jack built.
4. This is the cat that worried the rat that ate the malt that lay in the house that Jack built.

Each instance of "that" is followed by a sentence that has been inserted or embedded into the one before it. Sentences similar to the ones we have indicated give a fairly clear indication that speakers may build up sentences into more complex ones, and that there is no longest sentence in the language. We can just add another word or embed another sentence. That a young child, perhaps not yet in school, can understand such "This is the house that Jack built" sentences reflects an ability that cannot be taught. It can only be learned. What is significant is that the child who can understand sentences similar to the above must already have a sophisticated grammar of his language.

In order to account for complex structures and sentences we need to look to PSR # 5, which specifies an optional recursive S. Sentences similar to the following set consist of two sentences, one of which is embedded into the other:

1. John thought *that the senator was a fool*
2. *For John to cheat Gertrude* was unthinkable
3. *John's protesting* alerted the assembly
4. The boy *who laughed* is my brother

The portions of each sentence that we have italicized are sentences that have been embedded. The embedded sentences are then

1. The senator was a fool
2. John cheat Gertrude
3. John protest
4. (The boy) laughed

Sentence embedding reflects the ability of speakers to create longer and more complicated sentences. For sentence 1, a possible underlying structure, abbreviated here, would be the following (triangles are incorporated to signify the sentence that has been embedded):

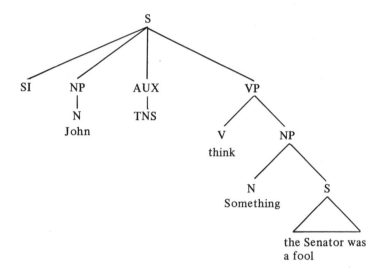

The constituent sentence, "The senator was a fool," is embedded into the NP of the main sentence, "John thought (something)," employing a transformation that is called a *that* (or factive) transformation.

Sentence 2 has the following abbreviated structure:

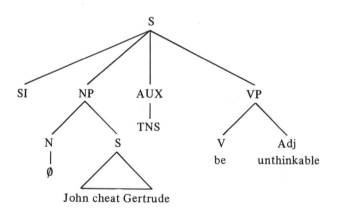

The sentence, "John cheat(s) Gertrude" becomes a part of the main sentence through a transformation that may be called the *for-to* or the infinitive transformation: "for John to cheat Gertrude."

Sentence 3 has the following abstract structure:

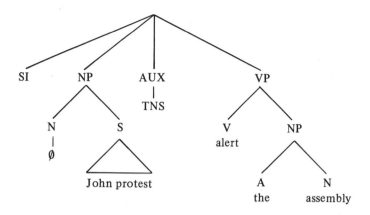

The underlying sentence, "John protest(s)," is embedded into the main sentence by using the *possessive + -ing* or gerundive transformation (which involves attaching the possessive marker to *John* and the *-ing* marker to *protest*): John's protesting.

Sentence 4 has the underlying structure:

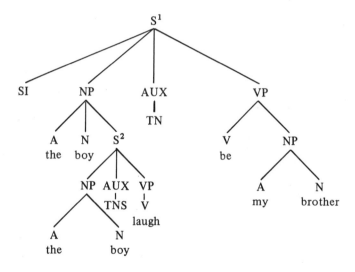

The sentence, "The boy laughed," is embedded into the main sentence with the use of the relative clause transformation. Let us examine more closely the deep structure of sentence 4, to determine exactly what is involved in relative clause embedding. We have two sentences: sentence 1 is the "frame" (or main) sentence and sentence 2 is the constituent sentence. In order for the relative clause transformation to apply there must be two sentences with identical NP's, one of which will be replaced by *which, who(m)*, or *that*. The "lower" NP is replaced by *who* in the sentence which appears on the surface as, "The boy who laughed is my brother."

Additional Transformations

We have listed in this chapter a fragment of a transformational component that serves to reflect the ability of a language user to construct negative, question, reflexive, and passive sentences, and that also enables him to make more complicated structures through the use of sentence embedding. Other than the transformational component that we have listed and explained above, there remain additional transformations that serve to conjoin words, phrases, clauses, and sentences. These transformations also involve, as did the embedding transformations, two sentences. The results from such transformations are the following set of examples:

1. *Apples and oranges* are my favorites
   N + N
2. The man and the boy pleased the woman
   NP + NP
3. He washed the dishes and she waxed the floor
   S + S

This exhausts our explanation of some of the attributes of the syntactic component of generative-transformational grammar. We might imagine that even this rather brief presentation has exhausted our reader. We hope, however, that our reader is left with the impression of how complex and how symmetrical and beautiful the wonderful world of language is.

We have learned, in summary, that the study we call linguistics involves learning a new language, similar in many respects to the language of mathematics and logic, from which generative-transformational grammarians have borrowed. Anyone who wants to pursue the study of language in this modern context must first learn the language associated with this study.

Since the appearance of the revolutionary *Syntactic Structures*, there have been extensive revisions proposed by language theorists. One revision is the important attempt by Charles Fillmore of the University of California (Berkeley) to account not only for syntactic relationships but for semantic relationships as well. We will cover semantics in the next chapter.

LANGUAGE VIEWED THROUGH OTHER MODELS

In a work of this sort, a few words ought to be said about other significant linguistic theoretical models. The reader is encouraged to use the bibliography in order to learn more about the models briefly discussed here.

TAGMEMICS: Originally known as "gramemics" or "grammemics," this model developed out of Bloomfieldian Structuralism, incorporating a number of its concepts and approaches, although with significant modifications. One of tagmemics' main points of difference with structuralism is its rejection of binary constituent analysis, in which the constituents or parts of an utterance are "sliced" into related groups, until each item is paired with another with which it is closely related. Instead, tagmemics prefers to analyze the constituents though "strings," consisting of closely related segments. The basic unit of analysis is the *tagma*, which in an utterance comprises a string replaceable or substitutable by any similar string. Here is a simple example:

The boy	/	saw	/	a telescope.
Subject		Predicate		Direct object

In the above example, the string within or before each slash is a tagma, whose slot could be filled by strings of similar class and relationship, such as:

| The girl | / | bought | / | a dress. |

As may then be seen, in this model "slot" or "function" and "class" or "set" are essential notions expressing the relationships. In the above samples, each of the tagmas (or strings) before the slashes also corresponds to a *tagmeme*. Two types of tagmas are distinguished:

1) Those which are essential constructions in a given type of utterance, called "nuclear" or "obligatory" (as are all those presented above) and 2) optional constructions or complements, considered "peripheral." For example, to any of the above models one could add a temporal tagma, such as "last week" or a locative one, like "in Boston".

Archibald Hill, in *Linguistics Today*(277) terms tagmemics: " . . . one of the very vigorous schools of American linguistics." Without a doubt, more languages of the world have been described through the tagmemic model than any other. The reason for this is that it has been utilized in general (although not always) by the Summer Institute of Linguistics, an interdenominational organization of Protestant missionary-linguists, active in many parts of the world, particularly in Latin America, Africa, and Asia. Undoubtedly the leading theoretician has been Kenneth L. Pike, the "father" of the school, who divides his time between the SIL and the University of Michigan. The reader is also encouraged to explore the contributions of Robert Longacre, Peter Fries, Edward L. Blansitt, Jr., and William Merrifield, among others.

STRATIFICATIONAL GRAMMAR: Stratificational Grammar was developed by Yale's Sydney Lamb, who based it partially on the Danish Hjelmslev's *Prolegomena to a Theory of Language*. Very briefly, this model holds that in language there are at least four *strata* (some even posit six):

> sememic
> lexemic
> morphemic
> phonemic

Grammatical functions are divided between the lexemic and morphemic strata, while the sememic one, at the top, basically refers to semantics, or meaning.

The structures of all strata are interconnected by a network, with branches extending both upward and downward. Rather than rules, stratificationalists rely upon "tactics", or the combinatory arrangements which are grammatical in any given language. Diagrams analyzing sentences resemble flow charts. This is not accidental, since Lamb gleaned many of his insights through experience with Russian-English mechanical translation, in which such charts explicitly detail the steps involved in rendering an utterance from one language to another.

There are types of algebraic or other formulations which may be employed by stratificationalists for the sake of speed and simplicity, in place of these complex diagrams. Practitioners include Henry Gleason, David Lockwood, Adam Makkai and others. A promising forum for this and other "minority" models (although TG is by no means excluded) is the young Linguistic Association of Canada and the United States (LACUS), which publishes the journal *Forum Linguisticum*.

DEPENDENCY GRAMMAR: This model grew out of the syntactic theories of Lucien Tesnière, a Frenchman. Dependency grammar (or valence grammar) holds that structures contain a *nucleus* (or *governor*), which may have *dependents*. The central nucleus of the clause or sentence is a verb; the nouns are called *actants*. The first actant refers to the subject, the second, to the direct object and the third, to the indirect object. The other (basically adverbial) elements are termed *circonstants*. Diagrams, known as *stemmas*, resemble transformational trees, in the Chomskyan tradition.

In recent years, dependency grammar has attracted increasing attention in the German-speaking world, with such figures as Hans-Jürgen Heringer, who introduced modifications. Among American practitioners is David Hays of the State University of New York (Buffalo).

SYSTEMIC GRAMMAR: The father of this school is Michael A. K. Halliday, who owes some of his ideas to J. R. Firth, who we will mention briefly below. In systemic grammar, the elements of clause or sentence structure are *subject* (S), *predicator* (P), *complement* (C) and *adjunct* (A). One might say that the complement corresponds to direct and indirect objects, while adjuncts largely correspond to adverbial constructions (or peripheral tagmemes, in tagmemics.)

In systemic grammar, a type of string constituent analysis is employed, like that used in tagmemics. The main differences between the two are terminological. Basic to the model is the concept of a systems network to show the interrelations of the constituents of a sentence. Proceeding from left to right, and becoming increasingly explicit, the diagram indicates the respective "entry conditions" and the available choices. These are mostly "either/or" conditions. For instance, given the entry condition "clause," this must be either "transitive" or "intransitive"; given the entry condition "verb," this must be "active" or "passive" (although in some languages other choices are also present).

Although Halliday himself is deeply interested, as was Firth, in the social dimension of language, he does not explicitly bring this into his theoretical formulations. Aside from this, however, he also pursues sociolinguistics, and is responsible for contributing the term *speech register*, roughly equivalent to the styles to which a speaker may shift according to the needs of the situation.

FIRTHIAN CONCEPTS: As the first linguist in the School of Oriental and Slavic Studies, University of London, Firth exercised a strong influence on colleagues throughout the British Isles from the 1930's through the 1950's. Falling under the influence of the anthropologist Bronislaw Malinowski, he came to articulate his belief in language as a social process, at that time regarded somewhat askance by American structuralists. By his concept of *restricted language*, he appears to have meant the social context where certain types of language might be employed.

J. C. Catford, now in the United States, has said that few scholars on the British Isles (probably not excluding himself) could be said to be "pure Firthians." Firth's prose was rather complex to grasp and much remained vague. He deigned to concern himself with such aspects of applied linguistics as the theory and practice of translation and pedagogy, often disdained by theoreticians.

MARTINET'S FUNCTIONAL SYNTAX: As set forth in Martinet's *Eléments de Linguistique Générale*, language is divided into two components, termed *articulations*. The first articulation, whose basic unit is the *moneme*, corresponds roughly to the morpheme in other models. The second is the *phoneme*, paralleling the concept as it is known in other schools. Moreover, functional syntax considers that human speech consists fundamentally of the *minimum utterance*, with more complex sentences merely constituting expansions of it.

Certainly one of the most productive scholars in our field, Martinet's influence is world-wide. He enjoys a numerous following, particularly in Spanish-speaking countries.

STRING GRAMMAR: As has been pointed out by Blansitt and Ornstein (1969), this model and tagmemics, both developing from structuralism, have much in common. Although both reject binary immediate constituent analysis, tagmemics tends to be more oriented toward anthropological linguistics, while string grammar has been primarily developed for automatic sentence recognition in major world languages, particularly as applied to scientific writings. In this model the "elementary sentence" is considered to consist of three components: subject, verb and object—the latter subsuming both direct and indirect object, as well as adverbial and other complements. String grammar is utilized in the Courant Institute of Applied Mathematics at New York University, with Naomi Sager heading a governmentally-funded project. Zellig Harris, the developer of the model, continues to be a practitioner of it.

VI. QUESTIONS AND ACTIVITIES

1. Why is there no "longest" sentence in any language?

2. Go through the rules of syntax in this chapter and generate five well-formed sentences. Are there sentences that can be generated from these rules that are ill-formed (some rule of English grammar is broken)?

3. What are the differences between function words (preposition, article, etc.) and content words (nouns, verbs, adjectives, adverbs)? Why is it possible to send a telegram without using function words?

4. In the sentence, "Send money today. Broke," what words have been deleted?

5. Write a telegram using ten words or fewer.

6. She said, "I love exciting dates." Is this sentence ambiguous? How would you paraphrase the two meanings?

7. "The goat is too hot to eat." What do you know about this sentence?

8. "John married Barbara." Is this sentence ambiguous? What could you add to this sentence and the ones above to resolve the ambiguity?

9. Draw tree diagrams for the following sentences:
   Jack kicked the can.
   Gertrude shot the snake.

10. What are the derivational morphemes in the word *antidisestablishmentarian*? What is the base? Is it free or bound? If you reach *establish* in your analysis and wish to call it the base, go to a good dictionary and see whether the word can be broken into still smaller constituents.

11. Draw a tree diagram for "I hate spinach." Draw a possible diagram for the sentence "Mother knows that I hate spinach." Draw a possible diagram for the sentence "Father believes that mother knows that I hate spinach."

    Can you make a generalization about English syntax based upon the above?

*   *   *

As the "other models" have only been briefly described, merely attempt to answer as many as you can of the following questions. All that can reasonably be expected are, of course, some general notions about them:

1. In your own words, try to give some idea of the notion of the tagmeme (or tagma) in tagmemics.

2. What particular group has utilized tagmemics to describe some hundreds of languages in the world? (Some linguists feel sure that the tagmemic model has thus been applied more than any other.)

3. In stratificational grammar, what are the "strata"? How are they connected?

4. Where has Tesnière's Dependency Grammar aroused particular interest?

5. In Halliday's systemic networks, what is the general function of the "entry condition"?

6. In Martinet's Functional Syntax, is the "phoneme" similar to the same term as utilized in other models? How about the "moneme"?

7. Comment freely on your reactions, both positive and negative, to any three of the models described.

VI. FOR FURTHER REFERENCE

(See also Chapters IV and V)

Adams, Valerie. 1973. *An Introduction to Modern English Word Formation*. London: Longman.

Bach, Emmon. 1968. *An Introduction to Transformational Grammar*. New York: Holt, Rinehart and Winston.

Blansitt, Edward L. Jr. 1967. "On Defining the Tagmeme," in Don G. Stuart, ed.: *Linguistic Studies in Memory of Richard S. Harrell*. Washington, D.C.: Georgetown University.

_____ and Jacob Ornstein. 1969. "Tagmemics and String Grammar." *Anthropological Linguistics* 11:167-176 (June).

Catford, J. C. 1969. "J. R. Firth and British Linguistics," in A. A. Hill, ed.: *Linguistics Today*. New York: Basic Books.

Davis, Philip H. 1973. *Modern Theories of Language*. Englewood Cliffs, N.J.: Prentice-Hall.

Fries, Charles C. 1952. *The Structure of English*. New York: Harcourt Brace Jovanovich.

Garvin, Paul L. 1969. "The Prague School of Linguistics," in A. A. Hill, ed.: *Linguistics Today*.

Grinder, J. and Suzette Elgin. 1973. *Guide to Transformational Grammar*. New York: Holt, Rinehart and Winston.

Halliday, Michael A. K. 1973. *Explorations in the Functions of Language*. London: Edward Arnold.

Harris, Zellig S. 1962. *String Analysis of Sentence Structure*. The Hague: Mouton.

Hays, David G., ed. 1966. *Readings in Automatic Language Processing*. New York: Elsevier.

Heringer, Hans-Jürgen. 1971. "Ergebnisse und Probleme der Dependenz-grammatik." *Deutschunterricht* 22.4: 42-98.

Hill, Archibald A., ed. 1969. *Linguistics Today*. New York: Basic Books.

Jacobs, Roderick A. and Peter S. Rosenbaum. 1967. *Grammar 1 and 2*. Boston: Ginn and Company.

_____, eds. 1970. *Readings in English Transformational Grammar*. Waltham, Mass.: Blaisdell.

Jakobson, Roman and Morris Halle. 1975. *Fundamentals of Language*. 2d. ed. rev. The Hague: Mouton.

Lamb, Sydney M. 1966. *Outline of Stratificational Grammar*. Rev. ed. Washington, D.C.: Georgetown University Press.

Lees, Robert B. 1964. "Transformation Grammars and the Fries Network," in Harold B. Allen: *Readings in Applied English Linguistics*. New York: Appleton-Century-Crofts.

Lester, Mark. 1971. *Introductory Transformational Grammar of English*. New York: Holt, Rinehart and Winston.

Liles, Bruce L. 1972. *Linguistics and the English Language*. Pacific Palisades, Calif.: Goodyear Publishing Company.

Lyons, John. 1970. *Noam Chomsky*. New York: Viking Press.

Makkai, Adam and David G. Lockwood. 1973. *Readings in Stratificational Linguistics*. University, Ala.: Univ. of Alabama Press.

Marchand, H. 1966. *The Categories and Types of Present-Day English Word-Formation*. University, Ala.: University of Alabama Press.

Martinet, André. 1960. *Cours de Linguistique Générale*. Paris: Armand Colin.

Muir, James. 1972. *A Modern Approach to English Grammar*. London: Batsford.

Nida, Eugene A. 1949. *Morphology: The Descriptive Analysis of Words*. 2d. ed. Ann Arbor: University of Michigan Press.

Pike, Kenneth L. 1967. *Language in Relation to Unified Theory of the Structure of Human Behavior*. 2d. ed. rev. The Hague: Mouton.

———. 1970. *Tagmemics and Matrix Linguistics Applied to Selected African Languages*. Santa Ana, Ca.: Summer Institute of Linguistics.

Sager, Naomi. 1972. "The Sublanguage Method in String Grammar," in Ralph W. Ewton Jr. and Jacob Ornstein, eds.: *Studies in Language and Linguistics II*, El Paso: Texas Western Press, University of Texas.

Sledd, James. 1959. *A Short Introduction to English Grammar*. Chicago: Scott, Foresman and Company.

Tesnière, Lucien. 1959. *Eléments de Syntaxe Structurale*. Paris: Klincksieck.

Thomas, Woen and Eugene Kintgen. 1974. *Transformational Grammar and the Teacher of English*. 2d. ed. New York: Holt, Rinehart and Winston.

VII. Semantics: The Study of Meaning

WORDS, WORDS, WORDS

Semantics is the study of meaning. In reading history, we may discover that scholars seem always to have been singularly fascinated with the subject of meaning. Hsün Tzu, a Chinese philosopher, said more than 2,000 years ago that even names have no fixed meaning. "It is only by agreement that we apply a name. Once agreed, it becomes customary, and the standard is thus fixed. . . . A name has no fixed actuality; it is only a product of such agreement."

We may thus infer from Hsün Tzu's observation that the only useful definition is the one which all can accept. What happens, though, if we cannot agree on a definition? In the interest of clear understanding, we must agree to disagree. We submit, also, that one definition is not necessarily "better" than any other, and suggest, too, that it can be misleading to accuse someone of "misusing" a word or term. For example, the concept and the various meanings associated with "democracy" have caused much confusion in recent times. A Soviet citizen may ask us, "What do you mean, 'democracy'? The people of the United States are not the beneficiaries of a democratic state since they do not own the means of production." But we may counter that "democracy" has little to do with "means of production" or the ownership of such means. "Democracy" consists of government constituted by freely elected representatives who govern with the consent of the governed. The semanticist asks us to accept the fact that we and the Soviet citizen are employing the same word with entirely different meanings. When we cannot agree on a definition we can only cease to employ the word in question and explore alternative words for expressing our message. Although this may at times be awkward, we should, however, note that it may prevent useless arguments. By dropping or clarifying any word we cannot agree on, such as "democracy," we can eliminate a source of misunderstanding—for, as long as we continue to argue about the correct meaning of "democracy," we inhibit understanding and communication.

If there is no such thing as a "correct" definition, what is the purpose of the dictionaries, we may ask ourselves? A dictionary is a history of the meaning of words; it is not a lawbook. If we do not know the meaning of a word, a dictionary can tell us how the word has been employed in the past. *Time* magazine phrased it beautifully in reviewing a newly published dictionary: "When he set out in 1746 to write the first great English dictionary, Samuel Johnson intended his definitions to be laws that would firmly establish meanings. But usage thumbs its nose at laws; the dictionary nowadays is more a *Social Register* of words than a Supreme Court of language."

Time surely states the modern case. Choice of words is a matter of fashion, custom, tradition, learning and environment. "Correct" definitions are like "correct" clothes. They are the ones in favor with the people with whom we associate. Insisting on dictionary definitions is a type of snobbery, no better than insisting that all of our friends must share our values.

Even when we can agree on definitions, problems remain. In the sentence: "He sat in a chair," the meaning of "chair" is clear and matter-of-fact. But we say a murderer "got the chair" and the word suddenly has a very different meaning. We may "address the chair" or "approach the chair" at an organized meeting. And if someone talks about "calling a chair" it probably means nothing to any of us. In some remote hill towns of the Far East, however, the sedan-chair is still a normal way to travel. There we could call for a chair, just as we in the United States can call for a taxi. "Calling a chair" and other uses of "chair" make sense in particular contexts.

Words defy strict compartmentalization in other ways, too. What a word refers to in the world of facts is called its *denotation*. If we do not know the denotation of a word we simply fail to understand it. The word "chair," for instance, would denote little to an African Bushman or to anyone else who had never seen or used one. The connotation of a word supplements its denotation. The same individual in the world of facts may be called "American Indian," "noble savage," or "red varmint." Since all these terms are applied to the same individual they have the same denotation; they all point to the same person in the world of facts. This may be difficult to accept because the three expressions do not have the same nuances. They differ in their *connotation*. Although the three terms point to the same referent—the same person in this case—there are three entirely different connotations involved. Of course, only the term "American Indian" is an objective description. The American Indians were neither noble savages nor red varmints. They were, and are, good and bad, trustworthy and treacherous—they are human, in other words.

Differences in connotation can lead to utter confusion, even to international incidents. According to Edmund Glenn of the State Department's Language Services Division, a reference to the "expanding economy" of the United States in an international congress produced a violent burst of Soviet opposition. The United States delegate was nonplussed, especially by the attitude of his European allies. The French delegation supported the United States publicly but privately criticized the mistake of backing the Soviets into a corner by such a "rigid and overbearing" attitude. The problem arose from the translation. The Russian translation, *rasshiraysshchayasya ekonomiya*, means "expanding economy" but it has a connotation of an economy that is expanding because of its own inherent characteristics. This interpretation runs counter to the Marxist insistence that capitalism carries the seed of its own destruction and will inevitably collapse of its own weight. The Soviet delegates, of course, were steeped in Marxist doctrine; to them the phrase was no less than rank heresy.

The original phrase in English had no such connotation. It simply referred to the American economy, which is in fact expanding. The Russian phrase, moreover, was the best simple translation. A more accurate translation would involve an explanatory footnote or circumlocution.

The moral of this incident is plain. If we are to translate accurately, or even to work accurately in a second language, we must pay close heed to secondary meanings and connotations. As was noted with the word "chair," the simplest word may not have the same meaning to any two different people.

CHARACTERISTIC FLAVORS

An object borrowed from another culture often brings its name with it: "moccasins" or "pemmican" in English, for instance, or *teburu* (table) and *taipuraita* in Japanese, or *beisbol* and *jonron* (home run) in Latin-American Spanish. Occasionally even the borrowing of an abstract concept occurs between languages. In such a case, the new word often seems especially typical of the culture that furnishes it. The French word *éclat* seems to mean much more than the English "sparkle." As a result, the word has been adopted, at least at the literary level, not only into English but also into most other European languages.

As another example, the Spanish "guerrillas" of the Peninsular Campaign who fought against Napoleon were by no means the first partisan fighters. Many populations before and since have resisted aggression long after their organized armies have been defeated. But something special about the effectiveness of the Spaniards, or English interest in the outcome of their struggle, carried their name solidly into the English language. So much is this true that the word is no longer written with italics as a more foreign word such as the previous *éclat*.

A final example is the English concept of "fair play." This word has carried over into several foreign languages. Other people know perfectly well what is fair, of course, but just as *éclat* is peculiarly French, the idea of fair play seems peculiarly Anglo-Saxon. Pictures of German workers show them carrying signs with the word "unfair." This word has entered the German language, just as *éclat* and "guerrilla" have entered the English language.

LANGUAGE AND ITS CULTURE

Anthropologists have long been conscious of the relationship between a language and its culture. When we are face to face with a radically different culture, such as that of the American Indian, we find ourselves in a new world of strange concepts. Appreciation of this fact led to the *Whorfian Hypothesis*, which takes its name from Benjamin Lee Whorf, who suggested that a person's native language defines the way he perceives and interprets his world. Whorf was interested in determining the possible concepts that a language can express. One possible concept is "snow." "Snow" can have various meanings in those cultures which experience snowfall. We, of course, say "snow," but an Eskimo may ask, "Which 'snow'? Falling snow, snow on the ground, snow in blocks for building igloos, or what?" Similar relationships are expressed with our concept for "water." We have a separate word for water while it is falling from the sky—"rain." At any other time, it is merely water. The Japanese do not have a general word for "water." The Japanese language obligates its speakers to specify whether the water is cold (*mizu*) or hot (*oyu*).

Whorf found that the Hopi Indian language had one word for "object moving in the air"—*masa'ytaka*. We could ask the Hopi, "What do you mean by your term *masa'ytaka*—a dragonfly, an airplane, or a pilot?" All would be called *masa'ytaka* in Hopi. The Hopi is constrained by his language to use one word for anything that flies, as long as it is not a bird—for which he uses another word.

These examples are just a few of the many which may give rise to confusion among speakers of different languages. Our reactions to the concepts and connotations of languages other than English are not logically based, however. The Eskimo's various words for "snow" may seem unreasonable to a culture that has only one word for the concept. Yet when English speakers live in the Arctic they may begin to use different words, also. *Satrugi*, a word borrowed from Russian (meaning wavelike ridges of hard snow formed on a level surface by the action of the wind), is an extremely useful word to those engaged in Antarctic exploration.

We may have similar reactions to languages that divide the color spectrum differently than we do. The Russian language employs two words for "blue": *siniy* for dark blue and *goluboy* for light blue. "Blue is blue," might be our reaction, yet we do the same thing for the red part of the spectrum. When red becomes pale enough we call it "pink." In English, "pink" is so different from "light red" that the latter term is used for a color that is known as "burnt ocher," a bright, brownish-red color. But technically and even logically the *siniy-goluboy* difference is similar to the contrast in intensity as between our "red" and "pink." A color is *siniy* on the painter's palette until he mixes enough white with it. Then it becomes *goluboy*. It is the same with "red" in English. When the painter mixes enough white with "red" on his palette, it becomes "pink."

What of the occasional complaint that we hear that the Eskimo language has too many words for "snow" or the Russian language has too many words for "blue"? We must finally admit that these are complaints of prejudice, caused by our familiarity with English. After all, any division of the color spectrum into colors is arbitrary. A cylinder, for example, could be painted with a white ring around the top, a black ring around the bottom, and the rainbow colors running vertically between them around the cylinder. By careful blending, all of these colors could be spread into each other without any visible border between any color or the next, or between the lighter and darker shades of each colors. In other words, all of the hues of the rainbow and all of their shades and tints merge into each other without any definite borders.

Any division of this merging continuum into separate colors is also arbitrary. It would indeed be surprising to discover that any two unrelated languages make exactly the same divisions. We should also not be too surprised if we find that some languages make as few as three major divisions while others make distinctions that are not found in English.

A single name for colors in the "cool" part of the spectrum—indigo, blue, and blue-green—is common. Chinese has such a word, which may also refer to our gray or black, and the color also carries an idea of the thing being described. The word, *ch'ing*, would not be applied to colors for dyes. For paper and paint there are separate words. But *ch'ing* sky is blue, *ch'ing* grass is green, *ch'ing* mountains are purple, *ch'ing* cattle are black, and *ch'ing* horses are gray.

Kinship terminology (names assigned to the members of the family) is another source of difference. It may be difficult for us to understand how some African languages do without a common term for a male parent. Their words for "my father," or "his father," or "your father" are all different. In English we do not say "brother and/or sister" as a single word. There is the word "sibling," of course, but this word is usually used in a technical sense. Old English had a word for "sibling" but the word disappeared from the language after the Norman Conquest. German still retains the word in the form of *Geschwister*, an everyday word used in contexts such as *Hat er Geschwister*? ("Does he have any brothers and sisters?"). German psychologists naturally use this word in concepts like "sibling rivalry," but to translate these terms into English, the obsolete word "sibling" was resurrected.

Or again, for one last example, we may find it strange that Navajo uses different words to describe the action of handing something to somebody. The following words all have the same first syllable, *san-*, but the rest of the word varies according to the shape of the object passed:

sanleh:	long, flexible, like string.
sanlin:	long, rigid, like a stick.
sanilcos:	flat, flexible, like a piece of paper.

TRANSLATION AND BETRAYAL

Rhetorically, we may ask ourselves, "Is a perfect translation possible from one language to another?" How difficult would it be to translate English language concepts into Hopi and Navajo? Even translating from English to Russian is difficult, and English and Russian are related languages. The task of the translator is complex. Between any two languages, denotations and connotations can vary tremendously. The translator must tread a narrow path between literal translation and free composition. Differing connotations between words that are literal equivalents force him one way, but if he goes all the way, he ends up with a new composition in the second language. Any translator will tell us that there is no simple answer.

Bible translation offers many examples. A phrase, "from the heart," occasionally is rendered, "from the liver" or "from the throat" or even "from the belly," depending on the language being used. To a Chinese the "Apostle's Creed" makes good sense only if the ascended Christ sits "on the left hand of God, the Father Almighty."

The problem is compounded when faced with the task of translating the literature of one language into the literature of another. Boris Pasternak and Aleksandr Solzhenitsyn electrified the world with their books containing an implied tone of criticism of the Soviet Union. Yet when a book of Pasternak's earlier poems was reviewed by the *New York Times*, the reviewer, while admitting that the poem had been competently translated into English, still maintained that they were little more than an echo of the originals. We should hardly expect more. (The translator just cannot satisfy everyone's notion of what is a good translation. The Italians put it well: *Traduttore–traditore*, "Translator–traitor.")

PRELINGUISTIC APPROACHES TO SEMANTICS

A book of special importance to the discipline of semantics was *The Meaning of Meaning*, by C. K. Ogden and I. A. Richards. The book is difficult even for the linguist, yet it has increased the interest of linguists in semantics. The authors state that the basic referents in the semantic system of any language are vastly fewer than the total vocabulary would suggest, since simpler synonymous expressions are available. They claim that a study of these referents or *basic irreducible designations*, as they called them, would lead to a much clearer understanding of meanings.

One activity to which their theory led is known as "content analysis." After World War II a large body of German propaganda was subjected to this process. In short, the analysts tried to pierce through the fog of what was written to determine the real meaning of the statements. It was claimed by some that content analysis applied to the speeches of Hitler and his colleagues could have aided in preventing World War II. Today, we can only recognize this claim as hindsight and conjecture, at best.

Another important contribution to the study of meaning and human reactions to words and other symbols is the book, *Science and Sanity*, by the late Count Alfred Korzybski. This book is the source of an approach to the study of meaning called "General Semantics." Some adherents of Korzybski promise just as much as the adherents of content analysis and claim that semantic reconditioning can solve almost all of the world's problems. But most students of general semantics make no such claim, nor do such authorities in the field as Wendell Johnson, S. I. Hayakawa, Harry Weinberg, and the late Irving J. Lee.

SEMANTICS AND LINGUISTICS

We have been examining the elusive notion of meaning and have referred to some of the earlier attempts to explain it—theories which we have termed "pre-linguistic" because they were never part of a general theory of language. It has not been until recently that linguists have attempted to include in a theory of language an analysis and explication of meaning. A theory of language must explain and include not only general principles of phonology, morphology, and syntax, but also meaning.

The revival of interest in meaning closely approximates the rise in importance of generative-transformational theory. Although Chomsky does not include a semantic component in his first grammar of English (*Syntactic Structures*), even maintaining that "semantic considerations play no role in the linguistic analysis of syntactic structures," later grammars based upon a generative-transformational format include a syntactic component. Since 1957, meaning has increasingly become more important in linguistic research, and this research has taken several paths. One path is described by Chomsky in his *Aspects of the Theory of Syntax*, which stands as a major modification to the grammar contained in *Syntactic Structures*. Within *Aspects*, Chomsky draws upon the earlier research of Jerrold Katz, Jerry Fodor, and Paul Postal.

In *Aspects*, syntax remains as the central component of the grammar, with the semantic and phonological components "interpreting" the output of the syntactic rules. This version of generative-transformational grammar is now called "standard theory," to distinguish it from other generative-transformational models which were later offered as modifications or even as substitutes to the theory as contained in *Aspects*. As modifications to generative-transformational grammar continued, the model of grammar as contained in *Aspects* would be called *standard theory* or *interpretive theory*.

Serious questions concerning the primacy of syntax were raised by linguists soon after the publication of *Aspects*. These linguists questioned the central role of syntax and insisted that "at the heart of an adequate theory of language must be an adequate theory of semantic structure." The advocates of modification including George Lakoff, James McCawley, John Robert Ross, Charles Fillmore, and Wallace Chafe, among others. They postulated that semantics, instead of syntax, would be the primary component of a generative-transformational grammar and went as far as to insist that syntax was not a "well-motivated" component of a grammar. They would argue, moreover, that semantic structures specified the shape of syntactic structures. Lakoff, McCawley, and Ross call their version of generative-transformational grammar *generative semantics* while Fillmore and Chafe call theirs *case grammar*. In recent years, however, Chafe has moved away from Fillmore's version of case.

Interpretive semantics, generative semantics, and case grammar are the labels which we will employ when we point to some of the differences among these three versions of generative-transformational grammar.

INTERPRETIVE SEMANTICS (Standard Theory)

The benchmark article that placed semantics within the mainstream of a theory of language was Katz' and Fodor's article "The Structure of a Semantic Theory" in which they state that "A semantic theory of a natural language is part of a linguistic description of that language," and must be included as a component of a generative-transformational grammar. Katz and Fodor attempt to maintain distinct and separate ("automonous" is the label which has wide currency) levels of syntax and semantics. They submit that "Linguistic description minus grammar equals semantics." Syntax provides data to the semantic component which then interprets (gives meaning to) the sentence.

One reason for adding a semantic component to a grammar was the existence of two kinds of ambiguity—*structural* and *lexical*. Structural ambiguity can be revealed by deep syntactic structures. For instance, the ambiguity in the surface sentence, "Flying planes can be dangerous," is the result of two different deep structures which happen, in this case, to have one surface form. In one sentence, someone is flying planes; in the other, there are planes which are flying. A different kind of ambiguity could not be explained by referring back to deep structures but could only be explained by appealing to the senses of the lexical item. The sentence, "The suit is too light to wear," is often cited as an example of this type of ambiguity. "Light" can mean "not heavy" or "not dark in color." A desire to characterize lexical ambiguity and to provide a reading (meaning) for each sentence generated led to the inclusion of a semantic component in a grammar of a language.

Katz' and Fodor's semantic component consists of a dictionary of lexical items and a set of projection rules (reading rules) which amalgamate the meaning(s) of the lexical items into the readings (meaning) of each sentence. The dictionary contains three kinds of information about each lexical item in the language:

1. *Information on the grammatical category of each lexical item.* While some lexical items may occur in two or three different syntactic environments (for instance, as either a noun or verb), other words may occur in only one. "Play" is an example of the first (noun or verb) and "entry" an example of the second (noun).

2. *General semantic information.* In *Aspects*, Chomsky says that a word consists of a bundle of distinctive semantic markers or features. For instance, if we look at the nouns "dog," "girl," "nationalism," "oatmeal," "chair," "Fido," "George," and "Boston" we can see that while the words are from one syntactic class (noun) they will differ in their semantic designations. The

features associated with these words are the following (although not all features are associated with each word): *common, count, animate, human,* and *mass.* D. Terrence Langendoen observes that these features, which are semantic in nature, "do not represent properties of the universe but innate properties of the human mind itself and of the human perceptual apparatus." These are universal features, in other words, common to all languages.

An individual word will reflect the present (+) or absence (-) of these features and the features will govern the role of the word in a sentence or constrain its appearance before or after verbs. If a word is *+ common,* then it is spelled with a small letter — except when it appears as the first word in a sentence ("dog" is an example); if the word is *-common* (a *-common* word is a proper noun) then it is spelled with a capital letter ("George"). The feature *count* refers to the fact that some words may appear with a numerical counter or indefinite article in front of them. We can count chairs and we can say "one chair, two chairs, three chairs," or "a chair," and so on. "Oatmeal" and "sugar" are among the many *-count* words. We cannot say "one oatmeal, two oatmeals, three oatmeals," or "an oatmeal," or "one sugar, two sugars, three sugars," or "a sugar," except in a specialized sense. "Nationalism" and "pluralism" are also *-count* nouns. We cannot say "one nationalism, two nationalisms, three nationalisms" or "one pluralism, two pluralisms," and so forth. However, there is a distinction to be made in the category of *-count* nouns. "Oatmeal" and "sugar," *-count* nouns, are also *+mass* nouns, while "nationalism" and "pluralism" are *-mass* nouns. *+Mass* nouns are *concrete*: we may actually touch, feel or smell "oatmeal" and "sugar," while the *-mass* nouns, such as "nationalism" and "pluralism" cannot be touched, felt, or smelled. Animate nouns may be classified into nouns which are *+human* (girl) and those which are *-human* (dog).

Implicit in the use of features to classify nouns into semantic categories is the notion of absence of redundancy. Certain features do not have to be explicitly stated. A *-common* noun is a *+proper* noun and must be spelled with a capital. It would be redundant to categorize a noun as both *-common* and *+proper.* *-Common* is sufficient to give us all the proper nouns in the language.

We have already pointed to the feature that separated "oatmeal" from "nationalism." We do not have to specify any other feature than *-mass.* *-Mass* also says that "nationalism" and "pluralism" are *abstract* nouns; and we know that an abstract noun is *-concrete.* The *-mass* feature implies *+abstract.* We have listed in the following matrix a number of nouns with their features specified.

FEATURE(S)	EXAMPLE(S)
+common	girl, dog, chair, oatmeal, nationalism
-common	George, Fido, Boston
+common -count	oatmeal, nationalism
+common +count	girl, dog, chair
+common -count -mass	nationalism

FEATURE(S)	EXAMPLE(S)
+common -count +mass	oatmeal
+common +count +animate	dog, girl
+common +count -animate	chair
+common +animate +human	girl
+common +animate -human	dog
-common -animate	Boston
-common +animate -human	Fido
-common +animate +human	George

These semantic relationships can also be portrayed on an inverted tree diagram:

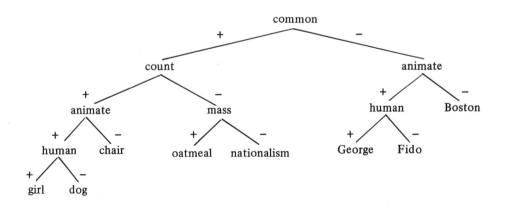

Thus, "girl" has the bundle of semantic features labeled *common, count, animate, human*. These features aid in explaining feelings or intuitions about relationships within sentences that we can judge to be semantic, as in the following sentences:

1. My toothbrush kicked the vase.
2. He amazed the injustice of that act.
3. Colorless green ideas sleep furiously.

By any standard, when we hear or read these sentences they are anomalous, or a bit weird—resembling sentences that we might find in literary works, especially in modern poetry. Semantic rules have been broken, since we "know" the verb "kicked" must have a +*animate* "doer," that after the verb "amazed" there must be an *animate* noun. Some speakers would even insist that after "amazed" the feature *animate* is not specific enough; the noun must also be +*human*, since the sentence, "He amazed the elephant with his performance," is not a possible sentence for them.

3. *Semantic Distinguishers*. In addition to indicating the possible syntactic category of each lexical item, along with its set of semantic markers, the Katz and Fodor dictionary also distinguishes the various meanings that each word has. For instance, the word "light" in isolation can mean "not heavy" or "not dark." There are many words which have more than one meaning, and these meanings are distinguished by the dictionary.

Projection Rules

A semantic component as developed by Katz, Fodor and Chomsky contains a set of *projection rules* which scan the deep structures generated by the syntactic rules to give the meaning(s) of each sentence. These rules combine or amalgamate the senses of each lexical item specified in a tree-structure, reading from the bottom of the tree to the top; a reading for each sentence is a combination of its lexical items. In the sentence, "The suit is too light," the projection rules correctly indicate that there are two distinct meanings for the sentence, depending upon the meaning of "light." The rules also indicate that only one possible meaning for "light" is possible in the sentence, "The suit is light enough for Mary to carry." Projection rules, then, add to the capacity of the semantic component to assign meanings to sentences.

ALTERNATIVES TO STANDARD THEORY: GENERATIVE SEMANTICS

We have been describing a semantic component that is now termed *interpretive*, one which assumes that there is a distinction between syntax and semantics. Linguists whom we have already mentioned argue that the distinction between syntax and semantics is artificial, arbitrary, and even redundant. James McCawley, in his article "Where do Noun Phrases come From?" suggests "that there is no natural breaking point between a 'syntactic component' and 'semantic component' of grammar such as the level of deep structure as seen in the *Aspects* model." *Generative semanticists*, as they are called, and *case grammarians* (discussed later) maintain that syntax is determined by semantics (syntax "clothes" meaning). Instead of having rules which generate deep syntactic structures which are then interpreted by semantic rules, these linguists would have a grammar generate abstract semantic structures which determine various syntactic structures.

Generative-semanticists (and case grammarians) believe that their way of perceiving the speech act comes closer to portraying the capacities of the language user. The speech act, they maintain, begins with concepts which are then encoded into syntax. Thus, semantics is the focus of language; they hope to find that semantic concepts are universal, while syntax and phonology are language-specific.

There are a number of arguments which are employed in attacking the adequacy of interpretive theory. It is not our purpose to discuss them all, but to present the following in order to give our reader a sense of the conflict.

1. *The passive transformation argument.* In interpretive theory, transformations are "meaning-preserving." No transformation can change the deep structure meaning of any sentence. For example, the passive transformation preserves the meaning of the active:

> Active: The dog bit the man.
> Passive: The man was bitten by the dog.

Although the passive transformation does not change the meaning of the active sentence above, it does change the meaning of the following sentence:

> Active: Everyone loves someone.
> Passive: Someone is loved by everyone.

The counter-argument, to summarize briefly, is that some transformations *do not* preserve meaning, and that interpretive theory therefore contradicts itself. Generative semanticists sought to prove that this was a major flaw in interpretive theory.

2. *Syntactic Configurations.* Some sentences which consist of the same meaning cannot be related syntactically:

> The boys piled the wagon with hay.
> The boys piled hay onto the wagon.
>
> The acid dissolved the metal.
> The metal dissolved in the acid.

These sentences, similar in meaning, could not be related in a grammar that held that syntax was the primary component.

3. *Verbs and Adjectives.* Verbs and adjectives derive from one constituent class, although on a more abstract level. The traditional definition of a verb, as a word expressing "action" or "state of being," correctly captures the semantic distinction between two kinds of verbs. By reinterpreting this intuition, we can say that a verb is either +*stative* ("state of being") or -*stative* ("action").

Verbs therefore can fit into two *paradigms* (patterns), depending upon whether they are +stative ("own," "know," and "resemble") or -stative ("look," "paint," and "wash"). Verbs which are +stative cannot appear in imperative sentences:

> Own that house.
> Know that book.
> Resemble that picture.

-stative verbs can appear in imperative sentences:

> Look at that tree.
> Paint that house.
> Wash that car.

Another test which determines the category of verb is the "progressive" test. +stative verbs cannot occur with the progressive (a form of the verb "be" and the inflection "-ing"):

> I am owning that house.
> She is knowing that fact.
> They are resembling that picture.

-stative verbs can:

> I am looking at that house.
> She is painting that bike.
> They are washing that car.

Adjectives are similar to verbs in the above respects, as some can be categorized as stative while others cannot (a fact that has pointed to the existence of languages without adjectives). +stative adjectives cannot occur in imperative sentences:

> Be tall.
> Be short.

-stative adjectives can occur in imperative sentences:

> Be noisy.
> Be good.

+stative adjectives cannot occur with the progressives:

> He is being tall.
> She is being short.

-stative adjectives can:

> He is being noisy.
> He is being bad.

The features that adjectives and verbs share have led generative semanticists to the conclusion that there is an abstract constituent called a *verbal* which includes both verb and adjective. These facts about the similarity of verb and adjective were not (and according to generative semanticists, could not be) characterized by interpretive theory.

4. *The nature and relationship of words.* Another characteristic of generative semantics is that its proponents insisted that deep structures had to be far more abstract than they were in *Aspects*. Words not phonetically related were so close in meaning that they must be derived from the same constituent class of word; the notion of "word" is much more abstract in this analysis. The sentence, "Gertrude killed Pete," provides an example of how abstract this analysis can be. The simplified tree-diagram for this sentence is:

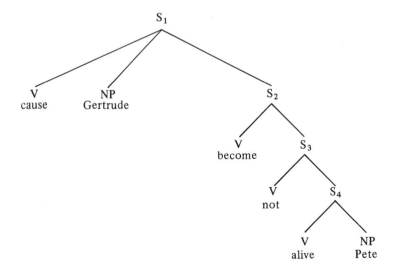

As each sentence is lifted, or *raised*, into the sentence immediately above it, different word-constructs are formed. Sentence 4 (S_4) is raised into Sentence 3 (S_3), and "not alive" is read in the sentence as the following:

> Gertrude caused Pete to become not alive. ("Not alive" equals "dead")
> Gertrude caused Pete to become dead.

Sentence 3 can then be raised into Sentence 2 producing:

> Gertrude caused Pete to become not alive. ("to become not alive" equals "die")
> Gertrude caused Pete to die.

Finally, Sentence 2 is raised into Sentence 1:

> Gertrude caused Pete to become not alive. ("caused Pete to become not alive" equals "kill")
>
> Gertrude killed Pete.

5. *Various functions within the sentence*. In interpretive theory, the function of a lexical item is determined by its position in the deep structure. A challenge to this notion was most notably led by Charles Fillmore, who said that other considerations are involved in determining the roles of lexical items in the surface structure. This leads us to a discussion of *Case Grammar*.

CASE GRAMMAR

Charles Fillmore argues in his article, "The Case for Case," that semantic features and syntactic features may be combined; he uses "the term *case* to identify the underlying syntactic-semantic relationships." Fillmore hypothesizes that "The case notions comprise a set of universal, presumably innate concepts which identify certain types of judgments human beings are capable of making about the events that are going on around them, judgments about such matters as who did it, who it happened to, and what got changed."

Case relationships in some older stages of Indo-European (the parent language of English) such as Indo-European itself, Sanskrit, Greek, and Latin were signaled by suffixes (inflections) placed on nouns. What was signaled by placing suffixes on nouns in the above languages is signaled by word order and prepositions in English. The case relationships for English, and presumably for other languages as well, include:

Name of Case	Definition	Example (case is italicized)
Agent (A)	Instigator of action. Must be +animate.	*Sam* opened the door. The door was opened by *Sam*.
Instrumental (I)	The –animate force involved in the event as stated or named by the verb.	The *key* opened the door. Sam opened the door with a *key*.
Dative (D)	Indicates animate being affected by events named by the verb.	Sam sees *Bill*. Sam gave the book to *Bill*.
Factive (F)	The object or being resulting from the state or action indicated by the verb.	Sam built a *chair*. God created the *universe*.

Name of Case	*Definition*	*Example* (case is italicized)
Locative (L)	Location as specified by the verb.	The book is on the *chair*. *San Antonio* is warm. Sam ran to the *store*.
Objective (O)	The most neutral semantic case. The case of anything represented by a noun whose role in the action or state identified by the verb depends on the meaning of the verb itself.	Sam sees *Mary*. Sam opened the *door*.

Fillmore uses the cases to classify verbs. The verbs "open" may appear with *objective*, *instrumental*, and *agent* cases. "Open" would appear in Fillmore's theory within a "case frame."

[open O (I) (A)]

Parentheses point to the fact that the (I) and (A) do not have to be specified in a sentence containing "open." The objective case, with no parentheses, has to appear, however. This is a constraint on the use of "open." Let us examine the following sentences containing "open" as the verb.

The door opened. [open O]

Here we have the objective case occurring in first position in the sentence. We "know" that "someone" or "something" had to open the door, and we "know" this without having the agent specified.

John opened the door. [open O (A)]

We have the obligatory O, which appeared in first position in the previous sentence, appearing here after the verb, with the agent "John" (the "someone" (A) appearing in the first position).

The key opened the door. [open O (I)]

In this sentence, the objective case appears along with the instrumental (I), with the (I) occurring in first position.

John opened the door with the key. [open O (A) (I)]

All three case relationships are explicit.

We can see from these examples that syntax and semantics are closely related. Syntax can express semantic relationships and semantic relationships can be expressed by positions in sentence or by a preposition. Fillmore believes that the above cases [A, O, D, I, L, F] are the absolute minimum for any language, but he also says that there may be other case relationships. Case relationships, to sum up, express the experience of the speaker as to:

1. who did what,
2. who it happened to, and
3. what got changed.

With case grammar, our analysis of the systems of language ends. Research continues, of course, into the various systems which fit a theory of language, and we can look forward to grammars that come ever closer to approximating the knowledge that native speakers bring to the task of learning, speaking, and understanding the languages of their environment.

VII. QUESTIONS AND ACTIVITIES

1. Euphemisms abound for "toilet" (which is itself a euphemism). What are some of them? Can you judge them in terms of acceptability for various kinds of social functions and interactions?

2. Why does a language have euphemisms? During the Viet Nam war occasionally the phrase "surgical strike" was employed in place of "bombing." What are other euphemisms associated with war?

3. "That bachelor is pregnant." Knowing what you do now about nouns and their features, what additional feature must be associated with "bachelor" (one that we did not discuss in this chapter)?

4. What "case" is assigned to the following noun? The *mirror* cracked.

5. What semantic features are associated with the following nouns?

fact	frog	Kissinger
horse	linguist	nationalism
lid	teacher	oats
Georgetown	Lassie (the dog)	

   Can "oats" ever appear in the singular? In what contexts?

6. The language of the Eskimo has a number of terms for snow, depending upon the kind of snow, and whether it is falling or on the ground. English has one word for snow but various words for rain, some of which are regional. Name some of them. Why are there more words for various kinds of rain in English than there are for snow?

7. Instead of "first class," "second class," and "third class" accommodations, airlines now have "first class," "tourist (coach)," and "economy." What are the reasons for these changes in labels?

8. "Detente" was a term used during former President Ford's administration to describe the relationships between the Soviet Union and the United States. In 1976, Mr. Ford decided not to employ the term, and in fact had it excised from his public addresses. What can account for the former President's action?

9. "Bread," "butter," "milk," and "sugar" are a few of the many mass nouns. We normally do not count them as we count non-mass nouns—for example, "chair" and "table." If we want to count mass nouns, we have to employ a phrase. What are these phrases? Name some other mass nouns that have to be counted in this way.

VII. FOR FURTHER REFERENCE

Allen, J. P. B. and Paul Van Buren, eds. 1971. *Chomsky: Selected Readings*. London: Oxford University Press.

Austin, J. L. 1962. *How to Do Things with Words*. Cambridge, Mass.: Harvard University Press.

Carroll, Lewis. 1946. *Alice in Wonderland* and *Through the Looking Glass*. New York: Grosset and Dunlap.

Chafe, Wallace. 1970. *Meaning and the Structure of Language*. Chicago: University of Chicago Press.

Fillmore, Charles J. 1968. "The Case for Case," in Emmon Bach and Robert T. Harms, eds.: *Universals of Linguistic Theory*. New York: Holt, Rinehart and Winston.

Hayakawa, S. I. 1964. *Language in Thought and Action*. Rev. ed. New York: Harcourt Brace Jovanovich.

Hechinger, Fred M. 1974. "In the End Was the Euphemism." *Saturday Review/World* March, 50-52.

Jacobs, Roderick A., and Peter S. Rosenbaum, eds. 1970. *Readings in English Transformational Grammar*. Waltham, Mass.: Blaisdell.

Katz, Jerrold J. and Jerry Fodor. 1963. "The Structure of a Semantic Theory." *Language* 39:170-210.

Korzybski, Alfred. 1933. *Science and Sanity: An Introduction to Non-Aristotelian Systems and General Semantics*. Lancaster, Pa.: Science Press.

Lakoff, George. 1970. *Irregularity in Syntax*. New York: Holt, Rinehart and Winston, Inc.

_____. 1971. "On Generative Semantics," in D. Steinberg and L. Jakobovits, eds. *Semantics: an Interdisciplinary Reader in Philosophy, Linguistics, and Psychology*. New York: Cambridge University Press.

Langendoen, D. Terence. 1970. "Roles and Role Structure," in *Essentials of English Grammar*. New York: Holt, Rinehart and Winston.

Leech, Geoffrey. 1974. *Semantics*. Harmonsworth, England: Penguin.

Liles, Bruce L. 1972. "English Sentence Structure," in *Linguistics and the English Language*. Pacific Palisades, Calif.: Goodyear Publishing Company.

McCawley, James D. "Where do Noun Phrases Come From?" in R. Jacobs and P. Rosenbaum, eds.: *Readings in English Transformational Grammar*. Waltham, Mass.: Blaisdell.

Nilsen, Don L. F. and Alleen Pace Nilsen. 1976. *Semantic Theory: A Linguistic Perspective*. Rowley, Mass.: Newbury House.

Ogden, C. K. and I. A. Richards. 1930. *The Meaning of Meaning*. 3rd ed. New York: Harcourt Brace and World.

Osgood, Charles E. 1971. "Explorations in Semantic Space: A Personal Diary." *Journal of Social Issues* 27:5-64.

Perlmutter, David M. 1971. *Deep and Surface Structure Constraints in Syntax*. Holt, Rinehart and Winston, Inc.

Postal, Paul. 1970. "On the Surface Verb 'Remind'." *Linguistic Inquiry* I: January, 137.

Searle, John R., ed. 1971. *The Philosophy of Language*. London: Oxford University Press.

_____. 1969. *Speech Acts*. Cambridge: Cambridge University Press.

Sledd, James and Wilma R. Ebbit. 1962. *Dictionaries and THAT Dictionary*. Chicago: Scott, Foresman and Company.

Whorf, Benjamin Lee. 1956. *Language, Thought, and Reality: Selected Writings*. Cambridge, Mass.: Technology Press of M.I.T.

VIII. Writing Systems of the World

THE PLACE OF WRITING

"Put it in writing" is a familiar request, as is "Drop me a line." Yet almost half of the world's adult population cannot fulfill these two simple requests, since in many communities of the world only a small minority are literate. An example of a country that has a low level of literacy is Nepal in South Asia, where only one of every ten adults has the ability to read and write. In such societies the ability to read and write is a mark of status. And in some areas of Africa, the public scrivener is still a well paid and highly respected person. Even in the United States, there are many illiterates and semi-literates. Literacy societies have sprung up in various urban centers to teach reading and writing; and the three branches of the military have found that sometimes they must teach these skills to new enlistees. Writing and reading, then, are not universal traits; and while we do not have to teach children to talk, we usually have to teach them to read and write.

How did the art of writing first develop? Probably no one will ever know just when and where the first person made a mark that had meaning. However, when this occurred, it was an instance of written symbolization. If these marks functioned then as they do today, we can call them "written symbolization of a verbal symbolization." Writing serves partially to capture in a semipermanent form a verbal message, although there are differences, as we have said, between writing and speech.

The earliest records that we have of marks intended to communicate are inscriptions on caves, rocks, artifacts, or articles of daily use. The inscriptions occasionally resemble actual drawings of objects; these are sometimes crude approximations but they leave no doubt as to what they were meant to accomplish. The earliest records of writing are to be found on clay, bone, shell, and stone, yet it is not always clear what the early "writer" meant to convey.

ORIGINS OF WRITING SYSTEMS

There exist many myths among the peoples of the world about the origins of writing, or *orthography*. The ancient Egyptians, the Mayans of Mexico and Central America, and the Japanese all have myths that attribute their writing systems to divinities. Originally, the Egyptian system of *hieroglyphics* (meaning "sacred stone writing") was based upon pictorial or facsimile representations. Thus, to indicate "man," "woman," "sun," and similar concrete concepts the Egyptians merely drew pictures of these objects. But since there is much that cannot be presented pictorially—for example, concepts such as love, hate, honor, pity—attempts were made to revise the writing system so as to include a way to represent these abstract notions.

The story of how the Egyptians expanded their system for writing is worthy of note. In Egyptian, for instance, the word for *sun* was *re*. The symbol for *sun* came to be employed not only for the star but occasionally for the written representation of any word in which the sound *re* occurred. The Phoenicians, neighbors to the Egyptians, generalized the Egyptian writing system further. Five thousand years ago, the graphic shape which had earlier represented an entire word in Egyptian evolved into a symbol which was employed for the initial consonant which began that word.

ORTHOGRAPHIES OF THE WORLD

SEMITIC

The Hebrew orthography still reflects traces of its pictorial origin. The *a*, called *aleph*, originally stood for the head of an ox. The *b* is referred to in Hebrew as *beth*, which is the word for "house." The letter *g* is known as *gimel*, for "camel," the head of which is represented by the Hebrew version of this symbol. An example of Hebrew writing follows.

יהדות ליטא

...המפליא בתולדותיהם היא העובדה שעל אף התמורות

המדיניות, החברתיות והרוחניות שעברו עליהם, הצליחו

לשמור על אופים המיוחד. הם לא נבלעו ולא נטמעו

בתוך קיבוצי יהודים אחרים... הם שמרו על הומו־

גניות. על מסורת רוחנית מיוחדת, תכונות מוסריות

משלהם וכל אלה נצטרפו יחד לכלל אורח חיים ספציפי.

יתר על כן, בתוקף סגולותיהם אלו זכו יהודי ליטא,

MODERN HEBREW

The Semitic writing system spread with the growth and spread of Islam. The contemporary Arabic symbols show little if any obvious resemblance to the earlier Semitic script from which they are historically derived. The most important reason for the discrepancy might be explained by the fact that all Arabic script is based upon a cursive, or handwritten, form. The Arabic writing system spread even farther than the Arabic language. With some modifications and adaptations it serves today as the mode for writing Persian, Pushtu, Urdu, and Hindi. Formerly it was the system for Turkish, Malay, Hausa, Swahili, and most of the languages of Muslim peoples in what is now the Soviet Union. This script has had at least some use wherever the Moslem religion has spread. Some historically interesting cases are seen in its use for Somali in East Africa, Malagasy on Madagascar, and Sulu in the southern Philippines. Only the Roman and Cyrillic alphabets can claim wider use.

قسم دراسات الشرق الأوسط

جامعة تكساس أوستن

ARABIC (MODERN AMERICAN USE)

The Semitic system of writing served as a partial basis for the earliest Greek alphabet. The Greeks, however, made an important stride in that they were the first to record vowels. Only consonants were recorded in the writing systems employed by the Phoenicians and Jews.

The Roman, or Latin, alphabet developed mainly from the capital letters of the Greek alphabet. From these letters a large number of variants evolved, such as the Irish and Gothic alphabets. The Irish alphabet was first used around the 12th century and was employed until the 16th century, when the less ornate Roman form took its place. The use of German Gothic, however, continued in the Scandinavian countries until the 19th century; and in Germany today, it is still employed about half of the time, and alternates with the Roman form.

Another variant of the Greek alphabet became the basis for the Coptic and Ethiopic systems of writing. The latter is in current use in Ethiopia and Eritrea today. Coptic survives, for religious purposes only, among the minority of native Christians in Egypt.

ARMENIAN

An Armenian legend credits the invention of the Armenian letters, by Mesrop Mashtots in the 4th century, to divine revelation. There was clearly a human component involved in the origin of this alphabet, as Mesrop had studied the Greek system of writing, and many of the capital letters in Armenian show a clear resemblance to the small letters in the Greek alphabet. The Georgian alphabet, employed in the Soviet republic of Georgia in the Caucasus, may have been adapted from the Armenian system.

«Այգուն,այգուն իմ խղճի մոտ
Լուսաճպիտ մինչ առավոտ
Երգէ պլպուլն իմՄիսվկանայ
Կիլիկիա, Կիլիկիա:«

Հայոց Բագրատունեաց Հատատութեան անկումէն յետոյ,
Կիլիկիոյ բարձունքներուն վրայ պապստան գտնող Հայ իշ-
խաններ սկսան տակաւ գօրանալ։Իուքինեան իշխաներէն
Լեւոն Բ. իր քաջութեան եւ արիութեան շնորհիւ կարձա-
նանայ Թագաւորական գահին ու կրելայ հիմնադիրներէն
Ռուբինեան Հարստութեան:

ARMENIAN

CYRILLIC

Still another variant of the Greek alphabet is the Cyrillic or Slavic alphabet, which was devised by the monks Cyril and Methodius, who were sent from Constantinople to convert the Slavs to Christianity. This alphabet is used by the Russians, Serbs, Bulgarians, Ukrainians, and Byelorussians, and has been adapted to serve for many other languages spoken in the Soviet Union.

Природой здесь нам сужено,

В Европу прорубить окно.

CYRILLIC: RUSSIAN (PRESENT SPELLING)

RUNES

One of the more intriguing variations of the alphabet is the runes, used by the early Germanic scribes. The runes, supposedly possessed of magical power, were scratched in armor, on horns, and on obituary stones. Their exact origin is unknown, although Greek, Thracian, and

Etruscan and Latin sources have been suggested. In Wagner's *Siegfried*, the Dragon Slayer climbed a mountain surrounded by fire and awakened a sleeping Valkyrie, Brünnhilde, with a kiss. Brünnhilde was a daughter of the gods and therefore skilled in all forms of magic, including the runes, which he asked her to teach him.

SANSKRIT AND SYLLABARIES

Another derivation from the Semitic system is the ancient Devanagari of India in which Sanskrit is written. The Devanagari in turn was the ancestor of the present-day alphabets of India and of various systems employed to record some Southeast Asian languages, such as Thai and Burmese. A few of these are rather more complicated writing systems, with each symbol representing a consonant or group of consonants followed by a vowel.

One of these, the writing system of Ceylon, has more than 300 symbols and makes the English alphabet, with its 26 letters, seem quite simple. However, the system employed in Ceylon is clearly not an alphabet, but a syllabary. One symbol stands for one syllable, consisting of one or more consonants and a following vowel. In contrast to a syllabary, an alphabet employs one or more symbols for each consonant and one or more symbols for each vowel.

तत्सवितुर्वरेंण्यं भर्गो देवस्य धीमहि।
धियो यो नः प्रचोदयात् ॥१०॥

DEVANAGARI: SANSKRIT

Even though syllabic writing systems may appear to be less efficient and more cumbersome than our more familiar alphabetic system of writing, some newly created writing systems have been of the syllabic type. The best established of the syllabary systems is employed in northern Canada by the Cree and the Eskimo. In this system the basic shape of the letter represents a consonant sound, and the way it is turned indicates what vowel follows the consonant.

pē ta̅ w   pi to š
"he brings it"   "differently"

Another region of the world where a syllabary was introduced was southwestern China, among the non-Chinese of that region. The Pollard script for the language called Miao is now dying, a result of the standardizing influence of the government of the People's Republic of China, which insists that there be no foreign writing systems employed there.

MIAO: HWA DIALECT, POLLARD SCRIPT

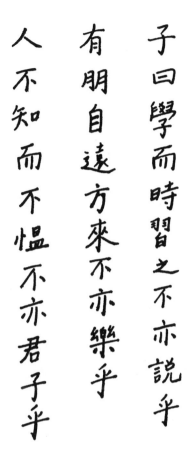

CHINESE

SIGNS FOR WORDS

The descendants of picture-writing systems (also called ideographic writing) have by no means vanished. Both China and Japan, and, to a certain degree, Korea, still make use of the Chinese characters. Similar in purpose to the ancient Egyptian system, the Chinese symbols were designed originally to represent certain concrete objects. What makes the Chinese writing system particularly difficult is the number of combinations of elements that a learner must memorize. For instance, the symbol for "good," 好 , consists of elements meaning "woman" and "son." The character for "love," 愛, *ai* consists of four elements meaning "claws," "a roof," "heart," and "move slowly." *Nang*, "nasal stoppage," written 齉 , consists of eleven identifiable separate units or combinations, a total of 38 strokes. The symbol is the most complex character listed in *Matthews' Dictionary*, the standard reference on Chinese character writing.

Very early in their history the Japanese adopted many features of Chinese culture, including its system of writing. Instead of one pronunciation for each character, Japanese has three, or more, pronunciations for each. One pronunciation is the Japanese version of the Chinese pronunciation of the symbols as of the date first borrowed (the Go-on pronunciation). Another pronunciation reflects a later pronunciation (the Kun-on pronunciation); the third way to pronounce the character reflects a Japanese pronunciation. The Chinese character 人 , *jen* is pronounced in various Japanese compound words as *nin* (Go-on), *jin* (kun-on), and *hito*. This last pronunciation is the Japanese word for "person." 門 , *men* is "door" or "gate" in Chinese.

The Japanese pronunciation is *mon* (Go-on), or *to*. *To* is used in the Japanese word *kado* (the *t* voices), and is the Japanese word for "gate."

It is rather obvious that to master a writing system such as Chinese or Japanese takes years and years, even for the native Chinese and Japanese. To read Japanese we must memorize at least 1,850 characters and their various pronunciations. To read Chinese we would have to memorize even more characters. Because of the extreme amount of memorization involved for anyone wishing to learn how to read these languages, attempts have been made in the past to simplify the Chinese and Japanese writing systems; but change has been difficult and slow, since both cultures take enormous pride in the artistic and esthetic appearance of the graphs. At present, the People's Republic of China appears to be attempting to simplify the characters employed in everyday communication by reducing the number of strokes for the more complex ones. The People's Republic has also made a number of attempts to institute a Romanized (alphabetic) writing system. The April 10, 1972, *Asahi Evening News*, an English language paper published in Japan, reported that Kiro-Mo-Jo, the President of the Academy of Sciences and Vice-Chairman of the National People's Congress, said that Chairman Mao was urging that the "Chinese characters . . . be reformed and that reform . . . take the form for the rest of the world—romanization." He added, however, that it would be difficult to adopt the ideas of "certain Japanese friends who recommended the amalgamation of the simplified characters of the two countries."

There have been previous successful attempts to reform the writing system of Japan. Approximately thirty years ago, the Japanese, under the urging of General Douglas MacArthur, who was then Chief of Occupational Forces in Japan, simplified the system, reducing the basic character inventory from 5,000 characters to a more manageable 1,850. This one reduction encouraged and provided the opportunity for a greater number of Japanese to become literate.

The Japanese, however, do not employ only Chinese characters in their writing system. While Chinese makes use only of characters, the Japanese have developed two additional sets of symbols called *hiragana* and *katakana*, which are syllabaries. These symbols are employed to indicate grammatical forms, such as verb suffixes. For instance, *kaku* is the base of "to write." The past "I wrote" is expressed as follows: *kakimashita. Kaki* is symbolized by the character (書き) and *mashita*, which indicates the past tense, has three syllables (*ma-shi-ta*) and is symbolized by three syllabics (ました). *Ma* is ま; *shi* is し; and *ta* is た.

JAPANESE: CONVENTIONAL (KAISHO), GRASS (SOSHO), HIRAGANA, KATAKANA

The Koreans, unlike the Chinese and Japanese, employ an alphabet that is just as efficient as the Greek or Latin, with letters that resemble Chinese characters. Interspersed among the Korean script are large numbers of Chinese characters that are still used to represent older Korean words. Still, the move toward the use of an alphabet is an important innovation.

Direction of writing also differs among the world's writing systems. The Roman, Greek, and Cyrillic alphabets are written from left to right. The Arabic and Hebrew syllabaries, by contrast, are written from right to left. The Chinese and Japanese systems are written from top to bottom and then from right to left.

PROBLEMS AND HORIZONS

No writing (or orthographical) system, regardless of the direction in which it is written, is totally efficient in representing speech. Intonation, which can often reflect a speaker's attitude, receives only rudimentary representation in English with the use of commas, periods, question marks, and exclamation points. And tone of voice can be inferred only from parenthetical remarks or third-person narrative: "he said ironically."

In literate societies writing develops to a certain extent on its own. Often writing has an influence on speech—most noticeably when "spelling pronunciations" develop—such as the pronunciation of the *t* in *often*, or even the *b* in *subtle*. Writing will at times convey information that the spoken version of a message leaves out, as for example, when English writing distinguishes *pear* from *pair*, *right* from *write*, and *pale* from *pail*, to mention only a few. Writing systems employ certain conventions that are unrelated to what we do in speech. Examples of this in our own system would include the use of capital letters, italics in printing, and much of our punctuation.

In this era of rapid communication the trend has been more and more to a simplification of writing systems. Alphabet reform has been an extremely lively issue in world affairs. In his program of modernization, Kemal Ataturk adopted the Roman alphabet for Turkish, in place of the Arabic syllabary previously employed in that country.

With all due admiration for the beauty of the writing systems of Japan and China, they both take an inordinate amount of time to master. Yet we must admit, for China especially—with its many dialects—the character system can be read throughout the nation with the same meaning. This occurs even when one speaker of Chinese cannot understand a speaker of another dialect.

Tone is also difficult to indicate in an alphabetic system. Vietnamese, for example, has attempted to solve the problem in its use of an alphabet, by writing symbols over and under the vowels to indicate the proper tone, leaving tone number one unmarked. Thus, in Vietnamese one writes:

$$\text{ma} \quad \text{má} \quad \text{mà} \quad \text{m\~a} \quad \text{m\=a} \quad \text{ma}_{\circ}$$

The above syllable has six different meanings according to its tone quality. Nevertheless, there remains another problem. The Vietnamese language has at least ten different vowels, the exact number depending on the dialect spoken. The Latin vowel letters are rather insufficient to indicate all the vowels, and the result is that a letter may have both a mark for tone and another (a diacritic) mark that indicates that pronunciation of the vowel, as in the following:

$$\text{rằng} \quad \text{giảm}$$

From time to time, there have been attempts to change English spelling. George Bernard Shaw made a provision in his will for an award to be made to the inventor of the best new system. President Theodore Roosevelt attempted to employ the resources and power of his office to institute a new, simplified, more phonetically based writing system. No public enthusiasm has been exhibited for such changes. To the contrary, Morris Halle and Noam Chomsky (*The Sound Pattern of English*) maintain that the present spelling system, discounting the irregularities, is a good system for English. And although movements for spelling reform occur, there appears little likelihood for spelling reform in the near future. Edgar Sturtevant once suggested that the best way to reform English spelling would be to quit teaching it.

One observation is certain: when a country adopts an orthography, it is extremely reluctant to change. Charles F. Hockett notes: "The language changes as languages always change; but for some reason peoples are more conservative about writing systems than about any other human institution that can be named—even religion."

The tendency for writing systems to become more conservative with time deserves comment. Few advances were made in the writing process until the printing press was developed in the 15th century by the German inventor Gutenberg. At that time, it became possible to make thousands of copies of any book. Previously, each book had to be laboriously copied by hand, and each copier varied the spelling of some of the words. Even proper names were given various spellings, as attested by the different ways that Shakespeare (Shakspear, Shakespear) spelled his own name. The printing press changed this attitude toward spelling. Henceforth, there would be one, and only one, way to spell a word, and any deviation from the norm, however logical it might be, was a certain sign of ignorance.

Nineteenth and twentieth century technology further revolutionized written communication. First came the telegraph, capable of transmitting messages around the world in a split second. Then the typewriter, which was developed late in the 19th century, greatly increased the speed at which a book could be copied. And now we have the electric typewriter, and typewriters that can be linked to mechanical scanners. Although typewriters are efficient for alphabetic systems, with their very small inventory of symbols, they are inefficient to transcribe the complex systems employed in Japan, China, and Korea.

Modern technology is bringing tremendous changes to written communication, thanks to such processes as offset printing, multilithing, mimeography, and the ubiquitous Xerox machine. Computers and input-output electric typewriters ensure storage and retrieval of vast amounts of information in a fraction of the time formerly required. Thus, librarians and researchers are developing the new science of information dissemination and retrieval, skills that are now a vital part of a librarian's training.

Daring advances are now commonplace in the discipline of space communications. We have learned to use the moon as a point from which signals can be ricocheted over vast distances. Telestar, an earth satellite, has led to international television programs broadcast simultaneously from one source to various places around the globe.

The first mark on an object, the first attempt to record and preserve a message, has led to this age, in which we can scarcely do without the medium of writing.

VIII. QUESTIONS AND ACTIVITIES

1. The Japanese child must learn at least 2,000 symbols to be highly literate. It takes him most of his public school years to learn them. How many years does it take an American child to learn the alphabet? Who would you rather be: a Japanese child who must learn the alphabet or an American child who must learn the symbols of Japanese writing?

2. Cite ten general spelling regularities in English. Cite ten words that do not conform to any rule and must therefore be memorized.

3. What is shorthand? How does it differ from regular writing?

4. Why is it that *solemn* is spelled with a final *n*; *damn* with a final *n*; and *sign* with a final *gn*? Are these spellings arbitrary or rule-governed?

5. Why is there so much emphasis in our culture on spelling correctly?

VIII. FOR FURTHER REFERENCE

Chomsky, Carol. 1970. "Reading, Writing, and Phonology." *Harvard Educational Review* May, 40:287-309.

Diringer, D. 1948. *The Alphabet*. New York: Philosophical Library.

_____. 1962. *Writing*. New York: Praeger.

Francis, W. Nelson. 1974. "Language, Speech, and Writing." *Spelling Progress Bulletin* 14:00-00.

Garvin, Paul L., ed. 1963. *Natural Language and the Computer*. New York: McGraw-Hill.

Gelb, I. J. 1963. *A Study of Writing*. Rev. ed. Chicago: University of Chicago Press.

Hays, David G. 1967. *Introduction to Computational Linguistics*. New York: American Elsevier.

Hockett, Charles F. 1958. *A Course in Modern Linguistics*. New York: MacMillan.

Irwin, Keith Gordon. 1958. *Man Learns to Write*. London: Dobson Books.

Kavanagh, James F. and Ignatius G. Mattingly, eds. 1972. *Language by Ear and Eye*. Cambridge, Mass.: The MIT Press.

Mey, Jacob. 1971. "Computational Linguistics in the 'Seventies." *Linguistics* 74:36-61.

Venezky, Richard L. 1970. *The Structure of English Orthography*. The Hague: Mouton.

Walpole, Jane R. 1974. "Eye Dialect in Fictional Dialogue." *College Composition and Communication* 25:191-96.

Wang, William S-Y. 1973. "The Chinese Language." *Scientific American* February, 228:50-63.

IX. Other Systems of Communication

GESTURES, BODY LANGUAGE, OR KINESICS

In recent years much attention has been directed toward the variety of gestures people make. While some gestures are universal to all cultures, others are unique to one. We might assume, for instance, that the nodding of the head in an up-down motion means "yes" to all people, and similarly that the shaking of the head from side to side means "no." But in India the converse is true: up-and-down means "no" and sideways means "yes." In the United States we shrug our shoulders if we are puzzled, slap our forehead if we forget, lift our eyebrows if we wish to question the veracity of a statement or position, wink one eye for intimacy, and so on. A fascinating study of gestures, or as it is technically called, *kinesics*, is to be found in Julius Fast's book, *Body Language*, and in E. T. Hall's *The Silent Language*.

Meaning is conveyed in many non-verbal ways. We are all accustomed to divining another person's meaning without a word being spoken. The hero says to the heroine, "Don't say anything—I understand." And we may drive along a road and suddenly see a sign; or arrive at a busy intersection where the traffic officer makes a signal for us to stop, then signals when it is safe to drive on. A car ahead makes a left turn, but before it does, the driver stretches out his left arm and points in the direction in which he intends to go. This is communication, and yet not a single word has been uttered. But that is not the extent of this kind of communication. A wife strongly hints that she would like to go out, so her husband takes her to a movie, where the ushers make signs to one another to find two seats together.

And this by no means exhausts the repertoire of ways in which messages can be sent. There appears to be no language in which speakers do not make use of gestures, or *pasimology*, as it is called. Athletic games such as baseball, boxing, and football have a definite set of hand symbols understandable to participants from any part of our country. The American Indians often made use of a code of gestures for intertribal conferences. In 1936 such a conference was called in Oklahoma, and pictures as well as a record of the gestures used may be consulted in the Smithsonian Institution in Washington.

We have all heard others, particularly southern Europeans and Mediterraneans, criticized because "they talk with their hands." E. T. Hall, an eminent anthropologist, points out in his book *The Silent Language* that gestures are used by all peoples although they differ in form and meaning. The classic example of this is that a wave of the hand with palms down means "goodbye" or "go away" in America, but a wave of the hand with the palm up means "come here"—while just the opposite can be signified by these gestures in parts of Italy.

Although there is a myth that the Anglo-Saxon cultural pattern is undemonstrative this is not really so. We gesticulate far more than we imagine. If we try to talk without making any sort of movement of the hands, body, forehead, or face, we will probably soon find communication almost impossible. Another revealing experiment is to turn on the television but turn off the sound. You will notice that there is scarcely a moment when the actors do not make some kind of non-verbal symbol.

A number of attempts have been made to harness gestural symbols to the task of helping man solve his international communication problem. The most successful attempt so far has been in the International Sign Language for Tourists devised by the late Stephen Streeter, a Washington travel expert. This language consists of 72 symbols to express basic concepts such as "I'm hungry," "Send a doctor," etc. A manual is available with explanations in nine world languages.

In developing his International Sign Language, Streeter found that there were a number of booby-traps. For example, he learned that one of his symbols meant "go to the devil" in Brazil, while he was obliged to give a wide berth to others which might have been offensive to certain religious and ethnic groups. *The Silent Language* gives many additional examples of how ignorance of the symbols of various cultures causes misunderstanding even when we have mastered the mechanics of the language involved.

In the Far East, there is the traditional dancing language of China, Korea, Japan, Vietnam, Indochina, and Indonesia where hands, rather than feet (as in Western dancing), carry the message. According to Mario Pei, a prolific writer on language subjects, there are in those conventionalized gestures 200 symbols to express various states of love.

The Trappist monks, whose rule includes a particularly rigorous discipline of silence, have developed an elaborate set of gesture symbols to enable them to carry on necessary communication without speaking. This is, of course, a higher level of organization in the use of gestures. Most gesture communication represents the largely unconscious accompaniment to speech. We also find isolated conventional signs like the hitch-hiker's thumbed request for a ride. The football referee's hand signals represent a small system of deliberately organized signs. Most gesture systems are limited to use for special purposes. Only in a few cases do we find basic communication carried out by gestural means, such as in the sign language of the deaf. Normal conversation can be carried on with only occasional recourse to spelling out English words by means of special alphabet-letter signals. An investigation into the functioning of this system, using methods comparable to those employed in the investigation of spoken language, has been inaugurated recently by the American linguist, William C. Stokoe, Jr., who says: "A symbol system by means of which persons carry on all the activities of their ordinary lives is, and ought to be treated as, a language." He has recently published a dictionary of this language and is in the process of bringing out other badly needed works.

People often ask why sign language did not originally develop instead of speech. Darwin attempted an answer to this question by pointing out that it was a matter of efficiency, basically, since gestural language demands the use of hands while oral speech leaves the hands free for other tasks. Gestural language also requires light while oral speech can proceed in the dark and at some distance from the person being addressed. It is obvious when one examines the matter that, compared with oral speech, manual (and other systems of) communication has many disadvantages which limit its range of expression. And of course it now appears likely that man was born to speak.

CODES

One of the most interesting forms of language is the whistle speech of the natives of Gomera in the Canary Islands, by which the islanders communicate for miles. Meanings in it are carried by modulations in the whistling pattern. Similar systems have been reported as being in use in the French Pyrenees and Haiti.

Another intriguing "language" is that of the drums, a standard medium of communication in many parts of Africa south of the Sahara. So effective is this that natives are able to communicate from one village to another through the drumbeats. From all indications, however, the inroads of modern communication, including radio, loudspeakers, and television, are taking their toll of these primitive systems of communication.

Drum signal messages often follow the tonal patterns of words they represent. Mazateco, a language of Central America with an elaborately complicated tonal system, is also associated with a form of whistle speech, in which ups and downs of pitch that ordinarily go with words are whistled.

While systems such as these derive from the spoken language, others derive from writing; Morse code and semaphore signals are examples. In these the basic units stand for letters of the alphabet:

	a	b	c	d	e
International Morse Code:	• —	— • • •	— • — •	— • •	•
Semaphore flag:					

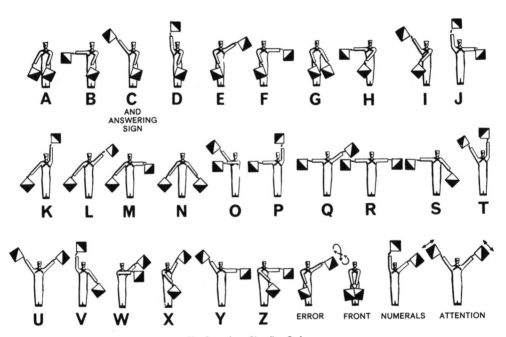

The Semaphore Signaling Code.

To this brief list may be added cable code and the international weather reporting code, elaborated by the Methodological Division of International Civilian Aviation, which operated according to five-figure groups.

Then there is the language of flowers, which, particularly in the days of chivalry, had definite meanings according to how the flowers were arranged. In past centuries, flicking a fan in a certain way had a definite meaning in the language of love. The language of bobby-soxers from an era long past reflects a certain kind of communication: the bobby sox straight up meant "available," one fold meant "going steady," rolled down meant "taken," beads knotted at the neck meant "dated," and so on.

Engagement and wedding bands also exercise communicative functions. They have their "grammar rules" too, for if a woman in America wears a certain type of ring on the third finger of her left hand she is probably engaged or married. In certain African tribes marriageable girls have definite styles of headdress and married women another. These are all systems in which only a small number of possible messages need to be kept straight. Perhaps as most typical we might cite the storm-warning flags hoisted at Coast Guard stations. Their meanings are: storm winds from the northeast; storm winds from the northwest; storm winds from the southeast; storm winds from the southwest; winds dangerous only to small craft; and HURRICANE!

We can see that signaling systems exist all around us. Some we do not even suspect. For example, beggars and vagabonds have a way in which they write on the walls of a house which warns their brethren either to avoid or approach it: "hostile" or "soft touch."

Codes can be, and actually are, devised constantly for special purposes. For instance, the message of the fall of Troy was sent to Greece by lighting an immense fire on hill after hill. A bonfire is still a symbol of "help, come rescue us" on land and sea. In a recent movie, police planning a raid agreed on a series of symbols, the first of which was the Chief of Police lighting a cigarette. Translated, the message was, "Begin the raid." Of course, we all remember Paul Revere's famous lanterns: "One if by land and two if by sea." Finally, graffiti, appearing often in the most unexpected places, as well as in restrooms, run a wide gamut of messages and sentiments, ranging from love and friendliness to pornography, hostility, and threats.

MORE DIFFUSE SYSTEMS

The pictorial form of communication is less tangible but very real. We all know the cliché that a picture is worth a thousand words. Actually, pictures are messages. People who know art can look at a picture, just as one listens to a speech or reads a letter, and interpret the message through the various clues given. Art interpreters refer to clues given by color, texture, shadings, tone, and arrangement. Abstract art was a reaction against the traditional pictorial realism and favors paintings and designs that are abstract. Instead of delivering an unmistakable message, it merely suggests objects, moods, or concepts. However, pictorial representation may be the oldest written language known to man.

Music has also been called a language. Styles and patterns vary—as we quickly notice when listening to native Chinese music consisting of only a few chords, as compared with the current hard rock—but the musical scale is a real alphabet, understood by musicians throughout the civilized world.

Music is even more symbolic than art and more subjective in interpretation, for the same musical selection that communicates a sense of joy to one person may bring a message of sorrow to his neighbor. The appeal of music is so universal that a 19th-century Frenchman devised an international world language based on the musical scales, and called it "Solresol." If this language had persisted, we might today walk into a restaurant and sing out in Solresol, "A hamburger with French fries and a malt, please."

A language of fabrics is used by the *cognoscenti* in the textile field; and even today schools in Japan teach the language or art of *ikebana* (flower arranging) and the language of the highly ritualistic tea ceremony.

Each time that we stop for a traffic light we are responding to one of a vast complex of non-verbal systems that we use to send messages to one another. We know that there are more than 4,000 different verbal languages, and if it were possible to enumerate non-verbal systems of communication, we might discover an even greater number.

IX. ACTIVITIES AND QUESTIONS

1. Describe ten gestures that accompany speaking, for instance, shrugging the shoulders.

2. How close can we get to a person when we are talking to him? Ask a person of another language whether the distance is the same in his culture.

3. What sorts of gestures do children learn early?

4. What are some of the differences between male and female gestures?

5. Demonstrate five nonverbal ways that we can use to indicate that a person is "out-of-his-mind."

6. Are there any gestures that have more than one meaning?

IX. FOR FURTHER REFERENCE

Birdwhistell, Ray L. 1970. *Kinesics and Contexts*. Philadelphia: University of Pennsylvania Press.

Burling, Robbins. 1970. *Man's Many Voices: Language in its Cultural Context*. New York: Holt, Rinehart and Winston.

Engel, Walburga von Raffler. 1975. "The Correlation of Gesture and Vocalizations in First Language Acquisition," in Adam Kendon, Mary Ritchie Key, and Richard M. Harris, eds: *Organization of Behavior in Face-to-Face Interaction*. The Hague: Mouton.

Fast, Julius. 1970. *Body Language*. New York: M. Evans.

Green, Jerald R. 1968. *A Gesture Inventory for the Teaching of Spanish*. Philadelphia: Chilton Books.

Key, Mary Ritchie. 1970. "Preliminary Remarks on Paralanguage and Kinesics in Human Communication." *La Linguistique*. 2:17-36.

Hall, Edward T. 1959. *The Silent Language*. New York: Doubleday.

Jakobson, Roman. 1972. "Motor Signs for 'Yes' and 'No'." *Language in Society* 1:91-96.

Ruesch, Jurgen and Weldon Kees. 1956. *Non-Verbal Communications: Notes on the Visual Perception of Human Relation*. Berkeley: University of California Press.

X. One Language for the World?

THE LANGUAGE BARRIER

The Old Testament described the multiplicity of languages as an affliction visited upon mankind, and history is replete with misunderstandings resulting from language barriers. Examples are at hand: A Venezuelan shipper sends an order for automobile spare parts to Italy—and is shipped tractor parts instead. The British Foreign Office uses the word *requerir* ("to demand") incorrectly—and the incensed French government demands an apology. American tourists in a Far Eastern city attempt to communicate in sign language—and are severely mauled because their gestures are interpreted as insults. People drown in a sea disaster (the *Andrea Doria*) because they cannot understand rescue directions given in a language other than their own.

Why not merely devise a universal language acceptable to all? Surely we were better off during the Middle Ages, when everything of international importance was expressed in Latin. And since then, a world language has been one of man's most persistent dreams. No fewer than 600 plans for a universal language have been proposed by men and women seeking a solution to the problems of communication. The parade of language planners has been a colorful and varied one and has included learned scholars and dilettantes, scientists and even crackpots.

Descartes, for example, speculated about a language so perfect in its symbolism that it would be impossible for human beings to err in it. In the 19th century a man named Sodre invented Solresol, a universal language based on the musical scale. And in this century some scholars devised Translingua Script, which makes use of numerical codes. For example, a tree would be known in every country by the number 31 and a man by 10 and so on.

Several billion people have, however, remained blissfully unaffected by the hundreds of schemes that have been devised to free them from their linguistic imbroglio. Most of the languages that have been invented have never traveled much farther than the walls of the inventor's own study or at least beyond a handful of devotees. Only a few of the remainder have made any kind of impact at all.

VOLAPÜK

The first constructed language to enjoy mass appeal was *Volapük*, devised in 1879 by a German monsignor by the name of Johann Martin Schleyer, a man whose linguistic prowess became legendary—he was reputed to have spoken more than 70 languages. Schleyer created Volapük (meaning "world speech") out of English, French, German, and the Romance languages, with reliance upon his native German as a source of word basis. The Lord's Prayer in Volapük appeared as follows:

O Fat obas, kel binol in süls, paisaludomöz nem ola! Kömomöd monargän ola! Jenomöz vil olik, as in sül i su tal! Bodi obsik vädeliki givolös obes adelo! E pardolos obes debis obsik, äs id obs aipardobs debeles obas. E no obis nindukoläs in tentadi; sed aidalivolös obis de bad. Jenosöd!

Volapük appeared at a time when the world was particularly receptive to a world language. It was the rage of Europe from 1879 to 1889, and societies were formed in which pastry cooks hobnobbed with archdukes in a fraternal effort to master the new "world" language. In the United States, the American Philosophical Society (founded by Benjamin Franklin) considered supporting the language, but eventually decided that it was too difficult. Some Parisian department stores even gave their sales personnel lessons in the new language.

The success of Volapük was, however, shortlived, largely because of the difficulty of its grammar, with complicated case-endings and a sound system that included the front round vowels, symbolized in German by *ü* and *ö*. The language collapsed in 1889 at an international conference of Volapük speakers when enthusiasts, attempting to deliver speeches in the language, found it too "cumbersome" to use.

ESPERANTO

After Volapük, a new language appeared—*Esperanto*, the creation of Dr. Lukwik Zamenhof, a Polish doctor reared in the city of Bialystok where Poles, Lithuanians, Ukrainians, Germans, Russians, and Jews lived together in uneasy hostility. The idealistic doctor came to feel that the basis of tension among peoples resulted from language, and that a universal language would bring peace and understanding.

Zamenhof based his international language on English, German, and the Romance languages, with the heaviest reliance on the latter. Profiting from the experience of Volapük, Zamenhof aimed—quite successfully, we believe—at utmost simplicity in designing Esperanto. Nevertheless, Professor Richard E. Wood of Adelphi University, a leading linguist, polyglot and Esperantist, observes that the language is only Romance-Germanic in basic word stock, although it follows a largely independent pattern in word-formation processes, the coining of compound words, and the like. He adds, moreover, that, "the philosophical basis of Esperanto is independent (as was that of Volapük) rather than neo-Romance."

The rules of Esperanto can actually be learned in a few hours. To learn to use the language is quite another matter, however. The sound system is familiar for most Indo-European speakers and difficult for speakers of many Oriental and African languages.

Here is a sample of Esperanto:

Esperanto	*English*
La astronomo, per speciala teleskopo fotografas la sunon, la lunon, kaj la planedojn.	The astronomer, by means of a special telescope, photographs the sun, the moon, and the planets.
Modernaj delikataj instrumentoj permesas la detalan ekzamenon de la strukturo de la atomo.	Modern, delicate instruments permit the detailed examination of the structure of the atom.
La teorio de Einstein, la nova principo de relativeco, presentas komplikan problemon.	The Einstein theory, the new principle of relativity, presents a complex problem.

A few degrees greater in difficulty is the following technical passage, furnished by Professor Margaret Hagler of Lincoln Land Community College, Springfield, Illinois:

Esperanto

Ekologio estas la fako de biologio pri reciprokaj rilatoj inter vivantaj organismoj—kaj plantoj kaj animaloj—kaj ties ĉirkaŭaĵoj. Modernaj ekologistoj emfazis la studadon de la rilatoj de homaroj al iliaj naturaj kaj urbaj ĉirkaŭaĵoj. Ekologistoj asertas, ke la evoluo de moderna teknologio okazigis grandajn avantaĝojn, sed ankaŭ pliigis malpurigon de la aero, akvo, kaj grundo. Tamen la eldono de ekologiaj esploradoj igis plej grandan publikan scion de la graveco de tia fako.

English

Ecology is the field of biology concerned with relationships between living organisms—plant and animal—and their environments. Modern ecologists have emphasized the study of the relationship of human beings to their natural and urban surroundings. Ecologists point out that the development of modern technology has brought great benefits, but has also caused increased pollution of the air, water, and soil. However, publication of ecological research has led to greater public knowledge of the importance of this field.

Today, almost 85 years since its genesis and 67 years after the first Esperanto World Congress, which ushered in the period of its practical use, Esperanto remains alive. But many students consider it to be more of a philosophical movement than a language. Still, each year, Esperantists hold a Universal Congress. A wide range of programs in cultural and social activities is offered, as well as several score of specialized conferences, all in the *internacia lingvo*. In many places in the world, the wearer of the Esperantists' green badge (green for hope) can rely upon fellow members for assistance in getting around. At the various World's Fairs, for instance, Esperanto interpreters are available along with those in national languages.

One of the co-authors of this book was invited to participate in a newly formed "Seminar on Esperanto Language and Literature and Interlanguages," as part of the annual meeting of the prestigious Modern Language Association of America, held in New York in December, 1972; the seminar was attended by more than 50 persons, which gave evidence of the rather remarkable vigor of the Esperanto movement. The participants included a number of well-known linguists, and discussions were conducted on the future of Esperanto (and other interlanguages), on literary production in the language, and on the development of teaching programs. A modest number of high schools and colleges in this country offer the language, though mostly not for credit.

One of the more interesting papers at the seminar was that of Howard P. French, a professor of German at Southern Illinois University, whose remarks on "Esperanto and Academic Respectability" emphasized the need for a more scholarly image of the movement. Following French's paper, Margaret Hagler addressed herself to "Esperanto as a Poetic Medium." Finally, William Solzbacher, a policy officer at the Voice of America, pointed out that more than 50 scholarly publications in 15 countries now publish articles or summaries in Esperanto, and about 145 periodicals are printed entirely in the language. Fifteen radio stations in Rome, Vienna, Warsaw, Sofia, Valencia, Peking, Stoke-on-Trent, and Berne broadcast programs in Esperanto. In the 1960s the Voice of America employed Esperanto in four series of shortwave programs and received almost 2,000 letters in Esperanto from 91 countries. From one count, Esperanto is taught in at least 700 schools in 40 countries. When the University of Leningrad, years ago, broke a long-standing ban and announced classes in Esperanto, there was a surge of applicants.

Esperanto organizations today number about 110,000 actual members. Esperanto remains the only interlanguage that can claim a considerable literature, with some 8,400 titles that include original works as well as translations of the Bible, the *Divine Comedy*, and even *Winnie the Pooh*, recently translated by Professor Humphrey Tankin, former vice provost for Undergraduate Education at the University of Pennsylvania.

The seeming vitality of Esperanto is perhaps best reflected by the variety of spoken and written uses to which it continues to be put. The official Finnish tourist agency put out a guide to Finland in Esperanto, and the International Confederation of Free Syndicates in Paris distributes a pamphlet in this language. The July 11, 1966, issue of *Business Abroad*, a Dun and Bradstreet publication, in its article, "How European Businessmen Use Esperanto," pointed out that the Volkswagen, Gevaert, Philips, and Fiat concerns, as well as KLM Dutch Airlines, find Esperanto valuable for printed advertising matter. Recently, two publishers, E. P. Dutton in New York and the Channing Bete Company of Greenfield, Massachusetts, have reacted to an interest in Esperanto by preparing various new materials in it. The latter firm has produced a 14-hour cassette course.

As the above may suggest, Esperanto is intended to cut across ethnic, political, religious, and ideological boundaries. Its proponents point to the argument of its founder Zamenhof that its use shows neither favoritism nor prejudice to any politico-social group. They feel that, since it is not tied to any specific nationality, state, or culture, Esperanto has an advantage over culture-bound languages. Finally, they deny the notion that it seeks to replace national and ethnic languages, but declare that it merely provides a needed auxiliary communicative tool.

INTERLINGUA

As inevitably occurs, one group after another has broken away from Esperanto to form offshoots, such as Ido, Novial, and Occidental. Nevertheless, none of these has ever made much progress.

The only language that has seriously challenged Esperanto is *Interlingua*, presented to the world by the late American linguist Dr. Alexander Gode, whose work over a period of 20 years was supported by Mrs. Alice Vanderbilt Morris, who believed in a world language.

Interlingua is what its founder calls an "extracted" rather than a "derived" language. This means that a given word is generally taken in toto and subjected to little or no modification. Other constructed languages have generally altered words considerably to make them conform to prescribed patterns. The Interlingua vocabulary is taken from French, Italian, Spanish, English, and, to a much lesser extent, German and Russian. Only words that appear in at least three of these languages are adopted. When no word meets this requirement, a word is usually taken from Latin. Gode made attempts to construct the language as carefully as possible in an effort to arrive at what he calls "standard average European." Interlinguists claim that the language can be read with little or no previous study by educated persons. Its structure resembles Esperanto and can be learned in a few hours. A book comparing the difficulties of these two languages recently appeared. It was written by an Esperantist, and, not surprisingly, his conclusions were favorable to Esperanto.

Here is an example of Interlingua:

Interlingua	*English*
Professor H. Oberth, un del pioneros in le campo del rochetteria scientific in Germania e plus recentemente un associato de Dr. W. von Braun in su recercas de roccheteria al arsenal Redstone in Alabama, ha elaborate un vehiculo adoptate al exploration del luna. Un tal vehiculo debe esser capace a superar le difficultates extraordinari del terreno e del ambiente del luna que es characterisate per le absentia de omne atmosphere, per un gravitate reducite, per extrememente acute alterationes de temperatura, e per un superficie plus pulverose que ullo cognoscite in terra.	Professor H. Oberth, one of the pioneers in the field of scientific rocketry in Germany and more recently an associate of Dr. W. von Braun in his research on rocketry at the Redstone Arsenal in Alabama, has elaborated plans for a vehicle adapted for lunar exploration. Such a vehicle must be capable of overcoming the extraordinary difficulties of the terrain and surroundings of the moon, characterized by the absence of any atmosphere, by reduced gravity, by extremely sharp changes of temperature, and by a more dusty surface than any known on earth.

For the present at least, the aims of Interlingua are more modest than those of Esperanto. No real attempt has been made to promote it as a spoken language, although one of the authors heard and even understood a talk given in it at a meeting of the Modern Language Association of America. Its first objective is to gain acceptance as a medium of scientific and scholarly communication. It has done quite well in the 20 years of its existence, and by now, 20 journals make use of Interlingua, mostly for summaries. The Interlingua Division of Science Service, Inc., in Washington, D.C., attempts to promote Interlingua by offering to provide summaries and abstracts in that language for specialized journals and résumés for conferences of international research significance. (This organization also publishes an Interlingua version of *Science News Letter*.) By now there are several newsletters in Interlingua for subdisciplines in which no specific periodicals are available.

According to Gode, "The community of those who can be reached through Interlingua includes anyone with fair or full qualifications to grasp the technical import of the same message if presented in either French, Italian, Spanish, English, Greek, or Latin. In many scientific disciplines this makes for the possibility of complete and world-wide coverage through Interlingua . . . on the basis of what the reader knows and has known all along by virtue of his professional training."

Archibald A. Hill, in an article in *Texas Quarterly*, reviewed the status of constructed and simplified languages. Hill, who entitled his paper "Esperanto au Dubitanto" ("Hope or Doubt," in Esperanto), feels that a serious shortcoming of all the contenders so far is their failure to embody new insights and understandings from recent linguistic theory, particularly as regards phonological and suprasegmental features. Hill grants, however, that these constructed languages have a utility in limited-scope communicative tasks, such as serving as the language for learned and scientific papers at multilingual conferences. He concludes, though, that: "Auxiliary languages are not now, and to me seem unlikely ever to become, substitutes for natural languages, the media in which men have always expressed everything that is important to them. In an age when communication in depth, reaching into all levels of cultural activity, is a necessity for survival, anything which discourages us from the hard labor of language and culture study by offering a simple and easy kind of ersatz is a genuine and serious peril." This view by a respected linguist should temper all future attempts to construct artificial languages.

At the present time, the principal moving spirit of the Interlingua movement is Frank Esterhill, Executive Director of the Interlingua Institute in New York City (P.O. Box 126, Canal Street Station), where activities appear to be concentrated. He edits the Interlingua Institute Newsletter, performs translations and summaries (mostly of scientific work) and, possessing a knowledge of modern linguistics, appears frequently at scholarly conferences, or at panels where the relative merits of Esperanto and Interlingua are debated. Interlingua has been offered in the Division of General Education of York University and elsewhere.

OTHER APPROACHES

Another method of arriving at an artificial international auxiliary language has been suggested to the authors. The Russian linguist N. D. Andreyev believes that intermediary languages containing most of the features shared by the major natural languages will necessarily be developed in work on machine translation done by electronic computers. When the ideal intermediate language has been devised, Andreyev feels that it will be usable for human international communication.

Another suggestion recommends the simplification of existing languages. The best known of these attempts has resulted in *Basic English*, devised by the British philosopher, C. K. Ogden, and promoted in America by I. A. Richards. With its limited vocabulary of 800 words and 16 general-purpose verbs, "Basic" may sound easy. In reality, however, we have found that it requires skill to manipulate this small stock of words so that complex concepts may be expressed. Even to say "The watermelon tastes good," we are required to say, "The large, round, sweet vegetable has a good taste." Basic English reached its peak during World War II when it received a strong endorsement from Prime Minister Winston Churchill and the British Government.

Here is a sample of Basic English:

Basic English (New Testament)	King James Bible (Acts 4:32)
And all those who were of the faith were one in heart and soul: and not one of them said that any of the things which he had was his property only; but they had all things in common. . . . And no one among them was in need; for everyone who had land or houses, exchanging them for money, took the price of them, and put it at the feet of the Apostles for distribution of everyone as he had need.	And the multitude of them that believed were of one heart and one soul: neither said any of them that ought of the things which he possessed was his own; but they had all things common. . . . Neither was there any among them that lacked: for as many as were possessors of lands or houses sold them, and brought the prices of the things that were sold, and laid them down at the apostles' feet: and distribution was made unto every man according as he had need.

While Basic English appears to have lost the support of the British Government, the Voice of America's Special English (also with an 800-word vocabulary) has made some inroads. For example, in various parts of the world (such as San Andreas Island, Colombia, where Spanish is the language of instruction) people can learn English from those broadcasts. (Vocabularies and explanatory material are available to listeners upon request from the Voice of America headquarters in Washington.)

And progress has been made by the Federal Aviation Agency with Basic or Special English for international aviation communication, since its short vocabulary is useful for limited conversations such as those between air and ground. Unfortunately, the use of English in any form presents problems. Certain phonemes, such as /f/ and /s/ (both fricatives), do not transmit well and can be confused. Monosyllables, as in the case of *five* and *nine*, can be confused also. Moreover, there is scarcely an English phoneme that is not difficult to pronounce for one language group or another. Scandinavians have trouble with /j/ and the Japanese with /l/ and /r/.

Some scholars have vigorously opposed "constructed" or "simplified" languages, and advocate that a number of natural languages can assume the position of a world language. These languages include French, English, German, Russian, Spanish, Italian, Greek, Chinese, Latin, Hebrew, and even Yiddish. Only French and English have any real chance of acceptance in the Western world, because these two languages are actually functioning as second or foreign languages on almost every continent.

OTHER ATTEMPTS

Codes are being devised in other disciplines as well. Specialists in documentation, concerned with the worldwide collection and retrieval of information, have made increasing use of data processing machines and have developed international codes and symbols to control greater amounts of information than ever before.

One of the challenging by-products of "intelligent machine" research is the development of an international computer language. According to Bell Telephone research scientist John R. Pierce, an international computer language would consist of various forms of an "artificial, unambiguous, logical, mathematical language" understandable to all computer programmers.

Development of a "metalanguage," which would not be read or spoken by anyone but would merely be usable by computers that would "read" and "translate" it into any language desired, may become a possibility. Walter Sullivan, writing in the October 11, 1971, *New York*

Times, discussed the World Science Information System (UNISIST) in Paris. He touched upon its aim to "bring the many national and international systems for processing information into line so that information recorded for storage in one computer system can be fed into any other." At that same meeting, Dr. Harris Brown, foreign secretary of the National Academy of Sciences, pointed out that today's researcher is confronted by more than 35,000 journals in at least 50 languages, with the likelihood that in the future, he might have to reckon with 8,000,000 fellow investigators and a pool of 350,000 scientific and technical journals in various foreign languages.

PROSPECTS

And so the search continues. Esperanto and Interlingua advocates argue that their "languages" are easy to learn. They point out that since these "languages" are not identified with any specific nation, they are free of political overtones that make other languages—for instance, English and French—unacceptable to some countries, particularly the small, new nations. Yet, languages that are not rooted in a specific nation deprive their learners of access to the rich cultural heritage that the major languages afford. Others argue that a natural language such as English, German, Arabic, Russian, and Chinese is well worth learning since it provides access not only to a major culture but also to millions of people.

What remains of the prospects for a universally acceptable auxiliary language? Mario Pei, in his *One Language for the World*, says the answer will not come through creating new, artificial languages, since some natural languages are adequate for the task. Pei proposed that an international conference be called to discuss the merits of a number of languages and that one be adopted. Each nation would then pledge itself to teach that language in its school system. Pei believes that the world would become bilingual within a generation, and that bilingualism would sweep away many of the barriers that plague international communication today.

Since this second language would be taught mainly to children, the difficulties that adults might experience in learning it would not be a consideration. Pei suggests, for that reason, Mandarin Chinese—written in an alphabet—as his choice, however unlikely it might have seemed in yesterday's political situation. Although Pei sent copies of his book containing these suggestions to the heads of many governments, there has been no wholesale movement to date to take concerted action on this matter.

X. QUESTIONS AND ACTIVITIES

1. Children as well as adults can, if taught, learn a rule that will enable them to make English "deviant." "Pig Latin" is a deviation. Have someone demonstrate "Pig Latin" and then attempt to extrapolate the rule that is learned. What must an English speaker know to speak "Pig Latin?"

2. Why do certain languages become world languages? For example, French was often called "the language of diplomacy."

3. In Viet Nam, French was the second language, at least of the intelligentsia. Why?

4. In South Africa, Afrikaans is the official language. How did Afrikaans become the official language of an African state?

5. Is Esperanto growing in popularity or decreasing? What is your view of the future of "languages" like Esperanto?

6. What language would you propose as a world language? Why?

X. FOR FURTHER REFERENCE

Connor, George Alan, D. T. Connor, and William Solzbacher. 1948. *Esperanto: The World Inter-Language*. New York: Bechhurst Press.

Descartes, René. 1966. *The Meditations and Selections from the Principles of René Descartes*. John Veitch, translator. La Salle, Ill.: The Open Court Publishing Company.

Encyclopaedia Britannica. 11th ed. 1910-11. "Universal Languages."

Greenberg, Joseph, ed. 1966. *Universals of Language*. 2nd ed. Cambridge, Mass.: M.I.T. Press.

Hill, Archibald A. 1960. "Esperanto au Dubitanto." *Texas Quarterly* 3:150-55.

Pei, Mario. 1961. *One Language for the World*. New York: Devin-Adair.

Samarin, W. J. 1962. "Lingua Francas, with Special Reference to Africa," in Frank A. Rice, ed.: *Study of the Role of Second Languages in Asia, Africa, and Latin America*. Washington: Center for Applied Linguistics.

White, Ralph G. 1972. "Toward the Construction of a Lingua Humana." *Current Anthropology* 13:113-23.

XI. Implications and Applications: Social, Political, and Educational Consequences

"Language Riots in Assam! Scores Killed! Forty People Die! 40,000 Flee!"

It may be hard to believe the headlines printed in the international press in July 1960, concerning a region that many of us never knew existed. The speakers of Assamese (comprising about half of the nine million population of Assam) were rebelling against what they considered to be domination by persons of Bengali origin. When demands for adoption of Assamese as the official state language were not met by the Delhi government, the streets ran wild. The violence lasted for more than two months, and frantic appeals for national unity echoed throughout the land.

Bloodshed over language differences may startle us, yet from time immemorial people have been willing to risk their lives to defend ethnic and language rights. Language riots, we can see, are often the simple result of the competition among different language communities for predominance. Attachment to one's native language is a universal characteristic, and emotionalism is likely to flare up when one group is convinced that its language and culture are receiving less recognition and status than another. At the present time, when so many peoples are demanding self-determination, language rights have become one of the most visible issues of the day.

There is probably no greater example of the kinds of linguistic problems which exist than those of the Indian subcontinent. In 1946, after Great Britain released its hold on India, this vast area split into Pakistan and India. The language problem was immediate because of the number of languages and dialects which abound in that region. A sequel was recently written as the predominantly Bengali-speaking East Pakistan (or a large portion of it) broke away from Pakistan and became the new nation of Bangladesh.

Estimates of the number of major languages and dialects spoken today on the Indian subcontinent range as high as 500. However, after many years of British rule, English has become a convenient interlanguage, used both to communicate with people from other regions and to conduct official business; in reality, though, only an elite minority of about five percent are able to speak English. Independence gave the various language groups an opportunity to press their claims, while at the same time plans were being made by the government to abandon English entirely.

We believe that a glance at the diversified linguistic picture of the Indian subcontinent is essential if we are to gauge its import in other areas. No fewer than five main language families exist: Aryan or Indic (Indo-European), Dravidian, Munda, Tibeto-Chinese, and Mon-Khmer; for years the speakers of these languages have eyed one another with hostility. The largest and apparently the most important language family is Aryan, which has existed in India for the last 3,000 years and to which ancient Sanskrit and modern Hindi both belong. Dravidian is second in importance, covering roughly most of southern India and including the separate languages of Tamil, Telugu, Kanarese, and Malayalam. The speakers of Munda are much more economically primitive than the Aryans and Dravidians, although there is reason to believe that they may have been the first inhabitants of the subcontinent. The Tibeto-Chinese and the Mon-Khmer are fairly recent arrivals and are small in number and influence.

When India became independent, the government declared Hindi to be the overall "union" language, but it also granted official status to twelve other important regional languages of the country: Assamese, Bengali, Gujarati, Kannada (Kanarese), Kashmiri, Malayalam, Marathi, Oriya, Punjabi, Tamil, Telugu, and Urdu. In addition, Sanskrit enjoys official status and is employed as a classical lingua franca among highly educated Hindus. English exists, in effect, as a co-partner with Hindi as an interlanguage.

The preferred position given to Hindi, however, provoked linguistic jealousy among the Dravidians in the south. Even other Aryan speakers, such as the Bengalis, who think of themselves as the cultural leaders of India, felt that they had been forced to take the proverbial back seat. In Pakistan, the choice of Urdu, although acceptable in West Pakistan, was questioned in East Pakistan (from which it was separated by almost 1,000 miles), where Bengali was the vernacular. By now, of course, as a result of bloody conflict, chronicled in detail in the world press, the independent nation of Bangladesh has been created in East Pakistan, with Bengali remaining as the official language.

If there was, however, a single point which all linguistic factions agreed upon, it was that English must be replaced as the official language. (India in its constitution had committed itself to displacing English by 1960 while Pakistan specified no date.) But this was easier in theory than in practice as both countries find themselves today still leaning heavily on the language of their former British rulers.

Not so many years ago when Russian Premier Khrushchev visited India, he repeated the slogan, "Hindi Rusi Bhai bhai," or, "Indians and Russians are brothers." His listeners, particularly in the south, appeared confused because few could understand what he had said. And even in India's north, a considerable part of the population is not able to understand Hindi. Professor W. Norman Brown of the University of Pennsylvania noted at an educational conference in Pakistan that delegates from Bangladesh frequently complained that they could not understand speeches in Urdu. That this should obtain should not surprise us, however.

There are also tremendous obstacles to be overcome whenever the use of a new language is extended to old fields. All terminology, all reference books, all written precedents cannot be erased, forgotten, or translated overnight. It also should not surprise us that in India the courts, except on the lower levels, conduct their business even today in English only. Though terminology can be coined or borrowed from Sanskrit or Persian, it would be so new and unfamiliar that much of it would have little immediate meaning to its listeners. Indian and Pakistani lexicographers have simply not been able to coin and popularize new vocabulary rapidly enough to keep up with the needs of the country and its growing industrialization and intellectual development. Even in the universities, professors resort to the use of English almost entirely in their courses.

Insight into some of the major problems associated with multilingualism is treated in a field study by John Gumperz of the University of California. He studied at first hand the languages spoken in a fairly typical Indian village whose inhabitants, mostly illiterate or barely semiliterate, could speak a Hindi dialect. Yet they had difficulty in understanding technical presentations and lectures by speakers of the Hindi dialect spoken in Delhi. He found that few persons listened to the All India Radio news broadcasts because of their inability to understand the dialect and the terminology. India's Community Development Project is striving to mitigate these obstacles. Gumperz' study, however, illustrates how the striving for literacy may complicate the task of "language engineering" involved in encouraging or even requiring the use of one language by all the people of a nation state.

Selig S. Harrison may be slightly overstating his case when he comments in his book, *India: The Most Dangerous Decades*, that "Unless central educational controls can assure sufficient learning in English or unless Hindi is taught on a scale which now seems unimaginable, it is entirely possible that India will be led in not too many years by a generation of bureaucrats and politicians literally unable to talk meaningfully to one another on a national stage."

In the meantime, the linguistic cauldron continues to boil. For example, a few years ago in Orissa, state police were forced to use tear gas to disperse mobs, while other demonstrators stopped trains in Madras state. And in central India, upon learning that language problems were to be discussed, groups of demonstrators broke into the legislature of Madhya Pradesh state, throwing stones, articles of clothing, paper files, and miscellaneous objects at the legislators.

Several years ago the Sikhs, a sect numbering five million in Punjab province, agitated for their language rights. Fearing that they would be swallowed up by Hindi speakers, they continued to clamor for greater use of Punjabi, emphasizing their point with planned demonstrations.

The Sikhs finally settled for a language formula in which their native language, Punjabi, written in a special alphabet called Gurmukhi, would be used in grade school, while in the later school years Hindi would be the language of instruction. But conservative leaders, including Arya Samaj, preaching "Hindi for Indians," noisily protested this policy.

Many Indian students have expressed concern that India may dangerously weaken itself by granting too many small groups linguistic and cultural autonomy; they fear that India may fall prey to the dread specter of "balkanization," the splitting of a country into a patchwork of ineffectual rival groups, all competing for power. This fear, even with the recent disappearance of democratic government, remains strong today.

The states of the Indian subcontinent are finding it necessary to depend heavily on English in communicating not only with one another but with the rest of the world as well. There has not yet been time enough to translate texts and reference books. For this reason a special committee on higher education in India has steadily warned against a tendency on the part of the universities to replace English as a medium of instruction before these universities are equipped sufficiently to carry on instruction in the native languages. This same committee also pointed out that it is in the national interest to retain English as the second language in all universities, that any change should proceed in gradual stages, and that the government ought to provide for a proper foundation in English for secondary school students who plan to attend a university. Yet, English as a medium of instruction has virtually disappeared from the elementary and secondary schools, being retained only as a foreign language. While India's universities vary, in most cases there is a trend toward the increased use of regional languages.

Why, we may ask, does India appear unwilling to adopt English as a second language? The answer appears quite simple. It is primarily a matter of national or ethnic pride. To the people of the Indian subcontinent, English will always be the language of their former conqueror, the British Empire. At the same time, the Hindus, at least, have not forgotten that India has produced a highly advanced civilization and a philosophy and literature written in Sanskrit, the parent of modern Hindi-Urdu.

ISRAEL

Perhaps an even more striking example of language planning exists in Israel, with its immigrants from some 70 countries. Hebrew, a language not spoken for millennia, was "revived" and made the official language, an action related to the Israelis' consciousness of their past, a regard for the role of Hebrew in the development of Judeo-Christian tradition, and a desire to avoid any language reminiscent of former persecutors. Naturally, new terminology has to be coined or borrowed, but structure and basic vocabulary remain the same as in the Old Testament. Hebrew began to be "modernized" in the late 19th century and was becoming "sociologically complete" by the time it was officially adopted in 1946. Now used in all phases of life, it is probably one of the most rapid cases in history of the adoption of a language by a whole nation. English, however, is still spoken by virtually all educated people in Israel.

IRELAND

In decided contrast, however, is the sad case of modern Ireland, or Eire, which, on achieving independence in the 1920s, declared Irish Gaelic, spoken by only a small group in a few counties, co-official with English and a compulsory school subject. Societies have been formed in Eire to further the use of Irish. Literary competitions have been arranged and folk festivals are organized by the government. Nevertheless, while feeling no less Irish, the citizens of Ireland apparently do not feel a strong need for the ancestral language. It is doubtful that Irish Gaelic will ever replace English, which, although spoken by Cromwell and other anti-Irish Britishers, has been the principal language of Ireland since the 16th century and earlier.

AFRICA

Even though the Irish continue to employ English rather than the older Irish Gaelic, we still maintain that language—like religion—can become a symbol of solidarity or even emancipation when a people feel insecure, threatened, and unprotected; as, for instance, appears to be the case in parts of Africa, where today the flame of nationalism burns brightly. The desire for self-government brings political groups forward with demands for independence and the right to provide education in a native African language.

Africa south of the Sahara Desert represents a startling linguistic enigma. A few years ago an editor of an African daily was beaten in Uganda for using the "wrong" forms of the Luganda dialect, which had shortly before been standardized. This incident reflects the emotionalism attached to matters of language on that continent, where countries are desperately seeking a common language with which to communicate with their citizens, their neighbors, and the world.

The immensity of the language problems encountered in Africa can be grasped if we glance at a linguistic map of the continent. South of the Sahara alone there are 800 distinct languages. Instead of the neat, monolithic language families found in areas of western Europe or Latin America or even in India, the number of dialects and languages here may remind us of a crazy quilt. What makes matters even more difficult is that there are no languages which are spoken by a majority of the population. Swahili and Hausa, two of the larger language groups, are spoken by approximately eight percent of the population. In large parts of Africa many tribes in neighboring villages can communicate only through French, English, or in some instances, Portuguese or Arabic.

No one is more aware than Africans themselves of the obstacles confronting them in their quest for political solidarity, respectability, and technological progress. Nations such as those in Africa can neglect major Western languages at their technological peril, for according to some recent UNESCO figures, approximately 70 percent of all scientific writing is in French, German, and English, with English accounting for 62 percent of the total. Sociologist Janet Roberts remarks that, "The scientific and technical material needed to convert basically agricultural states to industrial nations is largely restricted to three or four languages, including Russian, in which a growing bulk of research is being printed."

Yet technological progress is only one face of the coin; the other is that of political, economic, and social solidarity, which is even more difficult to achieve when mutual intelligibility is not present, a fact recognized by Africa's leaders. On the eve of Ghana's independence, President Kwame Nkrumah said before that country's Parliament, "One of the most obvious difficulties which faces Africa south of the Sahara is the multiplicity of languages and dialects. Every one of us in this Assembly today has to conduct parliamentary business in a language which is not his own. I sometimes wonder how well the House of Commons in the United Kingdom, or the Senate of the United States, would manage if they suddenly found that they had to conduct their affairs in French or Spanish."

Let us glance for a moment at Ghana's linguistic composite. Its six and a half million people speak approximately 100 different languages, six of which are spoken by sizable populations. These are Twi, with almost three million, and Dagari, Ewe, Ga, Moshi-Dagbande, and Nzema, none of which is used by more than a quarter of a million people, while Hausa is understood in some areas as a lingua franca. Viewing this linguistic mosaic, the newly created state decided to adopt English as its official language. English is used in governmental and commercial situations with native languages employed for more informal exchange. Nevertheless, only a tiny minority, or an estimated 120,000, speak English, comprising an elite that has access to leadership and professional advancement.

If the African states are to become bilingual or trilingual, assuming that English or French will continue to be spoken, which native languages are to be selected? Here it is almost impossible to make choices without treading on tribal and group sensitivities. For example, the Nandis and Kipsigis of Kenya speak mutually intelligible languages but have refused to accept literature in the other's language because they "could not understand it." A committee established to solve this problem soon realized that the lack of comprehension stemmed from political rather than linguistic causes, and gave them both equal status under the blanket term "Kalenjin."

In Uganda, a mission committee attempted to solve the language problem of a northern province in which tribes refused to communicate with one another despite great similarity in languages. It created a composite language only to have one tribe whose language differed greatly reject it completely. Finally, the language did come into use and was known as the "church language." The Baganda of Uganda are extremely jealous and refuse to allow any other language to be given preference over their native Luganda, which at present shares official status with English. It is not strange, therefore, that even in Uganda, where political parties have had 20 years of experience under British tutelage, that Minister of Agriculture Joseph Mukasa once termed tribalism the greatest threat to that country.

It would not surprise us if the emerging African governments, themselves sensitive to problems of self-determination, were eager to accord as much autonomy as possible to separate ethnic groups and their languages. There have been some steps in this direction. Nigeria, for example, has been allowing regional governments to establish advisory councils for the ethnic minorities which before independence were demanding the creation of autonomous states. But there exists in this practice the danger of "balkanization." The number of languages in Africa obviously both aids and abets this threat. In Nigeria itself, an unsuccessful attempt to secede and establish an Ibo-speaking independent Biafra took place, and a certain number of Ibos in exile have not yet given up these aspirations.

There are at least two contradictory forces at work in Africa today. One is tribalism (or pluralism) and the other is nationalism. Africa's leaders vary, which means that views of self-determination for ethnic groups vary. For example, Nkrumah, Ghana's late "Osafegyo," favored pluralism, while Julius Nyerere, Prime Minister of Tanzania, stood opposed and urged unification.

All African states are striving for an ideal termed "Africanization"—in practice the replacing of Europeans by Africans in as many technical, social, and political positions as possible. But the accomplishment of this task depends greatly upon two factors—ability to speak and write a Western language, and education.

It is for reasons like these that "neutral" languages are of special interest. A few years ago Professor Gilbert Ansre of the University of Ghana at Accra conducted a language poll at his university. Of his respondents, almost 100 percent favored the continued use of English as the official language. Queries about other choices were inconclusive, with at least one student giving a reply that might be typical of the thinking of many young Africans. He said, "I won't like my language not to be chosen."

Other neutral possibilities in Africa are the pidgins and creoles. The best known is Swahili, a lingua franca which developed from a pidgin used by Arab slave traders and native Bantu peoples. There are 19 different dialects of Swahili today, with the recognized standard that of Zanzibar, erstwhile center of the slave traffic. But since it is not a tribal language, it is accepted as a useful means of communication in all of East Africa (although its former association with the slave trade still makes it repugnant to a few).

Another example of a lingua franca is Sango in the Central African Republic. Still others are Town Bemba in northern Rhodesia and Kitchen or Mine Kafir in South Africa, a means of communication that was employed by workers in the diamond mines. The point that has been made is that one or two of these mediums could be adopted as a common language only with the agreement of a number of African nations.

MULTILINGUAL STATES

Implementation of any language policy ultimately rests on the educational system and, as the experience of multilanguage states reveals again and again, conducting instruction in two languages imposes a heavy burden on any school system. This raises serious questions regarding language use in government offices and administrations—witness the past language riots by Flemish-speaking citizens of Belgium, protesting alleged discrimination by French speakers. And in Canada, similar agitation took place among French Canadians protesting the favored position of English. Although Canada is "officially" bilingual, only about thirteen percent of Canadians can actually speak both languages, and of these nine percent are French Canadians. A French separatist movement has existed for some time, and extremist elements have carried out several acts of violence.

Angry slogans of separatism have appeared in French Canada, proclaiming: "L'indé-pendence! Quebec out! Canada non!" Quite recently the Canadian government, wishing to make French a working language in the civil service, established a bilingual school in Hull, Quebec. Selected officials are sent to 10- to 12-week intensive courses in French or English, whichever is their second language. Half of the students will be native French speakers, and half English.

Meanwhile, tensions and incidents have continued as separatist movements remain a part of the Canadian political scene. The Canadian government has appointed a Royal Commission on Bilingualism whose published reports detail and define the findings of specialists on the problems of ethnic groups.

Not surprisingly, the Canadians find that in attempting to please one bilingual group the other may be displeased. In the national electoral campaign in 1972, Prime Minister Pierre Elliot Trudeau of the Liberal Party found that prairie farmers in the West tended to be displeased with the upgrading of the status of French. Voters in Neepawa, Manitoba, where very few speak French, questioned the value of having the words "Bureau de Poste" as well as "Post Office" lettered on the wall.

Canada, with its history, does seem to be on the path to becoming a true bilingual nation. The government acted in 1974 to make French coequal in status with English. And in an innovative educational experiment, children who live in Quebec and speak English at home have the opportunity to attend public schools in which the French language is the medium of instruction.

Another important multilingual area faced with similar problems lies within the borders of the Soviet Union. Much speculation exists regarding the loyalty to the regime of the numerous people who make up that vast state. With at least 200 distinct languages, the Soviet government has made Great Russian the language of *intercommunication*. This policy seemed to attract the interest of the leaders of India. When India received its independence, its government sent a commission to the Soviet Union to see how their government had "solved" the multilanguage problem. The Russian government had created alphabets (mostly an adaptation of the Cyrillic) for languages that had not been committed to writing and had established primary education in 60 regional languages. This policy has served the Soviet Union well, and is used as evidence that the Soviet Union is the friend of small and oppressed peoples. For example, in Rumania, near neighbor of the Soviet Union, the government created an alphabet (Cyrillic) for the language of the Gagauzy, a seminomadic Turkic group numbering about 100,000, and also established primary schools taught in this language. Such a limited number of people could hardly pose much of a threat to the government, and yet gestures such as this one are attractive to people bent on self-determination. Rumania, of all the East European nations, has the largest proportion and number of minorities, and the government provides primary education and radio broadcasts in Hungarian, Slovak, Yiddish, German, and Ukrainian. The main radio station in Bucharest also transmits programs in English, French, Russian, and even Spanish.

LINGUISTIC MINORITIES

In the Middle East there are four million or more Kurds, a seminomadic Indo-Iranian people, related to the Persians, and living in Iraq, Iran, Turkey, and Lebanon. The Kurds, who have staged more than one rebellion, seem determined to claim their own language and other privileges and are now in fact clamoring for the creation of an independent Kurdistan, where Kurdish would be the official language.

As in the case with the Kurds, language acquires a special significance for peoples who have no political homeland. And we have pointed out that agitation for language rights is often tantamount to a general appeal for improvement in status. More than one observer has pointed to the old Austro-Hungarian Empire where the ruling oligarchy and the "Ukrainophiles" struggled furiously over the use of the Ukrainian language in the schools and courts. This struggle was no mere argument over language. Rather, it was a bid by the Ukrainian peasantry to obtain a greater voice in national economic and political affairs.

While some language conflicts are acute and explosive, others are either mild, dormant, or merely irritants that potentially might be fanned into violence. Examples of these less volatile language conflicts can be found in Spain. The Basques are an intensely proud people and inhabit the Pyrenees around Bilbao (and across the border in France). While they are mostly bilingual, they hold tenaciously to their own language, which is spoken by very few outsiders. Separatist tendencies have arisen among them from time to time. In much greater numbers are the Catalonians, who live in Catalonia and Valencia, with Barcelona as the principal city. The Catalonians (whose language is closely related to Provencal, a language spoken across the France-Spain border) are also largely bilingual; they are hard-working, enterprising people who have more than once displayed strong separatist feelings and whose history includes periods of independence. If historical events had occurred otherwise, Catalonia might have become the political center of Spain, rather than Castile. The Spanish Republic had looked with favor upon the claims of these two ethnic groups, and there are signs that the present government is encouraging literary composition in these languages.

Once again, we cannot overemphasize that language claims are often reflections or an integral part of political, economic, social, and cultural conflicts within a country. John Gumperz of California warns that failure to specify the exact nature of the language conflict may result in a confusion between two rather different kinds of sociopolitical problems, commonly discussed and studied as problems associated with "language policy and planning." In one case, he notes, "a small elite using a literary language maintains a social control over a mass of illiterates, restraining access to power by artificially maintaining a language barrier." Medieval Europe with Latin and Greece with Katharevousa (classical) and Demotike (popular) forms are examples of these barriers. In the other case, two already literate groups may be struggling for political supremacy. Instances of this kind of dissension are the Hindi-Punjabi rivalry in Delhi and the rivalry in Norway between *riksmal*, the traditional literary form heavily influenced by Danish, and *landsmal*, which is based on a dialect of West Norway.

Students of nationality and language often despair, believing that animosity between people speaking different languages is inevitable. True, there is little basis for the belief that people who speak similar or the same languages will love one another. Wars among "brothers" and "sisters" are usually unparalleled in their ferocity, as witness our own Civil War, one of the most savage in all military history; or the Spanish Civil War; or the war between the Irish and the English, or the present war in Northern Ireland; or the conflicts between the Czechs and the Slovaks, the Serbs and the Croats, and the Indians and Pakistanis. Moslems speak the same or similar languages, and yet conflicts and tensions among them have often been severe.

We have cited this evidence to suggest that the study of language policies—a branch of the language sciences called *sociolinguistics*—consists of a large number of elusive and sensitive issues. Consequently, passions and feelings of those affected may on occasion run high. Various nations which predate the United States still continue to experience difficulties and problems concerning the selection of a national language or a language variety which will serve as the standard. And just as we have a number of language-related issues in the world requiring resolution, so too do we have a number of language-related issues in the United States, no less serious and no less demanding of action.

Linguists for years have been questioned: "What is linguistics good for?" In response, they have made serious attempts to apply the insights of the language sciences to the practical concerns of the everyday world. We now turn to a discussion of some of the implications of language study in this country and to a few selected applications of the insights from theoretical linguistics.

IN THE UNITED STATES: LANGUAGE VARIETY

We have discovered that in this country language has social, political, and, even more important for us here, educational consequences. Applied linguists have had much to say, suggest, and offer about how first languages and second languages ought to be taught. We will discuss second language teaching and learning in Chapters XII and XIII, and first language teaching here. By "first language teaching" we mean the activities in the classroom associated with teaching composition, reading, and a standard variety of English to the native speaker.

It is especially difficult to address ourselves to the notion of how linguistics can aid in education, as the term "linguistics" has so often struck fear in the heart of a teacher who has been repelled by the technical and engineering aspects of the science and has virtually no knowledge of how some of these theoretical insights can be applied to the immediate concerns of the classroom. In this regard, Robin Lakoff says, "While doing linguistics is often both an enjoyable and scholarly activity, it is also distressingly ivory-towerish; many theoretical linguists have assumed that their work has no direct relevance to the outside, or real, world, and often seem rather proud of the fact that anything 'applied' is of necessity soiled by its very usefulness. They console themselves by thinking that if indeed their work is not able to be a force for good, at least it cannot be a force for evil." She continues, "There is a sense of despair at the thought of working *in vacuo*, of training students to teach linguistics to students who will teach linguistics, etc. It is heartening, therefore, to see linguists now taking the first tottering steps toward relevance."

STANDARD AND NONSTANDARD ENGLISH

We will begin our description of some of these first "tottering steps" by noting that while linguistic science has been applied to the teaching of foreign and second languages for years, today there are new avenues of application being explored. Perhaps the most visible new application today is seen in its use in a native English classroom.

One of the perennial and traditional tasks of the English teacher is to maintain and teach the "standard" variety of English. This task, even in the 1950s, drew its share of criticism. Donald J. Lloyd then made the point that "There is at large among us today an unholy number of people who make it their business to correct the speech and writing of others." Lloyd was directing this "unholy" epithet, it seems, to all the English teachers of the nation.

Scholars such as Lloyd were among the first to confront the issue of "standard English" by pointing to the difficulty and perhaps impossibility of defining a standard. Everyone thinks that he knows what the standard is; few have a concrete notion of what it really is. Martin Joos addressed the issue of standard English variety in his monograph, *The Five Clocks*. In his study, Joos defines a number of spoken styles that each native speaker employs in appropriate social contexts. In effect, he describes a number of standards, and notes that the style that the speaker employs depends upon the context of the social situation and the familiarity of the speakers with each other. Among his styles are the following:

1. *Consultative style*: a style of speaking between strangers. Consultative style is not characterized by the use of slang or ellipsis.

2. *Casual style*: a style employed with friends and good acquaintances. In contrast to consultative style, casual style is denoted by the use of slang and sentences which may be truncated ("Believe me, it's fishy").

3. *Intimate style*: a style used between very good friends, between, for example, spouses or lovers. This style is denoted by excessive ellipsis, as in, "Don't say a word. I know what you mean." Communication can take place without excessive words because good friends can literally anticipate what is going to be said next.

4. *Formal style*: a style designed to inform, perhaps in the manner of a speech or presentation before a gathering of colleagues. This style is characterized by the use of full sentences and the avoidance of slang.

A style contains a number of characteristics (we have listed only a few). Each style can generally be defined on the basis of how much slang is employed, the proportion of sentences which are elliptical, and the amount of information provided to the person addressed—the more formal style requiring more information to be given to the addressee. By this model, Martin Joos seeks to prove that there are standards rather than *a* standard. Within this context let us continue our discussion.

One difficult problem for the schools in the past was in identifying, explicitly, just what constitutes the standard variety of English that should be taught. Paul Postal maintains that even "the standard which is taught is not very standard and may vary considerably from place to place." The concern with standard English, however defined, still occupies the attention of the schools today. Roger Shuy, Associate Director of the Center for Applied Linguistics, makes the point that "It has never been very clear what the schools can or should do about the speech of the students and it is not at all clear what direct good the study of social dialects has provided thus far." Perhaps it is only wishful thinking on our parts, but we do believe that the study of the varieties of English can sensitize the schools to the problems involved in teaching a standard.

In the past, children who did not speak a standard variety of English were often ostracized until they assumed the dialect spoken in the schools. The children who brought a nonstandard variety of English to the classroom were usually those whose parents were from the socially and economically disadvantaged class. For this reason, and also because of the stigma attached to the language varieties of the minorities, socio- and psycho-linguistic studies of language variation in the past 10 to 15 years have received enormous impetus and encouragement from anti-poverty and civil rights groups.

The varieties of English spoken by lower socioeconomic groups, both in urban and rural areas, have been studied by an increasing number of linguists and other social scientists in an attempt to determine the characteristics of nonstandard speech. Research into language varieties has truly revealed that certain varieties of English have had the effect of stigmatizing its users, socially and economically, and that these attitudes toward the users of the nonstandard have on occasion been perpetuated by the schools. An important investigator of language variation, particularly of the inner city, is William A. Labov of the University of Pennsylvania, whose book *The Social Stratification of the English of New York City* (1966) was as revolutionary, in the way that it perceived language variety, as any text on linguistics in the last 15 to 20 years. Labov, whose work concentrates upon the surface features of spoken English, has given definition to the concept of the *linguistic variable*. In recent years he and his colleagues have convincingly demonstrated that there is no one feature that uniquely identifies a person as belonging to one socioeconomic class or other. Most speakers use language features that have been identified as nonstandard. However, some speakers employ more nonstandard features than other speakers. What identifies the user as educated, as middle class, as uneducated, or as socially and economically deprived, is that in his or her speech the proportion of nonstandard features is higher or lower. The multiple negative ("They don't have none") or the dropping of "g's" (He's swimmin' ") are only two examples of features that have been identified as nonstandard. There are more, of course; some deal with syntax (question formation), and others with phonology (dropping of "r's"). The "more" or "less" is what is crucial for gauging the variety. Frequency of occurrence of nonstandard features is what Labov submits marks a nonprestigious language speaker.

Labov offered this hypothesis after investigating the speech of the lower East Side of New York City and the variety of English employed by a sizable proportion of blacks. There seems to be little doubt today that the Black English vernacular of the inner city has been the most studied of any American social variety of English. A veritable "Labovian" group of researchers has developed, dedicated to the investigation of social varieties of English in large metropolitan areas. These investigators include such scholars as Roger W. Shuy, Ralph Fasold of Georgetown University, Walter Wolfram, William A. Stewart, Joan Baratz, and Irwin Feigenbaum of the Education Study Center in Washington, D.C.

A parallel area of language variety research today is in the study of the varieties of Mexican-American English and Spanish. The Mexican-American constitutes the nation's second largest minority. Seven million bilingual Spanish-English speakers live in the five-state southwestern area of California, Arizona, New Mexico, Colorado, and Texas. Although the use of Spanish by students on school premises is no longer prohibited, a large number of bilingual and bicultural problems still remain and beg for resolution.

At the University of Texas at El Paso a Cross-Cultural Southwest Ethnic Study Center has recently been established with a grant from the Spencer Foundation of Chicago. The Center seeks to support research on regional minorities, particularly the Mexican-American, with a view to applying the data obtained for educational innovation and improvement. The Center is mentioned here as an example of the national movement toward the establishment of ethnic study departments, although the emphasis is upon research more than it is upon actual teaching. The Center has sponsored a number of activities, including an interdisciplinary survey of the linguistic and socioeducational characteristics of the entire UT-El Paso undergraduate student body, stratified into 16 subgroups according to Mexican-American versus "Anglo," age, sex, year of college, and place of birth. Since the enrollment of UT-El Paso consists of one-third Mexican-Americans, the results from this study may have important implications for "applied educational sociolinguistics."

Social scientists have joined linguists in probing the deeper implications of human language. Susan Ervin-Tripp, a psycholinguist, carries out research on several types of bilinguals. Her studies aim to assess the intimate interaction between language topic and listener, and the motivations for shifts in language and style of speaking. New frontiers in this kind of linguistic research are being opened in what is known as *ethnomethodology*, a discipline that focuses upon the conversational situation—what people do and the conversational rules they obey when they converse with one another. Leon Jakobovits, also a psycholinguist, studies what he terms the "syntax of conversational interaction" and draws upon the research of ethnomethodologists in his text, *Preliminaries to the Psychology of Ordinary Language*. We shall have more to say about the pragmatics of language use in our chapter on bilingual and second language education.

What people say and how they say it remains a topic of considerable importance to education today. Schools have (at least) two positions on the question of what variety of language to teach:

1. *The eradicationist position*: This position advocates teaching a standard variety by identifying the variables and characteristics of nonstandard varieties of English and prohibiting their use in the classroom and the school. There is considerable popular support for this strategy, not only from middle class white parents but also from some lower socioeconomic parents who believe that standard varieties of English must be learned if their children are to have the necessary linguistic equipment to escape the ghetto. The school, in this view, is an agent which encourages social and economic mobility; if students do not assume the language habits of the middle and upper middle class then they will be shut off irrevocably from a "better life."

A question has been raised, however, concerning the school's proper role: does the school have the right to correct a student who writes or speaks a variety of language employed in the ghetto or lower socioeconomic neighborhood? This question is fraught with implications. Organizations which represent English teachers have been drawn into the fray. The Conference on College Composition and Communication issued a policy statement in 1974 saying, "The school does not have the right to correct the linguistic habits of those who do not speak the school variety." The title appended to this policy statement is "Students' Right to Their Own Language." Perhaps this organization feels that it is "undemocratic" to attempt to eradicate a variety of English merely because it has low social prestige.

2. *The bidialectal position*: This opinion advocates "accepting" the variety of English brought to the classroom, but teaching the student the variety of English which is currently employed by the middle and upper middle classes. In other words, allow one dialect while teaching and encouraging the standard at the same time. Other nations teach a standard variety but accept other varieties if these are employed in the appropriate context. Great Britain is an example, where children may still employ their home language in their everyday affairs but must employ the standard in school.

Controversy over the bidialectal position arises from its implications. James Sledd, a vociferous critic of bidialectalism, says that the acceptance of two dialects, but only one for school, actually masks the wishes of the school to eradicate the variety which the child brings with him. Others have pointed to the pretense of accepting a dialect but rejecting it for school use—a practice, they believe, that is potentially damaging psychologically. Some feel that the policy is racist; the practice of accepting one dialect while rejecting the other does little to encourage and foster cultural pluralism.

The question of what to do with children who speak a dialect other than the one spoken in school has yet to be answered—if, indeed, it ever will. The study of language varieties, an example of applied linguistic research, takes into account the ways that people actually employ language and the reasons they employ it as they do, and will help to answer this question. This relatively new area of linguistic study is what we have labeled *sociolinguistics*. Psycholinguistics has also made a contribution. Research involving language varieties is open to anyone who is sensitive to how language is used and who exhibits an open mind concerning the uses of language in a society that prides itself on the fact that it is pluralistic.

The discipline of linguistics will have an ever increasing impact on education, especially as the curriculum in language turns away from the emphasis upon right versus wrong and standard versus nonstandard to an analysis, and appreciation, of why various socioeconomic groups, various occupations, and various age groups, actually employ language in all areas in which they function. In conclusion, may we remind our readers of the remarks attributed to the late Dr. Martin Luther King who, when queried about his change in language variety from white educated to black noneducated as he addressed a large assembly of black industrial workers, said, "If I didn't speak 'our' language, they wouldn't listen to me."

SPELLING AND READING

In recent years much attention has been directed to the failure of our schools to teach reading to all children. Many children were found to be reading behind their age group or not reading at all. Packaged reading programs were published by various textbook companies, each promising a success rate above that of the national average. Reading programs such as OPEN COURT and DISTAR were sold to school districts which were experiencing serious problems in reading, and the "Right to Read" project was begun.

Whether this attention to reading is effective or not is not our concern here. We only suggest, in passing, that other variables may likely be involved for the failure of children to learn to read. Most reading problems were found to be indigenous to low income neighborhoods, where children did not have enough to eat, where reading was not a prized activity of the home, and where homes, in fact, had no reading materials because parents could barely provide enough sustenance for their children. Linguistics cannot feed children, but we feel that it can provide some interesting insights into the spelling and reading processes which can aid the teacher in the presentation of reading and spelling data.

Linguists have long had an interest in language arts. Leonard Bloomfield published an article on spelling and reading in 1942, in which he attempts to correlate, in part, the letters of the alphabet with the phonemes of the language. He maintains that the regularities of the English spelling system should be displayed before the irregularities. He advocates, for instance, that beginning reading texts employ sentences such as "Jan planned her tan." Bloomfield's efforts resulted in some changes in reading data, but his suggestions were not an overwhelming success. His efforts were followed by those of Charles C. Fries (1962), who attempted to correlate structural linguistics with the problems of teaching reading. Yet with these efforts there remained the myth that English spelling was full of irregularities that outweighed its regularities.

It was not until linguists could "look beneath the surface" that they could maintain that English spelling, for the most part, was regular. Carol Chomsky, whose research into spelling and reading rests upon Halle's and Chomsky's book *The Sound Pattern of English*, says that "Good spellers, children and adults alike, recognize that related words are spelled alike even though they are pronounced differently. They seem to rely on an underlying picture of the word that is independent of its varying pronunciation." For instance, the lexical item "telegraph" is pronounced differently depending upon the suffix which is attached:

telegraph	/tɛ́ləgræf/
telegraphic	/tɛ ləgræfɪk/
telegraphy	/təlɛ́grəfi/

If we spell these related lexical items as they sound, we would lose the written identity that they share. Chomsky advocates that children can be taught these regularities if, at the same time, they are not taught that there is a one-to-one fit between the sound and the letter. This is occasionally maintained in reading programs which emphasize the surface relationship between sounds and letters.

Carol Chomsky proposes spelling lessons partially based upon the comparison of stressed and unstressed vowels in words which are spelled the same but are pronounced differently:

Unstressed (supply the missing vowel)	*Stressed*
pre--dent	preside
comp--able	compare, comparison
maj-r	majority

Consonants, too, may be pronounced differently depending upon their phonetic environment, and Chomsky would have her spelling lessons capture this relationship:

criticize	critical
medicine	medical
nation	native

Even in words having a "silent" letter, there are environments where this letter is pronounced:

muscle	muscular
bomb	bombastic
sign	signify

By portraying the deep and abstract relationship between letters and sounds, the writing system is made much more accessible to the student. There is even a reason for spelling words differently if they have the same sound but differ in meaning. For these words, which would be ambiguous in print, the system provides a convenient out:

site	cite	sight
pear	pare	pair
by	bye	buy

These are the relationships that are important in language, that allow students to relate one word to another. Yet a caveat is in order here: if the surface relationship between the sounds and the letters is emphasized—to the virtual exclusion of the regularities as revealed by an examination of the underlying structure of the sound-letter correlation—we may be impeding children from learning, in the most efficient way possible, the correspondence between the alphabet and the phonological system of the English language.

Some linguists have also made the suggestion that reading programs use language that is realistic and believable. They have also recommended that the stilted language sometimes found in primers be removed and replaced by language which is more natural.

Linguists have also made suggestions on how to test for reading proficiency—or, more accurately, how *not to* test. Among the tests that teachers employ to gauge reading progress is the "reading-aloud" test. Occasionally, linguists have found, children who can relate marks on paper to English sounds do not comprehend what they have read as well as they understand speakers who either "sound different" (who do not speak a standard variety of English) or who make mistakes (called *miscue* by Kenneth Goodman) while reading orally. Especially at a disadvantage in the latter process are children who do not speak the language variety employed in the school and whose pronunciation is different from that of the teacher. There is here a confusion, we suggest, of the linguistic and reading abilities of children with comprehension difficulties. Reading is, after all, extracting meaning from printed marks. Whether dialect differences constitute a hurdle for the beginning reader is not at all clear at the present time—although there are readers printed in black vernacular which attempt to bridge the gap between the students' variety of English and the language that they may find in primers. Nevertheless, as Rose-Marie Weber argues, ". . . there is little evidence to support the contention that dialect differences in English significantly increase the difficulty experienced in learning to read." But we have learned something about reading performance: it is risky to judge reading proficiency solely upon oral production.

There are several other applications of linguistics to first language teaching, and we have listed texts in "For Further Reference" that describe some applications that we have not included here. These applications include linguistics and the teaching of writing; theorists in composition have used a model of generative-transformational grammar to teach sentence-combining and sentence subordination. Especially important is the research of Kellog Hunt. Transformational-generative grammar has also been employed—notably by Richard Ohmann—to explain the intricacies found in various literary styles, to explicitly indicate the differences between and among the literary styles of Ernest Hemingway, William Faulkner, Samuel Johnson, and Edward Gibbon. Other linguists, also interested in style, have employed the phonological component of generative-transformational grammar to develop the concept of a metrical line. Exactly, what is metrical and what is not? What do critics mean, for instance, when they say that Chaucer writes in iambic pentameter?

Linguists also conduct research on the brain and on speech disorders, and their findings are of immense value to psychologists, psychiatrists, and speech pathologists.

One far-reaching and important application is in the teaching of second and foreign languages, on which our last two chapters will focus.

XI. ACTIVITIES AND QUESTIONS

1. Robert Hall, Jr., published a descriptive grammar of English in the 1950s entitled *Leave Your Language Alone*. He subsequently changed the title to *Linguistics and Your Language*. What is implied in the first title that is missing in the second? How might English teachers react to the first edition?

2. How do you react to a person who says, "I don't got none"? What is the basis of your reaction?

3. What is the social status of persons who, when asked, "Who is it?", answer, "It is I"? What would you answer? Is "It is I" taught as the "correct" response?

4. Why do socio-dialects exist? What are some linguistic traits of some socio-dialects that you know or speak?

5. Is it possible to teach a socio-dialect?

6. In 1976, airline pilots went out on strike in Canada. The strike was over the issue of which language the pilots and the ground controller could use to receive and give instructions for landings and take-offs. The pilots and the controllers wished to use both English and French, but the government decreed that only English was to be employed. Who do you think won in the dispute? Present an argument for or against the use of French in this situation.

7. Conflict caused by language policy continues to be in the news. In South Africa in the first half of 1976, 176 persons were killed and more than 1,000 were seriously injured as a result of rioting over the question of which language was to serve as the medium of instruction in the public schools. The government legislated Afrikaans but the blacks wanted English. What was the outcome? Which language won? What was the government's official policy as of July 1976?

8. Is there such a thing as "standard English"? How does the work of Joos and Labov contribute to the study and debate of this issue?

9. What theory of teaching reading and spelling do you favor? Why?

XI. FOR FURTHER REFERENCE

Bloomfield, Leonard, 1942. "Linguistics and Reading." *Elementary English Review* 19:125-130, 183-86.

Burling, Robbins. 1970. *Man's Many Voices*. New York: Holt, Rinehart and Winston.

Burr, Elizabeth, Susan Dunn, and Norma Farquar. 1972. "The Language of Inequality." *ETC* 29:414-16.

Cazden, Courtney B. 1972. *Child Language and Education*. New York: Holt, Rinehart and Winston.

Dasgupta, Jyotirindra. 1970. *Language Conflict and National Development: Group Politics and National Language in India*. Berkeley: University of California Press.

Dietrich, Daniel J. 1974. "Public Doublespeak: Teaching About Language in the Market Place." *College English* 36:477-81.

Dillard, J. L. 1972. *Black English: Its History and Usage in the United States*. New York: Random House.

Ferguson, Charles A. 1962. "The Language Factors in National Development," in Frank A. Rice, ed.: *Study of the Role of Second Languages in Asia, Africa and Latin America*. Washington, D.C.: Center for Applied Linguistics.

Fishman, Joshua A. and et al, eds. 1968. *Language Problems in Developing Nations*. New York: John Wiley.

Freeman, Donald C. 1970. *Linguistics and Literary Style*. New York: Holt, Rinehart and Winston.

_____. 1976. "Literature," in Ronald Wardhaugh and H. Douglas Brown, eds.: *A Survey of Applied Linguistics*. Ann Arbor: University of Michigan Press.

Fries, C. C. 1962. *Linguistics and Reading*. New York: Holt, Rinehart and Winston, Inc.

Gage, William W. 1971. "The African Language Picture." *Linguistic Reporter* 13 (Summer): 15-27.

_____. 1974. *Language in Its Social Setting*. Washington, D.C.: Anthropological Society of Washington.

Goodman, Kenneth S. and C. Burke. 1970. "When a Child Reads: a Psycholinguistic Analysis." *Elementary English* 47:121-29.

Gumperz, John J. 1969. "Communication in Multilingual Societies," in S. A. Tyler, ed.: *Linguistic Sciences and Language Teaching*. New York: Holt, Rinehart and Winston.

_____. 1967. "Linguistic Repertoires, Grammar, and Language Instruction," in C. J. Kreidler, ed.: *Report of the Sixteenth Roundtable*. Washington, D.C.: Georgetown University Press.

Hall, Edward T. 1976. "How Cultures Collide." *Psychology Today* July, 66-74, 97.

Hall, Robert A., Jr. 1966. *Pidgin and Creole Languages*. Ithaca, N.Y.: Cornell University Press.

Halle, Morris and Samuel J. Keyser. 1971. *English Stress: Its Form, its Growth, and its Role in Verse*. New York: Harper and Row.

Harrison, Selig S. 1960. *India: The Most Dangerous Decades*. Princeton, N.J.: Princeton University Press.

Haugen, Einar. 1971. "The Ecology of Language." *Linguistic Reporter* 13:19-26.

Hunt, K. W. 1970. *Syntactic Maturity in School Children and Adults*. Monograph of the Society for Research in Child Development 35: No. 1.

Hymes, Dell, ed. 1971. *Pidginization and Creolization of Languages*. Cambridge: Cambridge University Press.

_____. 1973. "Speech and Language: On the Origins and Foundations of Inequality Among Speakers." *Daedalus* 102:59-85.

Joos, Martin. 1967. *The Five Clocks*. New York: Harcourt Brace and Jovanovich.

Key, Mary R. 1975. *Male/Female Language*. Metuchen, N.J.: Scarecrow Press.

Labov, William. 1966. *The Social Stratification of the English of New York City*. Washington, D.C.: Center for Applied Linguistics.

_____. 1972. *The Study of Nonstandard English*. Champaign, Ill.: National Council Teachers of English.

Lakoff, Robin. 1975. *Language and Woman's Place*. New York: Harper and Row.

Lakoff, Robin. 1976. "Language and Society," in Wardhaugh and Brown, eds.: *A Survey of Applied Linguistics*. Ann Arbor: University of Michigan Press.

Landar, Herbert. 1966. *Language and Culture*. New York: Oxford University Press.

Le Page, R. B. 1964. *The National Language Question: Linguistic Problems of Newly Independent States*. London: Oxford University Press.

Lloyd, Donald J. 1951. "Snobs, Slobs, and the English Language." *The American Scholar* 20: Summer, 279-288.

Madsen, William. 1964. *The Mexican-Americans of South Texas*. New York: Holt, Rinehart and Winston.

Malmstrom, Jean and A. Ashley. 1963. *Dialects—U.S.A*. Urbana, Ill.: National Council of Teachers of English.

Malstrom, Jean. 1976. "First Language Teaching," in Wardhaugh and Brown, eds.: *A Survey of Applied Linguistics*. Ann Arbor: University of Michigan Press.

Mellon, J. 1969. *Transformational Sentence-Combining: a Method for Enhancing the Development of Syntactic Fluency in English Composition*. Urbana, Ill.: National Council of Teachers of English.

Ohmann, Richard. 1964. "Generative Grammars and the Concept of Literary Style." *Word* 20:423-39.

Rank, Hugh, ed. 1974. *Language and Public Policy*. Urbana, Ill.: National Council of Teachers of English.

Shuy, Roger W. 1967. *Discovering American Dialects*. Urbana, Ill.: National Council of Teachers of English.

Sledd, James. 1969. "Bi-dialectalism: the Linguistics of White Supremacy." *English Journal* 58:1307-15, 1329.

Stewart, William A. 1968. "An Outline of Linguistic Typology for Describing Multilingualism," in Joshua A. Fishman, ed.: *Readings in the Sociology of Language*. The Hague: Mouton.

Von Malitz, Frances Willard. 1975. *Living and Learning in Two Languages*. New York: McGraw-Hill.

Wardhaugh, Ronald and H. Douglas Brown, eds. 1976. *A Survey of Applied Linguistics*. Ann Arbor: University of Michigan Press.

Weber, Rose-Marie. 1976. "Reading," in Wardhaugh and Brown, eds.: *A Survey of Applied Linguistics*.

XII. Second Language Learning and Teaching: Gaps in a Crucial Area

APPLYING THEORY TO PRACTICE

Within the previous eleven chapters we have repeatedly and persistently referred to and examined the various attributes of language, the skills and capacities that a fluent speaker brings to the task of using his language, and various theoretical positions adopted by the linguist in his attempt to describe those attributes, skills, and capacities. In the two concluding chapters we will seek to identify and examine the relationship between formal language study and the teaching of language, in the broadest context possible. We will not confine our discussion in these chapters to the teaching of language as a subject, as for instance in a class entitled Spanish 1; we will also examine the recent experience of teaching language in a context that has been given the name *bilingual education*.

We may well refer to the recent changes in language education as a revolution. Just as there has been a revolution in the way that the linguist perceives language, so too has there been a revolution in the approaches, methods, and techniques of teaching language. And we maintain that these two revolutions are related; the revolution in pedagogy could not have occurred without the impetus of the revolution in theory.

Let us begin, then, with the following anecdotes, which we employ to preface a history of language teaching in the United States.

LANGUAGE UNPREPAREDNESS: AN HISTORICAL ACCOUNT

During the war in Viet Nam, an American Army squad was moving cautiously along a path separating two rice paddies when a villager ran up and attempted desperately to make himself understood: a Viet Cong unit was in the area. The squad was badly bloodied because no one was able to understand the friendly villager's simple warning that it was about to be ambushed. In Japan, after World War II, a woman scavenging for scraps around an Army perimeter was shot because she misunderstood an American sentry's gesture to move away from a restricted zone. Instead of moving off, she walked toward the sentry. The sentry did not know that his gesture to move off had exactly the opposite meaning for a Japanese. These two language incidents—one verbal, the other gestural—are significant, yet they were scarcely the first examples of language ignorance as the cause of such events.

The United States has always been language conscious, with a consciousness derived principally from an Old World concept that an educated person knows more than one language. Yet throughout the history of the United States, foreign language enrollments have risen and fallen. Periods of xenophobia, both before and after wars, have contributed to an irrational intolerance for foreign languages. World War I especially, with its strong wave of hysteria against everything German—and by extension anything at all foreign—is a case in point. Sauerkraut was renamed "liberty cabbage." And some 20 states, most of which had large ethnic populations, passed

148

legislation banning any language except English as a medium of instruction. (Such legislation was annulled by the Supreme Court in 1924, however.)

The isolationism of the years following the World War I extended well into the 1930s, and was reinforced by a view of the oceans as permanent, impregnable defenses. After World War II broke out, eleven million American men and women were deployed over a global battlefront—and found themselves handicapped by ignorance of the languages of their allies as well as those of their enemies. "Snafus," misunderstandings, and spilled blood were the result. Intensive programs to give GIs basic instruction in 40 languages were launched. It was a concerted effort, and highly successful in many cases, yet it could not overcome previous language handicaps.

THE FEDERAL ROLE

Emerging as a world leader after World War II, the United States found that it needed people proficient in foreign languages to conduct the day-to-day task of diplomacy and international business. The ability to speak the language of a country has always been important for the diplomat. Yet we still hear queries similar to the following: "What difference does it make whether we know more than the rudimentary phrases of the language of the foreign country in which we are to reside? There are few persons in places of power who do not know English." Perhaps the most appropriate rejoinder is this true story: When the United States first established a mission in a Far Eastern nation about 20 years ago, it had no one who could speak the official language of this state. It was necessary to rely upon native translators to read and digest the opinions of the leaders of this government as expressed in the press. The translators, out of their sense of deference to their employers, chose only those items that were favorable to the United States. When, finally, officers trained in the language, able to read periodicals and attend sessions of the lesiglature, were sent out, they found that the entire country was in the grip of a virulent wave of anti-Americanism. Thanks to the knowledge of several officers who knew the language, the United States was able to redirect its entire foreign policy in a strategic region of the Far East.

The acute need for language skills, as indicated by the above, motivated the government of the United States to establish its own language teaching facilities. In 1945, the Army began its Language School in Monterey, California, with the teaching of 29 Eastern and Western languages. The Navy established its Intelligence School, and the Department of State its Foreign Service Institute in Washington, D.C. The Naval Intelligence School has offered, usually, eight languages, while the Foreign Service Institute has provided instruction in more than 40. The Defense Language Institute, West Coast Branch, Monterey, California, with some 15,000 students and 500 instructors, is perhaps the largest full-time language school in the West. Members of the language profession generally consider that the scope and quality of the work being done at this school are extremely high.

The role of the Foreign Service Institute has been of special significance, particularly since it has accepted as students a large number of employees of the United States Information Agency, the Agency for International Development, and the Department of Agriculture. Yet, despite its genuine successes, Under Secretary of State Walter Bedell Smith in 1954 charged the Wriston Committee with presenting a plan whereby the Institute's work could be made even more effective.

The results of the Wriston report were of the utmost significance, since it expressed dissatisfaction with the relatively low language competence of the government's Foreign Service officers. On November 2, 1956, the Secretary of State approved a new language policy that is still in effect today: "Each officer will be encouraged to acquire a 'useful' knowledge of two foreign languages, as well as sufficient command of the language of each post of assignment to be able to use greetings, ordinary social expressions, and numbers; ask and give simple questions and directions; and recognize proper names, street signs, and office and shop designations."

These measures were followed by policy statements from the International Cooperation Administration and the United States Information Agency. In 1960, Congress made the following statement: "It is the policy of the Congress that Chiefs of Mission and Foreign Service officers appointed or assigned to serve in foreign countries shall have, to the maximum practicable extent, among their qualifications, a useful knowledge of the principal language or dialect of the country in which they serve."

The Defense Department has recently consolidated language efforts under a single Defense Language Institute, still located in Monterey, California. The Foreign Service Institute continues to expand, adding courses as needed. An African department was added in the last few years, and FSI continues to offer courses in Swahili, Hausa, and other African languages. As the number of black governments in African nations increases, the African department of FSI will become even more important in the years ahead. With the aid of the government, the Institute has undertaken a broad program of publishing its texts through the U.S. Government Printing Office.

"Language is ordnance" might well be considered a byword of government service today. Even the Marine Corps guards bound for duty overseas must take a minimum of 100 hours of the language of the country to which they are assigned. The Peace Corps also offers a successful example of language teaching, with 450 hours in language required of all volunteers. Thus far, instruction has been given in 72 languages, including Nepali, Nyanja (an African language), Farsi, Tagalog, and Quechua, an important Indian language of the South American Andes region.

Despite these encouraging examples of language teaching, the need remains great. Dr. James B. Frith, Dean of the School of Languages of the Foreign Service Institute, spoke to the 14th Georgetown University Roundtable Conference on Languages and Linguistics on "Language Learning in the Foreign Affairs Community." He pointed out at the outbreak of World War II there were only 58 countries in which the United States had embassies or legations. There are four times as many now. Although 12 languages might have been useful in 1941, it was actually possible to conduct all official business in French or English. Today, Dr. Frith emphasized, Foreign Service officers find themselves "eyeball to eyeball" with an increasing number of peoples and lands. Based on a systematic study of the language situation in the various countries to which the United States sends representatives, the Department of State came to the conclusion that Foreign Service officers might have a genuine need for between 97 and 154 languages.

LANGUAGE, GOVERNMENT, AND SCIENCE

Occasionally the cost of not knowing a language runs high. Not many years ago an article that appeared in a Soviet scientific journal on contact-relay networks went unnoticed in this country while a government-funded project was duplicating the identical experiment. Writing in the *Scientific American*, William Locke of the Massachusetts Institute of Technology estimated that the cost to the U.S. scientific establishment in duplicated research was extremely high. The Soviet Union not only places great emphasis on language study by their scientists, but also has facilities for rapid abstracting and translating of practically everything of technical importance appearing in foreign periodicals.

Recently, members of the Stanford Research Institute at Menlo Park, California, pointed out that one of the best and most effective ways for an American scientist to keep abreast of developments in his own field in the United States is to follow Russian summaries and abstracts. It is, of course, encouraging that serious attention has been paid to translation and that the National Science Foundation has taken important measures to assure rapid perusal of important research in Russian and other languages, and to make abstracts and translations available. But we must emphasize that if a researcher cannot scan and read materials in the original, an even greater time lag between researcher and reader usually results.

In an issue of the *Journal of Geological Education*, Dorothy B. Vitaliano of the U.S. Geological Survey at Indiana University presented a convincing case for more language power for scientists. She maintains that the researcher who cannot do his own reading in foreign literature has a tremendous handicap since translations are often expensive, out of date, and inept. In one paper on the internal combustion of the earth, the Russian word *kora* (crust) was consistently mistranslated as "core," while the Russian equivalent for "barren strata" came out "unpregnant beds." She concludes that, "Before dismissing as unrealistic the thought that the day might ever come when every American geologist—or every American scientist for that matter—will have a working knowledge of three other languages, remember that Europeans have long achieved this as a matter of course."

Scientists and others who had been pinning their hopes on an early breakthrough in machine translation—perhaps out of an understandable concern over the toil and strain of language study—might be less sanguine today. Mechanical translation is still in the embryonic state, although at least 15 centers in several countries are experimenting with methods and techniques (largely through the use of computers) for improving machine translation. Translations of scientific texts have been done by machine, but human translators are still less expensive—and more accurate. The so-called "intelligent" machines can do only what humans program into them. Until now the difficulties experienced have done more to inform programmers about the structure of language than to reduce the backlog of untranslated writings. A prominent theoretical linguist has even gone so far as to say that machine translation has drawn many capable scholars into activities of dubious value. He believes that a great deal more and better research could have been performed if even a fraction of the funds spent on machine translation had been allotted directly to basic research on linguistic theory.

FOUNDATION AND GOVERNMENTAL SUPPORT

Second-language teaching was also given impetus in those years immediately following World War II by the hysteria generated in educational circles as a result of the launching of Sputnik. Efforts were made to "upgrade" instruction in foreign languages as well as in science and mathematics. In this period new courses were introduced, in both language and area studies. The number of non-Western courses increased. Enrollments spiraled. Foundations, particularly Ford, Carnegie, and Rockefeller, made grants available for increasing the status of language teaching. An example of this encouragement was the Program in Oriental Languages, underwritten by the Ford Foundation and administered by the American Council of Learned Societies. This program supplied funds for new language and area courses in Eastern languages, as well as for the production of texts. In 1952 the Rockefeller Foundation awarded a $235,000 grant to the Modern Language Association of America for a six-year study of foreign language teachers' recommendations to strengthen and improve instruction at all levels of American education.

On the basis of the information thus gathered from this survey, the National Defense Education Act (NDEA) was passed by the 85th Congress, which authorized the expenditure of 700 million dollars for the improvement of instruction in language, science, and mathematics. Among NDEA's most positive accomplishments was the encouragement of the study of non-Western languages. In the first five years of the program more than 1,000 fellowships were awarded to graduate students for the study of more than 50 of the 83 languages on a "critical list" compiled for the Office of Education, ranging from Swedish to Yoruba, an important African language. The NDEA also supplied matching funds to 56 universities for establishing language-area centers in Slavic, Latin American, Oriental, and African languages. In 1960, according to figures from the Modern Language Association, there were 12,000 students learning critical languages, many of them at NDEA-supported language and area centers.

Support for foreign language programs was also made available in the form of matching funds for the building of more than 4,000 language laboratories in public schools and for financing the costs of state foreign language supervisors. Summer NDEA institutes held at colleges and universities gave more than 10,000 public school teachers the opportunity to study applied linguistics, and more important, to improve their fluency in the languages they taught. Finally, NDEA funds were granted for various kinds of research projects in linguistics and language teaching methodology. One project studied the accomplishments of two groups of students learning German, one group taught by the conventional or classical grammar-translation method (which emphasized reading and writing), the other by the audiolingual method (which emphasized hearing and speaking rather than reading and writing).

Rising enrollments, which begin in 1945, continued to increase for the next 20 years, after which they began to decrease. In 1955, halfway into this period, enrollments were still low and caused Secretary of State John Foster Dulles to observe: "The United States carries new responsibilities in many quarters of the globe, and we are at a serious disadvantage because of the difficulty of finding persons who can deal with the foreign language problem. Interpreters are no substitute."

Testifying before the 85th Congress in 1957, Dulles pointed out that fully one-half of our Foreign Service officers did not at that time have a "useful" knowledge of any second language, while of the incoming class of Foreign Service officers only 25 percent could speak any language except English with moderate fluency. We should point out here that by "useful" the State Department means a knowledge adequate to handle routine matters at a Foreign Service post.

In 1965, at the height of foreign language enrollments, it was estimated that more than 30 percent of all secondary and college students had taken a foreign language. Most popular during this era were Russian and other Slavic languages, Chinese, Japanese, Arabic, French, German, and Spanish.

PROSPECTS

The number of people studying the geopolitically significant languages has risen in the last generation, but on a relatively small scale. Czech, an important language of eastern Europe, rose in one five-year period from 90 to 154 enrollments, Arabic from 994 to 1,324, and Hindi from 106 to 281. More encouragingly, especially with the prospect of increased intercourse with the People's Republic of China, Chinese rose from 1,771 to approximately 10,000 today, with Japanese showing a similar increment to a total of 8,000. Hebrew, a favorite with Jewish students in this ethnic-minded era, has quadrupled in the last 20 years, now claiming 19,000 enrollments (the population of Israel is currently three million), but Hebrew also has a strong ethnic and religious significance.

In these days of shrinking public school and university budgets, we find it difficult to plead for the teaching of "exotic" languages that draw only a small number of students; yet the value of and need for small numbers of language-area experts is indisputable. Much of the teaching of these languages is done by Government and Defense Department organizations, the most important, as we mentioned, being the School of Language Studies of the Department of State's Foreign Service Institute and the Defense Language Institute. Nevertheless, the fact is that, for certain purposes, the nation's "overseasmanship" tasks must depend upon academically trained specialists whose commitment is a lifetime one, rather than a "duty-related" one, subject to change with little notice.

Just how well equipped is the United States with personnel able to speak important world languages? Approximately 30 years ago the American Council of Learned Societies in its survey of personnel in the humanities made an attempt through questionnaires to identify the individuals with a knowledge of non-Western languages and areas. The Center for Applied Linguistics has made similar studies.

Figures, however, are cold bits of information in comparison with the "real life" situations arising in encounters with the peoples of the world. Significantly enough, however, in such cases the needed language is not always a language like Tigrinya, Malagasy, or Burmese. The Department of State's Language Services Division, charged with supplying interpreters (as well as translators) for most official purposes, is at times hard put to furnish personnel in the less exotic languages. A good case in point is Portuguese. The Division would probably have to go to Brazil to recruit speakers well enough versed in both English and Portuguese to be able to perform interpretation at a conference or for escort-group functions.

We need to realize that for many languages we cannot indefinitely rely upon émigrés and refugees, yet at the same time we are faced with the fact that college graduates, for the most part, cannot pass the demanding interpreter examinations merely on the basis of their academic studies. We note here that although the regular staff of the Language Services Division is mostly American, it requires additional aid in the form of part-time contract personnel of foreign birth. The Division ordinarily will not consider anyone who has not lived for at least two years in the country where the language is spoken, since competent translation depends on both a knowledge of the language and a knowledge of the sociocultural background of its speakers. Interpreting is one of the most complex skills, as visitors to the United Nations will attest. Only one bilingual person in ten can pass the State Department's test for conference interpreting, be it simultaneous (in which he is required to interpret in unison with the speaker) or consecutive (in which he translates afterwards).

In this chapter we have attempted to present a few of the problems associated with language learning in the United States, the need for speakers of other languages, and the vicissitudes associated with past attempts at encouraging foreign language enrollments. We might, in conclusion, say that languages have not always been taught and learned successfully in this country, especially in our public institutions. The topic of our next and final chapter is devoted to a discussion of language learning and teaching, and the research associated with current trends, which can be subtitled, "the search for the right method."

XII. QUESTIONS AND ACTIVITIES

1. Which languages are usually offered in junior and senior high schools, and in colleges and universities? Are there any languages other than French, German, and Spanish offered? How popular are language courses? Are they required or can they be taken as electives?

2. How well can students use the language after one or more of these courses?

3. Cite some of the problems you feel might be associated with decreased language enrollment in the U.S. How might these problems be alleviated?

XII. FOR FURTHER REFERENCE

Alatis, James E. and Kristie Twaddell. 1976. *English as a Second Language in Bilingual Education*. Washington, D.C.: TESOL.

Andersson, Theodore. 1969. *Foreign Languages in the Elementary School: A Struggle Against Mediocrity*. Austin: University of Texas Press.

Burt, Marina K. and Heidi C. Dulay, eds. 1975. *New Directions in Second Language Learning, Teaching and Bilingual Education*. Washington, D.C.: TESOL.

Curtiss, Susan, Stephen Krashen, Victoria Fromkin, David Rigler, and Marilyn Rigler. 1973. "Language Acquisition After the Critical Period: Genie as of April 1973," in *Papers from the Ninth Regional Meeting, Chicago Linguistic Society*. Chicago: Chicago Linguistic Society.

Ervin-Tripp, Susan. 1974. "Is Second Language Learning Like the First?" *TESOL Quarterly* June, 111-27.

Lambert, Wallace E. and G. Richard Tucker. 1973. "The Benefits of Bilingualism." *Psychology Today* September, 89-91.

Paulston, Christina Bratt. 1974. "Linguistic and Communicative Competence." *TESOL Quarterly* December, 347-62.

Penfield, Wilder. 1953. "A Consideration of the Neuro-Physiological Mechanism of Speech and Some Educational Consequences." *Proceedings of the American Academy of Arts and Sciences* 82:201-14.

Pillet, Roger. 1974. *Foreign Language Study*. Chicago: University of Chicago Press.

Rivers, Wilga. 1964. *The Psychologist and the Foreign Language Teacher*. Chicago: University of Chicago Press.

_____. 1973. "From Linguistic Competence to Communicative Competence." *TESOL Quarterly* March, 25-34.

Slobin, Dan I. 1972. "Children and Language: They Learn the Same Way All Around the World." *Psychology Today* July, 71-74, 82.

Stevick, Earl W. "What Seems to Be What in Language Teaching," in *Adapting and Writing Language Lessons*. Washington, D.C.: Foreign Service Institute.

XIII. X, Y, Z's of Language Learning:
Bilingual and Second Language Education

RELEVANCE AND MOTIVATION

From 1945 until 1968, ten years after the NDEA, foreign and second language enrollments continued to increase; but after 1968, while university and college enrollments continued to increase slightly, enrollments in foreign language classes fell drastically and with unprecedented swiftness. Foreign language enrollments at the level of 30 percent of the total university and college enrollments in 1968 have fallen today to 20 percent of total student enrollments, and they appear to be sliding downward even further.

In the most popular languages—Spanish, French, and German, the languages that attract the most students—enrollments dropped by an average of 13 percent. Spanish enrollments are down by 7 percent, French 19 percent, and German 13 percent. These drops appear to reflect a general concern of students who believe that programs of study must be "relevant," a word that has found increasing popularity of late. Heretofore, high schools as well as most colleges and universities required at least two years of foreign language study for graduation. Students now cannot see why they should be required to learn what they may possibly never use. It has indeed been difficult to argue with this notion of relevancy, just as it is difficult for students to see the relevance of foreign language instruction if they are not living in a bilingual-bicultural community, and are not planning to travel or live abroad, or are not convinced by the argument that their learning of foreign languages will enable them to contribute toward world understanding.

Concrete instances of disenchantment have taken several forms. A candidate who advocated the removal of the language requirement for graduation was elected as student-body president at the University of Texas at Austin. A few years ago at the University of Nebraska, an ad hoc curriculum committee, composed of faculty and students, was formed to examine the language offerings and endorsed the elimination of a foreign language from the requirements of the Arts and Science College.

Parents, too, have voiced their concern about the language class, and it is not so unusual to hear a parent challenge: "Give me one good reason why my son, about to enter high school, should waste his time studying a foreign language. Three of my children took foreign languages in high school and college—and today not one of them can so much as order a cup of coffee in the language which he studied." Parents like this might join with Walter Pitkin, who said almost a century ago in *Life Begins at Forty* that language study is not worth the candle. In response to these criticisms the number of universities that retain the language requirement for graduation has dropped from a high of 89 percent in 1968 to 77 percent today. Universities and colleges have also gradually eliminated the language requirement for admission, thereby causing many secondary schools to cut back their range of language courses.

Admittedly, the students' demand for relevance has caused a change in curriculum; and admittedly, little has been done to justify a place in the curriculum for learning a second language. And we would agree that it is next to impossible to teach students to read, write, and speak a foreign language with any kind of skill in the traditional two-year, three-hours-per-week class. But we also need to point out that it is extremely difficult to teach students these skills even if the time is extended—and it has been—when there is no basic need to communicate in the language. We suggest here that it is extremely difficult to create this need in the typical classroom environment.

Even if we agree that bilingualism is impossible for the great majority of our students, other reasons for studying a foreign language come readily to mind, all worthy of consideration.

1. We learn about a foreign culture if we study a foreign language, especially if the teacher is a native speaker from the area in which the language is spoken. The Fulbright-Hays Act, designed to provide teachers and students with opportunities to study and to teach abroad, has as its purpose, other than the sharing of skills and research, acquainting foreign students and faculty with various cultures. Learning a language can lead to a kind of biculturalism, even without bilingualism. There are other ways to learn about a culture, but studying a language is one effective "window upon culture."

For example, John Gumperz, Director of the South Asia Language and Area Center at the University of California, Berkeley, went to India and Pakistan, where, together with several colleagues, he prepared sound films of people speaking in such typical situations as the market, home and family, and at work. These films provided valuable data on the way that these people actually used the language.

There is a growing tendency to pay more attention to the culture and background of the people whose language is being learned. Speaking at the Washington Area chapter meeting of the American Association of Teachers of Slavic and East European Languages, Professor Hugo Mueller of American University defined the study of a foreign language as the process of learning to "regard reality through another language," to understand the cultural elements involved in a given speech situation and the type of response that it would likely evoke from a native speaker. It is a fact, for example, that in the Hindi and other Eastern societies, one does not ask about the health of the members of the interlocutor's family. Modern texts for Hindi should alert students to this and supply conversational material that would be appropriate for a casual chat with a Hindi-speaking acquaintance.

2. There is, to be sure, the joy and wonder of being able to enjoy literature and to understand movies without surreptitious glances at the subtitles.

3. By studying a foreign language we become aware of our own language again (we perceive a different reality) as we become increasingly able to manipulate the language of the foreign culture. The grammatical structure of our own language, we learn, does not always conform to what we feel to be logical.

Here then are some perfectly valid reasons to support the study and teaching of foreign or second languages in the United States.

We have pointed already to the persistent notion that knowing more than one language appears to be a "cultural ideal." If we grant that for the above reasons languages should be taught (requiring study may be another matter, however), what are the factors that curriculum planners and teachers should consider and understand when establishing a foreign or second language program? The remainder of this chapter will be devoted to a consideration of that question.

APPROACHES, METHODS, AND TECHNIQUES

Edward Anthony, one of the world's foremost language-teaching theorists, maintains that language teaching can be viewed as a tripartite division consisting of an *approach*, a set of *methods* that follow from an approach, and a set of *techniques* that implement a method.

A language-teaching *approach* is a set of assumptions about the nature of language, language teaching, and language acquisition. We know from our past discussions that assumptions about the nature of language and about language acquisition differ. Structural theory and generative-transformational theory each embody a set of different assumptions about the skills and capacities of the typical language user, for instance.

A language-teaching *method* is based upon, and has as its source, a set of assumptions about the nature of language. A language-teaching *technique* is a "particular trick, strategem or contrivance used to accomplish an immediate objective." We must remember that "techniques carry out a method that is consistent with an approach." It will be useful to keep these distinctions in mind as we consider, and try to clarify, the nature of language teaching and language acquisition.

Our purpose here is not to advocate a particular approach, method, or technique—although our biases may creep through. Instead, we wish to indicate the particular set of assumptions, especially from language acquisition theory, that have influenced and directed language teaching practices in the last 25 years—a set of assumptions about *language* which are wedded to a set of assumptions about *learning behavior*. We believe that language teachers and curriculum specialists should be aware of both sets of theoretical assumptions. Even though it is our contention that a teacher should be aware of approaches, methods, and techniques, we do not advocate that this awareness should lead to dogmatism. Ronald Wardhaugh makes the following point in talking about theory: "We can never," he says, "ignore theory in talking about classroom practices, because good practices must necessarily be built on good theory. A good teacher," he maintains, "is someone who continually examines what he does, and continually tries to steer a course between doubt and dogma. Good teaching practice is based on good theoretical understanding. *There is indeed nothing so practical as a good theory*." With these preliminary words serving as background, let us now turn to the matter of *approach*.

The Chomskyan revolution in theoretical linguistics eventually spawned a similar kind of revolution in the teaching of language. There are two approaches which we will refer to: *the structural approach* (also called behavioristic) and the *generative-transformational approach* (also called cognitive). "Behavioristic" and "cognitive" are two terms employed by psychologists to codify, explain, and label a set of assumptions on learning. We will have more to say about these two terms as we proceed.

"Structural" and "generative-transformational" do not refer to methods, or even to techniques. They are terms that describe a set of assumptions or beliefs about the nature of language and language structure, from which language-teaching methods and techniques follow. Thus, approaches are important for the discipline of language teaching, since the particular approach the language teacher subscribed to would dictate which methods and techniques he would choose to employ in his classroom.

STRUCTURAL LINGUISTICS AND BEHAVIORISTIC PSYCHOLOGY

We have referred to the fact that World War II and succeeding events were primarily the cause for a strongly increased interest in foreign and second language teaching and learning, the impetus of which was not blunted until 1968, the year of student protest at the height of the hostilities in Viet Nam. Between these two wars, enrollments soared and structural linguists, employing their particular insights as to the structure of language, became very much involved in promoting the study of language: first, because they were language teachers during the war and thus had knowledge of a great many languages that held strategic value; and second, because they offered an alternative to the grammar-translation method that emphasized reading and writing; and third, because they advocated a set of methods through which the spoken language, in particular, could be taught. These methods, which were based upon a set of assumptions about the nature of language and learning, were called by a variety of different names, and it is not uncommon to find them referred to as "the linguistic method," "the Army method," "the mim-mem method," "the oral/aural method," "the pattern practice method," and perhaps most commonly, as the "audiolingual method."

Eminent linguists, including Leonard Bloomfield himself, wrote language-teaching texts that reflected many of the insights of structural linguistics and behavioristic psychology, and since these methods were designed to offer an alternative to the current grammar-translation method, textbooks that were predicated upon these assumptions found a ready and profitable market. In these methods, structural theory is related to, and is interwoven with, the psychological theory called *empiricism* or *behaviorism*: the belief that learning is a result of stimuli and the various responses to them. The set of assumptions that reflect and embody this view of learning had, as we shall learn, an important effect on the discipline of language teaching. Let us now examine those assumptions.

Assumption Number One: Language is primarily speech, not writing. This assumption was a reaction to classical or traditional grammar, which emphasized the primacy of reading and writing.

Assumption Number Two: Language is a set of speech habits largely learned through a process of conditioning and many repetitive drills, with emphasis upon mimicry and memorization of utterances and dialogues.

Assumption Number Three: The actual language should be taught, not merely the facts about the language being taught. Again, this assumption was a reaction to the traditional practice of emphasizing grammatical explanation.

Assumption Number Four: Language is what native speakers say, not what someone thinks they ought to say. This assumption was a reaction to rules that purport to prescribe "correct" speech.

Assumption Number Five: Languages are more different than they are alike.

Structural theory held, simply, that to teach a language one had to teach a set of language habits. In order for these responses to be learned certain habit-producing activities were advocated. These activities were: pattern-practice drills first enunciated by the teacher, mimicry of the teacher, and the memorization of dialogues. If only enough emphasis and time were spent upon these exercises, it was believed language fluency would soon follow.

The emphasis on the teaching of the spoken language would also take precedence over all other language skills, such as reading and writing—the classical concerns. In a representative text (*Beginning Japanese*) that remains popular even today, Eleanor Jorden voiced the opinion that "Language learning is overlearning. Through memorization of whole utterances and substitution within and manipulation of these utterances, a student achieves the fluency and automaticity that are necessary for control of a language. Language learning involves acquiring a new set of habits, and habits must be automatic."

Students were subjected to the spoken pattern drills of the *audiolingual*, or audio-oral, method, in which much emphasis was placed upon first hearing (stimuli) and then repeating (response). Pattern practice still remains an important aspect of the audiolingual teaching method. Robert Lado, who, along with Charles C. Fries, designed and wrote a number of language-teaching texts now famous the world over, says that in pattern practice drill "the student is led to practice a pattern, changing some elements of the pattern each time, so that normally he never repeats the same sentence twice. Furthermore, his attention is drawn to changes, which are stimulated by pictures, oral substitutions, etc., and this, *the pattern itself, the significant framework of the sentence*, rather than the particular sentence, is driven intensively into his habit reflexes." Students often found activities such as these boring and stifling, particularly when the entire lesson would consist of only these and related activities. Part of the current malaise existing in foreign language instruction can probably be attributed to this emphasis on the spoken language and to this set of methods and techniques employed to teach it.

To summarize, language lessons that reflect structural linguistic theory and behavioristic psychology contain dialogues to be memorized and a set of various kinds of "habit-producing" pattern drills. Until recently most language-teaching methods based upon linguistics were structural in orientation. Now generative-transformational theory and cognitive psychology promise to open up new vistas and alternatives to the language teacher. We turn to those now.

GENERATIVE-TRANSFORMATIONAL GRAMMAR AND COGNITIVE PSYCHOLOGY

All language teaching methods nowadays appear to have a linguistic and a psychological base. Noam Chomsky, in *Language and Mind*, has even suggested that linguistics can be considered a branch of cognitive psychology. At the same time that he urges the language teacher to question the insights of linguistics and psychology, as well as their application and relevance to the teaching of language, he also submits that "it is possible—even likely—that principles of psychology and linguistics, and research in these disciplines, may supply insights useful to the language teacher."

While keeping Chomsky's admonition in mind—that linguistics and psychology may not solve all of the problems that beset the language teaching profession—we believe, still, that these two disciplines, especially the varieties termed generative-transformational grammar and cognitive psychology, can provide useful "roadsigns" for those persons involved in teaching, evaluating, and writing language programs. Some of these roadsigns are ambiguous, however, and they may not become clear for some time to come. The process of acquiring language, or as it is called, *language acquisition*, is a useful point of departure.

LANGUAGE ACQUISITION

Under the topic of language acquisition there are a number of subcategories and trends, each one deserving more attention than it is possible to provide here. First, let us look at the nature of language acquisition and the theories which are employed to explain the process of language acquisition.

Structural grammarians, it is important to restate, emphasize the distinctiveness found among languages. Martin Joos said in 1957 that "Languages can differ from each other without limit and in unpredictable ways." By way of contrast, transformational theorists emphasize the similarities among languages, maintaining that while languages may appear to be very different, an analysis of their deep, abstract structures reveals they are more similar than they are different. Languages, these theorists submit, can only differ from each other in a limited number of ways.

That all languages share structures makes it simpler to account for the fact that children learn, without the benefit of formal instruction, the language(s) of their immediate environment. Chomsky's hypothesis about language acquisition is that every normal child is programmed with a capacity (a language acquisition device) to learn language, fluently, by the time he is five to six years old. That a child learns language(s) quickly, easily, and efficiently is observable by anyone who has lived in a foreign country with small children. And it is not uncommon to encounter children who have learned two or even more languages fluently, with native-like pronunciation. The processes that enable children to learn language(s) are still poorly understood and a great deal of current research—research that we label as *developmental psycholinguistics*—focuses itself upon discerning the language-learning attributes of the human species.

We can distinguish three areas of current developmental research:

1. Some research seeks to accumulate evidence which may demonstrate that children learn language by imitating the language patterns of adults. According to this theory, a child speaks an imperfect version of adult speech, and eventually reaches the model of adult speech through closer and closer approximation of it. The *imitative theory of language acquisition* has assumed less importance today, for reasons that we will explore below, and is being supreseded by other theories of language acquisition. A version of imitative language learning is developed by B. F. Skinner in his book, *Verbal Behavior*.

2. Another avenue of research is based upon Noam Chomsky's hypothesis about language acquisition. Chomsky theorizes that very basic linguistic concepts are native to the human species and that the young child arrives at the monumental task of learning a language already programmed with the knowledge of what language is. We find that Chomsky's theory consists of a syntactic component that is *generative* and phonological and semantic components that are *interpretive*.

David McNeil and others have done empirical research on the language of children, employing the theoretical constructs of language developed in *Aspects*. McNeil and his associates find that all children pass through the same states of language acquisition on their way to adult speech; the ages of children who reach a particular stage may vary, but never more than a few months. At approximately twelve months, children are speaking their first word; at 18 months, utterances consist of two to three words; and at two to three years, sentences can be heard. At the age of 18 months (the 2-3 word state) McNeil found that child language is as patterned, constrained, and rule-governed as adult language is; he also finds that children at this stage do not imitate the speech of parents or older siblings. Words at this early age do not occur in adult order nor in random order.

McNeil and others described the grammar that served to explain language behavior of 18-month old children as *pivot*. A pivot generative grammar will specify just those sentences that occur or might occur at various stages in children's speech.

The rules of pivot grammar, in brief, consist of the following:

• Sentence → Open + (Pivot)

Sentences of approximately 18-month old children consist of two classes of words: an obligatory *open* class and an optional *pivot* class.

• Open → a large number of words, including the following: boat, mommy, toy, come, shoe, milk, and sock.

• Pivot → a small number of high frequency words: allgone, big, my, and see.

Sentences generated by this brief sketch of a stage of young children's grammar might consist of the following set:

> boat
> shoe
> see toy
> allgone milk
> my toy

Thus, children's language is *not* a copy, however imperfect, of adult grammar. Pivot grammar had its own set of rules, from which new sentences could be generated.

3. While Chomsky's and McNeil's notion of the principles of language acquisition is based upon the primacy of syntax, a more recent explanation and set of hypotheses rest upon the primacy of *semantics*. In this view, the essence of language is *meaning*; the child has something

meaningful to say, and syntax merely "clothes" meaning. Thus, in this theory semantics becomes *generative* and syntax becomes *interpretive.*

Lois Bloom, in her study of early language acquisition, finds that a sentence with the same syntactic shape, such as "Mommy sock," can have various meanings, each meaning dependent upon the context in which the sentence is uttered. We can think of a number of possible meanings for the sentence, "Mommy sock," including the following:

> That is mommy's sock
> Bring me my sock
> The sock fell (off the table)
> Is that Mommy's sock?

What is perhaps the most important development in this area of language acquisition is that Jean Piaget's research on the intellectual and cognitive development of children can be correlated with generative semantics. Piaget's research identifies various stages of intellectual and cognitive growth and development, and these states can be linked to the various stages of language acquisition of the young child. Bloom submits, "Piaget's contention that language depends upon, as a logical consequence of, the prior development of relevant cognitive structures is strongly supported by the result of research in early language development." Bloom further makes the point that "children learn precisely those words and structures which encoded their conceptual notions about the world of objects, events and relations." Syntax, from this point of view, is not a crucial variable; *meaning* is.

Arguing for a semantically-based explanation of language acquisition, M. Bowerman says, "The structural component of the rules underlying children's early two- and three-word utterances may be semantic concepts like 'agent,' 'action,' and 'object acted upon,' rather than grammatical concepts like 'subject,' 'predicate' and 'direct object.' "

THE CRITICAL AGE

That children learn languages better, faster, and more efficiently than adults is a popular view. *Critical age factor* is a term employed by psychologists and linguists (including Chomsky and Lenneberg) to reflect the assumption that children do learn languages better, more easily, and more efficiently than adolescents and adults. The late Dr. Wilder Penfield of the Montreal Neurological Institute researched the psychological development of the brain and found that it is "specialized" in the learning of languages if the learning took place before the onset of puberty. After that age, he postulated, "gradually, inevitably, it seems to become rigid, slow, less receptive."

The *age factor* gives rise to the notion and the belief that the "language acquisition device" atrophies early in life, and that if language learning is to "take" children must be taught a language at an early age; this age "just happens" to coincide with the beginning of formal education. There were early advocates of teaching foreign languages in the elementary school even before current linguistic and psychological research. Among the early advocates was Dr. Earl J. McGrath, former United States Commissioner of Education, who in 1952, six years before the NDEA and five years before the publication of *Syntactic Structures*, helped to trigger the teaching of "FLES," as it was to be called. He observed that "for some years I unwisely took the position that a foreign language did not constitute an indispensable element in a general education program. This position, I am happy to say, I have reversed."

Support for McGrath's position of FLES came from psychologists Arnold Gesell and Frances L. Ilg of the Gesell Institute of Child Development, who declared that they were happy to see school systems providing opportunities for second-language learning in the elementary curriculum. They submitted that this practice "indicates a clearer recognition of the pattern and sequences of child development. The young child enjoys language experiences. With favorable motivation he is emotionally amenable to a second and even a third language. This holds true for nursery school and kindergarten age levels."

Since 1952, however, the movement to include foreign languages as a regular part of the elementary school curriculum has seen both success and failure—mostly failure. More than one million children were eventually introduced to a modern foreign language in the lower grades. Yet while some excellent FLES programs have existed, well over half of them were conducted after school hours, and outside the regular school curriculum. And many of these classes met for only 15 or 20 minutes, twice a week, with the students learning only a few phrases and songs. Moreover, and perhaps an even greater factor in their lack of success, language was taught as a subject. Children never learned *in* the language, as is done in some forms of bilingual education.

At the present time FLES appears to be moribund and, to A. Bruce Gaarder and others, it was not notably successful. The newest trend in second-language instruction and learning is reflected in various *bilingual* programs in the United States, a topic that we shall return to soon.

SECOND-LANGUAGE LEARNING

It may seem that our discussion of languages in the early grades has led us far afield from our discussion of language acquisition, or more specifically, from our inquiry: "Is second-language learning like the first?" There are a number of prominent scholars, psychologists, sociologists, and educators, as well as linguists, interested in finding an answer to this important question. Heidi Dulay, Marina K. Burt, Stephen D. Krashen, Jack Richards, Susan Ervin-Tripp, John McNamara and others all have been sorting through evidence, seeking to prove that it is the same or that it is not the same. While the jury is still out, evaluating all the evidence, what evidence there is seems to indicate that first- and second-language learning/acquisition is not qualitatively different (and some doubt there is any difference at all).

Research has focused upon the language learning skills and strategies of adults and children. Stephen D. Krashen and his fellow researchers believe that there is a natural developmental sequence to language learning in the adult, and these processes parallel the processes employed by the young child learning his first language. Their research leads H. Douglas Brown and others to suggest that "there is absolutely no conclusive evidence that the adult is cognitively deficient in his ability to acquire a foreign language." Susan Ervin-Tripp also finds in many important respects that development of communicative capacity in a second language follows the order found in mother tongue acquisition. One of these processes that eventually leads to fluency, which is found both in mother tongue and second-language acquisition, is the development of an "interlanguage," a language that is deficient from the fluent speaker's in many respects. The adult language learner, similar in strategy to the child in the process of acquiring his first language, will attempt to communicate before he has mastered sufficiently all levels of the target language—and this "imperfect" product is an "interlanguage."

Jack Richards, Marina Burt and Heidi Dulay have also suggested the close approximation of first- and second-language acquisition. They have examined the errors that second-language learners make and have compared them to the errors that first-language learners make. Structural linguists felt at one time that the errors made by language learners were due to interference from the first language. Richards, Dulay, Burt, and others now maintain that, in general, learner errors are due to language development factors rather than to the interference of the first language with the second. Contrastive analysis (as advocated by structuralists) is now being replaced by the notion of error analysis (which encompasses both language interference errors and developmental errors). While it is true that the phonological system of the first language usually leads to an accent in the second, it is not clear whether the morphology, syntax, and semantic structures of the first language produce errors in the same way. There is even the suggestion that developmental errors are sequential, and that all language learners, whether first or second, whether native speakers of Japanese, Polish, English, or any other language, experience the same kinds of difficulties and make the same kinds of errors in learning language—a hypothesis that serves to support the notion that there is a set of learning strategies and language skills shared by all.

"But I am not convinced," our reader might say: "There is a difference." We would agree that the older learner does experience difficulty that the younger does not. What the difference is, whether neurological (the Penfield, Chomsky and Lenneberg hypothesis), cognitive (learning strategies), or affective, we do not know as yet. We are not saying that the scholars we have cited above are correct in their premises, only that what they have discovered gives further evidence to support the notion of "universal learning strategy." And Joan Rubin, in her article, "What the 'Good Language Learner' Can Teach Us," recognizes the same ambivalence: while all people can learn one or more languages, some people seem to be more successful at it than others. She finds that successful language learners exhibit certain personality traits and employ identifiable strategies:

1. They are good, willing, and accurate guessers.
2. They are not afraid to appear foolish, so they take chances.
3. They are not afraid to attempt to construct sentences that they have never heard before.
4. They constantly look for new patterns in the target language.
5. They look for opportunities to practice, even to the point of seeking out native speakers.

As all good teachers know, there is much more to the learning and teaching of language than the appropriate approach, methods, and techniques. Rubin's research would attest to that, and leads us into a discussion of a topic of language teaching that has attracted much attention lately. If linguistics and psychology cannot provide us with answers to all of our questions that concern the difference, if any, between the adult and child language learner, what can? We suggest that the notion of the "affective domain" can give us additional answers.

THE AFFECTIVE DOMAIN

In a collection of papers given at the TESOL convention, there is a section entitled, "Human Relations, Affect, and Communicative Competence"; these three factors all pertain to the "affective domain," which includes a number of variables:

1. The emotional response of the student: his motivation; how he feels about himself, his peers, his teacher (the authority figure); his interactions with his peers and his teacher; how secure he feels; and even his reaction to his physical surroundings. His affective responses may be either positive or negative. For instance, a gloomy, unattractive classroom would be negative and would constitute a possible barrier to learning.

2. The student's reaction to the language that he is learning. He may experience "language shock." The language that he is attempting to learn may lack status; it may be, or may have been, the language of an oppressor; or it may sound so different from his native language as not to sound like a language at all—one that is worth learning.

3. The student's reaction to the culture of the people whose language he is learning. Sometimes students experience a reaction known as "cultural shock." A negative reaction to a culture may also cause a similar reaction to the language of that culture.

These are just a few of the variables in learning that have little to do with approach but may have a great deal to say about what methods or techniques will be employed in the classroom.

Motivation is an important criterion, and teachers always seem to talk about how to motivate students. Earl W. Stevick of the Foreign Service Institute makes the useful distinction between *instrumental* motivation and *integrative* motivation. *Instrumental* motivation in the classroom may be conditioned and directed by the teacher who awards grades, perhaps money and various prizes, sweets, the promise of employment or travel abroad; while *integrative* motivation "goes very deep—direct to the level of identity" and reflects a genuine interest in learning the language. Leon A. Jakobovits speaks to this point in his article, "The Psychological Bases of Second Language Learning," in which he submits that to spend "massive educational efforts in teaching FL's in the absence of genuine interest in that type of knowledge is not only futile but harmful." Affective factors, according to John H. Schumann, may indeed play a more vital and important role "than does biological maturation in problems associated with adult second language acquisition."

The reduction of tension in the classroom, perhaps with the teacher assuming a completely different role-relationship with his students, seems to have a corresponding effect on learning. A teacher has a tremendous effect on the learning climate in the classroom, and it is useful to report what one has said (from Ginott):

> I have come to a frightening conclusion. I am the decisive element in the class-room. It is my personal approach that creates the climate. It is my daily mood that makes the weather. As a teacher I possess tremendous power to make a child's life miserable or joyous. It can be a tool of torture or an instrument of inspiration. I can humiliate or humor, hurt or heal. In all situations it is my response that decides whether a crisis will be escalated or de-escalated, and a child humanized or de-humanized.

Two methods, in particular, that we will discuss below, Community Language Learning and the Silent Way, certainly have among their aims to reduce tension and the threatening aspect of the teacher in the classroom. Hopefully, the reduction of tension and threat will lead to more "receptive" learning (real learning) rather than to "defensive" learning (shallow or short-term learning), which is learning designed to avoid pain. But before we turn to methods and techniques, we will discuss one of the most important, to our minds, recent developments in education—*bicultural-bilingual education*.

BILINGUAL-BICULTURAL EDUCATION:
A RETURN TO THE PAST

"Thank God for the dispossessed American-Indian, for the disadvantaged Mexican-American, for the dislocated Puerto Rican! Without them (and the political leverage that they are only just beginning to exercise) there would be no publicly subsidized bilingual education (and, therefore, no semblance of public concern for cultural pluralism in American life) even today." So states Joshua Fishman in the foreword to William F. Mackey's book *Bilingual Education in a Binational World*.

Bilingual education is a recent educational phenomenon in the United States, or we should say, a recently *renewed* phenomenon. The United States was engaged in bilingual-bicultural education during the early part of its history. In 1774, John Adams wrote to his wife Abigail: "Above all ... let your ardent Anxiety be to mould the Minds and Manners of our Children ... Fix their ambition upon great and solid objects, and their Contempt upon little frivolous and useless ones. It is Time, my dear, for you to begin to teach them French." Yet after the outbreak of World War I, with its accompanying restrictions on immigration, the status of bilingual education began to change. Anyone who spoke any language other than English was suspect, at the least, for not being a "true American."

In recent years, however, bilingualism has become, according to Dell Hymes, a "sociolinguistic subject par excellence," and constitutes one of the newest areas of linguistic research. Mandated by the Bilingual Education Act (revised in 1976), by the Supreme Court Decision of *Lau vs. Nichols*, and by the Office of Civil Rights' Guidelines, public schools must provide initial instruction in the child's home language if he does not know English. We have come a long way from the "low prestige syndrome" suffered by the sons and daughters of immigrants in the United States, who experienced contempt in their bilingual or bidialectal community. Yet there are still problems in fostering minority languages, as some say pride in the minority culture may compete with national identification and prove detrimental to national unity.

These arguments provide evidence for the fact that bilingualism has many complex social, political, and psychological implications that must be studied, adding the research to the corpus of information on second-language learning and maintenance in the United States.

Bilingual education in the U.S. is not a unique phenomenon, since more than 100 nations of the world have bilingual programs. Bruck, Lambert, and Tucker assert that "living in North America, we frequently tend to forget that bilingualism and education in one's second language is the rule rather than the exception for most of the world's population." In these countries it is a way of life to attend schools where a second language is the medium of instruction.

Increasing attention has been paid to the study of bilingual communities in the world. Emeritus Professor Einar Haugen of Harvard University wrote a monumental study of Norwegian-English bilingualism in the United States. *Languages in Contact*, a text by Uriel Weinreich, presents a kaleidoscopic view of bilingual situations throughout the western world. New studies are constantly being published. Works by eminent researchers like Joshua Fishman, William F. Mackey, Wallace Lambert, G. Richard Tucker, Andrew Cohen, and Carolyn Kessler, to mention only a handful, are available for the reader, and we have listed some of these in the extensive "For Further Reference" section at the end of this chapter.

In Canada, an experiment in bilingual education is ongoing, and a large majority of English-speaking children in Quebec attend school where French is the medium of instruction. This particular model of bilingual education is called the *immersion model*. Instruction is available, more importantly, for most monolingual English-speaking children—not merely for the low socio-economic groups; in this way, this model differs from most bilingual programs which exist in the United States. (A notable exception, the Culver City Project, has attempted to replicate the Canadian experiment.)

The Canadian experiment in bilingual education began about ten years ago, when psycholinguists Wallace Lambert and G. Richard Tucker asked themselves, "What would happen if children were to attend kindergarten and elementary school where a foreign or second language was used as the major medium of instruction?" They, and a group of supportive parents, were mindful of the ineffectiveness of traditional foreign language instruction and even of FLES. The parents were also mindful and concerned about the current political situation in Canada, where both French- and English-speaking citizens reside and compete for political power. They also wanted to develop in their children a mutual understanding and respect for the French-speaking minority.

The experiment began when monolingual English-speaking children were placed in classrooms where instruction was carried on in French, and where teachers, although knowing English, responded and spoke in French. The *St. Lambert Bilingual Project*, as it was called, has become a prototype of a kind of bilingual-bicultural education, replicated in the United States and elsewhere; by most accounts, it is a tremendously successful model.

Another question which has been raised by many researchers and parents is, "If I put my child into a class where a second language is employed for instruction, will it make any difference to his or her cognitive development and growth?" In other words, does bilingual education work, and is it worth it? This remains a question, even into the tenth year of the St. Lambert experiment. Here are some of the research findings of the St. Lambert experiment and other projects administered by Lambert and Tucker on this question:

1. After several years of monitoring student performance, "no signs of negative effects in cognitive development" were found.

2. In math, or in any other of the "intellectual" subjects, there have been no significant differences in cognitive development.

3. There appears to be more cognitive flexibility demonstrated by the students: "What is particularly encouraging," Lambert and Tucker point out, "is that by grades four and five the

children's attitude toward French people appear to reflect more understanding, charity, and friendliness than is the case for the English-speaking control [group of children]."

An academic question that should perhaps remain moot is whether the cognitive skills and development of children are adversely affected by learning in two languages. Bilingualism has been a world-wide part of much education for such a long period, and English children, German children, and other children who participate in bilingual education are not known to be deficient in cognitive growth. There is, however, evidence gathered by John McNamara, in his study of bilingual education, that seems to indicate that Irish children *do* suffer cognitive lag. This lag may be explained by the fact that the Irish language has not been the national language of Ireland for long and is not spoken widely, rather than upon the weakness of any bilingual education program being administered in Ireland. Perhaps it is sufficient to postulate that children will do better learning a second language if the language is heard outside the school—as in Canada, where both English and French are used in everyday activities.

In the United States, bilingual-bicultural education has had a different thrust than in Canada. Bilingual education, or education in a second language, has not been based upon, nor has it evolved from, any research indicating the optimum chronological time to teach a language; it has also not been, in the main, a program for children from homes of the more educated or the more affluent (socially and economically) segment of the school-attending population. Rather, bilingual education in the U.S. has developed from the great concern that sizable minorities of young children are being deprived of their equal educational rights by having to attend schools where the language of instruction is not their home language. (It is rather ironic, we submit, that English-speaking Canadian children, by design, can attend schools where French is the medium of instruction, and that Canadian children appear to develop cognitively and socially as well, or perhaps better, than children who participate in monolingual education programs.)

There are other crucial differences, of course, between the Canadian experience and the experience of bilingual education in the United States. The emphasis in Canada is on the opportunity to *become* bilingual; in the United States, it is, in the main, to *educate* the bilingual. This distinction can be made a bit clearer if we look again to the philosophy of bilingual education in the two countries. In Canada, bilingual education is offered to the middle and upper socioeconomic classes (although lower socioeconomic classes do also participate). In the United States, bilingual education has been a *compensatory* program, implemented for the disadvantaged.

The experience of the United States in bilingual education is unique. Before any legislation was passed, children who spoke no English at home attended schools where there was little if no provision made to help them make the transition to the English-speaking environment. Teachers who often could speak the language of their students were required to speak only in English, and children were often penalized by the school administration for speaking their home language in class or at play. As a result, these children, because of their lack of English language skills, were retained or—worse yet—shunted off to classes for special education (designed for the slow learner and the mentally retarded). It is easy to see that the school was a hostile environment for these children, and it is no wonder then that the drop-out rate was in excess of 85 percent in some school districts.

The Bilingual Education Act, as Title VII of the Elementary and Secondary Education Act (revised in 1976), provides funds to school districts for use in funding bilingual-bicultural education programs designed for students who need aid in coping with the curriculum. An important Supreme Court decision, *Lau vs. Nichols*, requires school districts to provide instruction in the child's home language if he does not know English. A child therefore has the constitutional right, the Supreme Court has declared, to attend a school where his language will be employed to instruct him.

The interest that the federal government has demonstrated toward making the schools instruments of instruction for every child has resulted in the development of a number of different kinds of bilingual programs. In his article on the typology of bilingual education programs, William F. Mackey identifies many kinds. We shall distinguish two of the major types:

First there is the general type of bilingual program in which instruction is carried on in the child's first language, and the target language (the language to be learned) is taught as a subject. This may be called the *transitional model* of bilingual education, since there are specific classes to teach English until the time that the child can learn in English. At that time his mother tongue is replaced as a medium of instruction.

There is another general type of bilingual program, differing in a crucial aspect. In this type, both the mother tongue and the target language are employed as a means of instructing the child. If both languages are employed as mediums of instruction throughout the child's school career, *language maintenance* is one result. This program can also be transitional if one language, the school language, eventually replaces the mother tongue as the only language of instruction.

The distinction between the two general models is a qualitative one. In the first model, instruction is given in the language—language is treated as a *subject*, as arithmetic and social studies are. In the second model, language is employed as a *vehicle* of instruction, perhaps to teach arithmetic and social studies. William Mackey has always maintained that language treated as a subject will always remain a subject, learnable by few but not by many. One of the major reasons for the failure of FLES was that the target language was taught as a subject; it was never consistently employed to instruct.

THE YEARS AHEAD

Since we have a federally-mandated bilingual-bicultural education policy in the United States, let us now examine some of the possible difficulties that bilingual-bicultural education may face in the years ahead.

Perhaps the most serious problem is that bilingual education is mainly designed or intended for teaching the "different" language user rather than for creating a population of bilinguals. Albar Peña, former director of the Bilingual Education Office in H.E.W., says that this policy smacks of the *melting-pot* concept—a concept that says, in part, that everyone should become primarily English-speaking. As a result of this concept, there is a stigma attached to being bilingual, especially if one of the languages is the language of a segment of society which is economically deprived. Education aimed at the "disadvantaged minorities" is thus labeled *compensatory education*, geared to "rehabilitate" children so that they can enter and participate in the mainstream educational system.

A bilingual educational program of the compensatory type is a deficit model. To Bernard Spolsky, it is as if you are moving "people from one kind of monolingualism to another." Spolsky calls bilingual education practiced in this way "a gimmick for the disadvantaged," which, he maintains, is patronizing to the children who participate. Joshua Fishman argues that "compensatory-transitional bilingual education is self-liquidating at best and self-frustrating at worst: it is patronizing, apologetic, invidious, one-sided and unidirectional."

Bilingual education based on the compensatory model is thus basically a one-way street, and that is perhaps its most serious flaw. It is a two-way street in Canada where, in time, participants eventually consider themselves as both English and French-Canadian. In order for bilingual education to become more than compensatory in scope, we believe that the middle and upper classes must desire and be motivated to participate in it as well. As Fishman says, "It is the poor little rich kids who most desperately need bilingual and bicultural education. It is they who lack education for world-cultural realism and for global-cultural desiderata."

To succeed even more than it has, bilingual education should be much more than transitional. We believe that it can be. Bilingual-bicultural education, and the manner in which it can be implemented for the benefit of all societies in the United States, remains a topic of much concern. While the compensatory model has led the United States into the area of bilingual education, it has not as yet provided a viable educational opportunity for the majority. Perhaps as more is known about the benefits of knowing two languages, bilingual education will be offered for the many rather than for the few.

We leave our reader, in this first year of the third century for our nation, with this appropriate visionary statement from Fishman:

> In sum, my prediction is that when your great-grandchildren and mine celebrate the 300th anniversary of the U.S.A., there will still be non-Anglo ethnic maintenance and non-English language maintenance. They will find them changed. They will find them enriched. They will find them creative. They will find them stimulating. They will find them self-critical and critical of others. They will find them wonderful. They will find them part and parcel of America, just as they have always been. And they will find America richer because of them, more exciting because of them, and matured because of them, much as it has always been. Via bilingual education your great-grandchildren and mine can partake of this richness, this excitement, and this maturity. I pray that they will.

WHAT DID I SAY THAT WAS WRONG?

Christina Bratt Paulston tells a story about a recent visit that she made to her homeland, Sweden. Being fluent in Swedish, she had no difficulty in understanding the language or making herself understood. Where she had difficulty was in certain social situations, in which she used language that was inappropriate. Language, we find, also comes hand-in-hand with a set of social rules dictating how to use language in an appropriate manner. Paulston had invited dinner guests over for a typical American Thanksgiving feast. At one point, she had to leave her guests for a moment because she had to be in the kitchen. While she was attending to her culinary chores, another guest arrived who did not know any of the others. When Paulston returned to the room and asked her recent arrival, as any American would, "Have you met everyone?", the rather chagrined guest answered, "Of course I have." It is a rule of social etiquette in Sweden, but not in America, that one introduces himself to other strangers and does not wait to be formally introduced. In fact, it is obligatory that one Swede introduces himself to another, and a social insult (which reflects lack of good manners) if he does not.

Language, then, is not merely an array of well-formed responses to stimuli, but also an array of rules as to the appropriateness of these responses. Some matters that have to be taken into account when teaching or learning any language are the following:

1. The role of silence (Americans always want to fill the void, usually with small talk, while other cultures value silence—for instance, the Japanese).

2. Speaking volume and intonation (how softly, for example, does one speak in a restaurant?).

3. The use of formula utterances. "How are you?" does not really mean that the questioner is interested in the health of the person addressed. In fact, if given a long answer consisting of a list of facts about his health, the questioner might learn to avoid the person in the future—or at least to avoid asking the question.

4. How personal can we be? It has been said by many that Americans ask extremely personal questions of one another, and so they become adept at "missing the point" or avoiding direct answers ("How old are you?" can be answered by the evasive "Old enough to know better"). In Sweden, if one asks a direct personal question, the person is constrained to answer truthfully. It is a social rule in Sweden that one does not ask such personal questions.

Rules that we have been talking about are called *pragmatic* rules, and they must be learned along with the phonology, morphology, syntax, and semantics of any language. Spies have been known to have been tripped up on less.

CHOOSING WHICH LANGUAGES TO TEACH

Now that we have identified some of the factors that influence language teaching, what languages, if we had a choice, should be offered? In general, and following Earl Stevick's guidelines, the range of languages to be taught would be determined by what students find to be of deep interest. Charles A. Ferguson, former Director of the Center for Applied Linguistics, suggests that students would find useful any of the major "culture" languages, which provide the key to a rich written literature and which serve as mediums of communication for large segments of the world's population. They include: Arabic, Chinese, French, German, Hebrew, Hindi-Urdu, Indonesian, Italian, Japanese, Persian, Portuguese, Russian, Spanish, and Swahili.

Other factors in the choice of languages include the availability of instructors and ethnic considerations. In areas with a concentration of persons of a particular national origin, there could be interest in learning the ancestral speech. Many public schools in Hawaii prefer now to offer Chinese and Japanese. In parts of the Midwest and Pennsylvania, German and Scandinavian languages may be favored, while in the East, particularly in the industrial centers, the Slavic languages, Hungarian, and Italian may be of interest. Certain cities have for one reason or another attracted particular groups. Boston has the largest number of Armenians and Albanians; Cleveland, Ohio, of Hungarians, Slovenes, and Croatians; New Bedford, Massachusetts, of Portuguese; Indianapolis, of Bulgarians; and sheep raising areas in Nevada and California have drawn concentrations of Basques from Spain.

Most of the large cities have other ethnic groups. It is our belief that too little has been done to encourage the teaching of these languages on a regional basis. It also seems incomprehensible that the various languages of the American Indian are not offered more frequently—although it would be rather ironic to offer them as "foreign" languages.

Curiously, however, parents' support of ancestral languages is often weak or nonexistent, perhaps because of the fear that their children will remain too "foreign," that the language in question is not of "practical" importance, that the language represents an ethnic group that has not been prosperous or respected, or that these languages don't stand as much chance of being learned as the more popular ones. According to Theodore Heubener, a former supervisor of foreign language instruction in New York City, a city that leads in the number of varied ethnic backgrounds, neither parents nor students have in the past appeared to be much influenced by national origin, or availability of a language. This tendency may be changing, however. As we have already indicated, enrollments in Hebrew are increasing in the public schools as well as at Yeshiva University. By way of contrast, although Brooklyn has a fairly substantial Norwegian community, very few elect to study the ancestral language. In other states, for instance in Wisconsin, where there is a high Polish population, enrollments have never been high.

To attract the Polish vote, a state legislator in the 1930s set up a chair of Polish at the University of Wisconsin. A visiting professor from Poland was hired, a collection of Polish books was purchased, and excellent courses were organized. Yet in 1938 the annual enrollment for all courses amounted to only twenty. Recent interest in the Slavic world, however, vindicates the Wisconsin politician, and the university's Polish facilities are among the best in the country.

There are areas in the United States in which languages are being taught even though few, if any, native speakers of the language reside there. A few years ago in Utah, several high schools introduced Arabic, Chinese, and Japanese, mostly taught by Mormon missionaries with firsthand experience of the languages and cultures. From all indications, their efforts have been successful.

Inspired by these examples, one secondary school in Colorado has introduced Arabic, while several California schools are teaching Chinese and Japanese. Sometimes the initiative comes from the pupils themselves. A few years ago students of a New Jersey high school petitioned for an after-hours course in Swahili. The school board supported their request, an instructor was located, and this African language was introduced. However, Richard Brod of the Modern Language Association staff has expressed the opinion that such moves reflect more the results of social pressures than intrinsic interest in languages.

We realize that Eastern languages take a great deal of time to learn. Educators are now, however, making them available at the precollegiate level. Columbia University, with the aid of a grant from the Carnegie Foundation, has brought Chinese to New York City high schools. New York City has one of the largest contingents of Chinese living outside of China, and now that the People's Republic of China is participating in the United Nations, Chinese may become even more important and popular.

We present these examples to show that American students are interested in learning foreign languages. But we must also recognize that what is good, or interesting, or of value to a few students may not be for all. We merely suggest that there be made available more opportunities to learn.

We would also like to encourage the teaching of a course in secondary schools and colleges on "Languages and Linguistics in the World Today." It could, in simple terms, introduce young people to the basic facts of language knowledge and language performance. It would give a picture of the language families of the world, and some notions of sociolinguistic problems in domestic and international affairs. Such a course ought to help dispel any myths concerning language that the students had absorbed, replacing them with a realistic notion of the structure of language and its role in society.

CHOOSING A LANGUAGE-TEACHING METHOD

We have discussed various concerns of the language-teaching art, but we have not so far discussed how a good language learner becomes a user of the language that he is studying. Somewhere in the process of learning a language there must be, to cite Wilga Rivers, a transition from skill-getting to skill-using, or from linguistic competence to communicative competence.

We should ask ourselves just what sorts of language activities language users do during a normal day; some, but not all, are the following:

Elicit information from someone; express an opinion; report an event or any other "happening"; elaborate a statement; justify or make an alibi; engage in small talk (about the weather, for example); tell a joke; compliment someone; disagree with someone in an acceptable manner; refuse, politely, an invitation; make an excuse; tell a lie; appear to be objective (even when not).

In changing the focus of our attention from what the language learner has to do linguistically to the communicative acts that he will have to engage in, we must not permit our linguistics to get in the way. We should, according to Rivers, engage in interaction activities as soon as possible, perhaps even on the first day of instruction. While audiolingual practices emphasized the acquisition of the structure of the sentence, other methods that have been suggested recently are less linguistic-directed and more communicative-directed. The method that is called Situational Reinforcement® is an excellent example of a communicative-directed method. There are, in addition, several language teaching activity texts published by the University of Pittsburgh that list situations, and strategies for coping with them, in a conversational context; and these we have listed in our section, "For Further Reference."

We have suggested several times in our last two chapters that there may be ways to improve the teaching of language in our educational institutions. We have not suggested any concrete proposals on how improvement in foreign language teaching may occur, however. What we have said is that modern linguistic theory may provide useful insights into the language learning process. We are now in much the situation of a flying instructor, who has taught his students the theory of aerodynamics (what keeps an airplane in the air) and the various kinds of motor coordination needed to fly the airplane. Yet, if after these explanations they were told, "Go fly," they would still be at a loss as to what to do.

The following, then, is a "what the teacher can do" in the classroom to *facilitate* the learning of a foreign language. We refer to the teacher as a facilitator because we believe that what the learner does to learn a foreign language is far more important that what the teacher teaches. Hence a change in focus, as indicated by our terminology, from "teacher" to "facilitator."

There are various techniques and methods for teaching language on the market, some new and some old, some useful and some not. Some of the new approaches reflect current research in psychology as well as in linguistics. We do not advocate any particular brand of language teaching, but, on the contrary, we adhere to enlightened eclecticism, believing that methods and techniques must appeal to the student's interests, his needs, and his particular set of learning strategies. As in all discussions of teaching methods, there are caveats to be considered: methods and techniques are in the province of the teacher and better methods and better techniques can lead to better learning. But additional variables in the learning situation must also be considered:

1. Interest or perseverance of the student. How badly does he want to learn the language?
2. The time available for the task of learning.
3. The various language learning aptitudes of the students.

Another possible roadblock is that adherence to one method, without the possibility of variation, can lead to boredom in the classroom. As noted, language teaching methodology has been almost exclusively audiolingual (mimicry, memorization, pattern drills), and the adherence to this approach (coupled with unimaginative teaching) may have contributed to the recent reaction to the language requirement. Boredom is pain and the bored will take measures, some extreme, to alleviate it. In sum, it is our belief that for instruction to be effective, a variety of methods and techniques must be employed.

With these preliminary remarks serving as our guide, let us examine four current methods of teaching language. These range from the familiar audiolingual to the less familiar "Silent Way." We will be looking at the following methods: St. Cloud, Community Language Learning, Situational Reinforcement, and the "Silent Way."

ST. CLOUD

The St. Cloud method places emphasis on the spoken language and is a variation of the audiolingual method. The St. Cloud variation originated in France, where the Centre de Recherche et d'Etude pour la Diffusion du Français of the Ecole Normale Supérieure, located at St. Cloud, has been engaged in significant research. Their courses are based on what constitutes the most basic, frequently used, and culturally essential vocabulary and grammatical patterns of French. This study is explained in a book titled *L'Elaboration du Français Elémentaire: Etude sur l'etablissement d'un vocabulaire et d'une grammaire de base (Development of Elementary French: Study of the Determinations of a Basic Vocabulary and Grammar)*. A team of scholars, consisting of Georges Gougenheim, Paul Rivene, René Michea, and Aurelien Sauvageot, determined the frequency of words and grammatical constructions in a broad sample of spoken French. One of the most novel aspects of the study was the emphasis on the quality that some words have for readily coming to mind in discussions of a given topic. The basic vocabulary totaled 1,500 words.

The method developed at St. Cloud has been adopted by the General Office of Cultural and Technical Affairs of the Ministry of Foreign Affairs for the teaching of French as a second language. It has helped establish more than 40 audiovisual teaching centers in more than 20 countries. Their instructors have taken an orientation course at St. Cloud and are expected to employ the methods and materials developed at the Ecole Normale Supérieure. The language material is recorded on magnetic tapes, which are coordinated with filmstrips designed to show the meaning of the taped phrase or of the cultural situation in which it would be used; the appropriate name given these materials is *Voix et Images de France*. The use of filmstrips in this manner is noteworthy since, by and large, these have been neglected by American language teachers.

The basic St. Cloud course consists of 32 lessons. In a typical lesson the essential material to be covered is learned in the dialogue; sentences involving grammatical manipulations of the same material are introduced in the second phase; a final segment is devoted to sentences picked to highlight certain French sounds. As each frame of the filmstrip is projected on the screen, the instructor clarifies the meaning through mimicry, gestures, and drawings. There is a constant endeavor to maintain, through speech and pictures, a "transposed reality" in which the new language comes to seem an integral part of the situation. Next comes the stage of active repetition and memorization, with close attention to the pronunciation of the students as they repeat. After this the lesson enters the phase of using sentences that illustrate certain grammatical alterations or variations of dialogue material. The immediate goal of these manipulations is to lead the student to the point at which he can participate in conversation in the context of situations similar to those presented in the lessons.

In the United States, St. Cloud is represented by Rand-McNally. In the past, two-day orientation seminars, one-week workshops, and four-week institutes have been conducted by the Center for American and Canadian Teachers for those interested in applying the St. Cloud method at their schools. A certain number of scholarships are available to applicants from the United States and abroad. Materials have also been developed for German, Russian, Italian, Hebrew, and Swahili.

SITUATIONAL REINFORCEMENT®

Situational Reinforcement® (SR®) is the trade name for a method of teaching characteristic of many language materials published by National Textbook Company. There are four basic characteristics in the SR method and materials:

1. Emphasis is placed upon natural communication. Students are led to talk about familiar persons, objects, actions, and situations. They extend what they learn inside of the classroom to situations outside.

2. The situation in which the student is placed controls the complexity of the language structure presented. SR makes the point that natural learning of a language is not structured learning, that a student should not be forced to master present tense before past (as is often advocated in audiolingual materials) or the active before the subjunctive. At the onset of instruction, there should be a mixture of structures, as in natural speech. Emphasis is thus placed on situations in order to force the student to "think" in the language that he is learning, not merely to manipulate the structure of the language.

3. Gradual mastery of the language is emphasized. Structures, since they occur in situations, are continually reviewed, corrected, and reinforced, all within a context that is *real*. Reinforcement of the language by real situations eliminates the need for translation in the SR method.

4. An alternative response is accepted if it is appropriate and correct. Here, following Chomsky's observation that language is creative, is where SR reflects, to a great degree, the research of modern linguistics.

The basic unit of the SR method is the *Response Sequence*, which includes a sequential presentation and the use of commands, questions, and answers, focusing on language situations in which communication occurs naturally. A sample of a Response Sequence follows.

Unit 1.   Mr._____, pick up your pencil. [Student performs action]
          Ms._____, what did Mr. _____ do?
          He picked up his pencil.

Unit 2.   Mr. _____, write your name/the date/your address in your notebook.
          What's he doing?
          He's writing his address in his notebook.

Unit 3.   Where's he writing his address?
          In his notebook.

Unit 4.   What did he do?
          He wrote his address in his notebook.

Unit 5.   Where did he write his address?
          In his notebook.

After each unit is learned, all of the units are employed in a *conversation sequence.*

Mr. ___, pick up your pencil.
What did Mr. ___ do?
He picked up his pencil.
Mr. ___, write your address in your notebook.
What's he doing?
He's writing his address in his notebook.
Where's he writing his address?
In his notebook.
What did he do?
He wrote his address in his notebook.
Where did he write his address?
In his notebook.

"The aim," according to the Institute of Modern Languages, "is to guide the students into connected discourse with each other with minimum instructor involvement."

To recapitulate, SR calls upon the student to participate actively in the language to be learned in as typical a situation as possible and calls upon his ability to infer from the data the "rules" of the languages. As it stands, SR emphasizes reality with its setting of responses and participation and offers a method that emphasizes language performance. As such, it differs from classical audiolingualism, with its emphasis upon disconnected drills and patterns.

COMMUNITY LANGUAGE LEARNING

Community Language Learning (CLL) was developed by Father Charles A. Curran, a psychologist, and emerges from the premise that adults have a basic, primitive resistance to a new learning situation, and feel the need to protect their egos. CLL theorizes that students will learn much more effectively if their defenses are lowered, being then free to invest themselves in learning. A teacher, then, is trained to become a counselor-teacher in a potentially anxiety-provoking situation.

CLL places the responsibility for the data that is to be learned more on the student than on the teacher, who is called the "knower" or counselor. Students, and not the knower, initiate all language activity. From six to twelve students sit in a circle; on the outside of the circle there are one or more speakers of the target language. The emphasis is on conversation, carried on at first with the high dependence upon the informant or knower; but as time goes on students become more proficient with less and less dependence upon the knower. The "conversation" is carried on in the following manner:

1. A student who wishes to say something first utters the statement in his native language. The knower whispers the same sentence in the target language into the ear of the speaker, who repeats it.

2. The person to whom the speaker addresses his remarks now goes through the same process in responding, saying his response in his native language to the knower. The knower then whispers the equivalent into the respondent's ear, who repeats it to the questioner.

3. The activity goes on for 20 minutes, and is recorded on tape. Then the conversation is played back and analyzed.

This method of language instruction is clearly "student-centered." Activity is initiated by the student. He says what he wants to say. He monitors his own speech; he is actively engaged in communication. Highly dependent at first, he becomes less so as he increases in proficiency. Unlike audiolingualism, which we may call "teacher-centered," CLL forces the student to use his own mental powers to engage in conversation; in this way it is similar to SR, which is also highly dependent upon the students to actively participate in conversation. Moreover, underlying the CLL model are the assumptions that everyone needs to be understood and to belong. Therefore, in CLL the teacher-counselor establishes an atmosphere in which the "whole person" participates and in which a sense of community develops.

THE SILENT WAY

The Silent Way, based upon the research of Caleb Gattegno, is perhaps the greatest departure in language instruction that has been proposed in the last twenty-five years. Called "silent" because students rather than the teacher do more than 90 percent of the talking, the Silent Way has the following characteristics:

1. Only the target language is employed in instruction. The students' native language is not used.

2. Talk concentrates around a set of multicolored rods (blocks) of differing shapes and sizes. Students and teacher sit in a circle and the teacher passes a block to a student, commenting on its size, color, and/or shape. Initially, the teacher may call the block by its name in the target language. The student then passes the block on to another student, repeating what he has heard the teacher say. The block eventually returns to the teacher, who may then continue to pass the block around: but this time he may say something different, or he may send a different size or shape of block around. The teacher says his utterance in the target language only once, however.

Although conversation is initially rather simple, and may consist of only a few words or phrases, communication becomes more complex, to the point where relationships between and among blocks are discussed. Students are urged to talk, to the teacher as well as to the other students, about the blocks.

3. To an extent this method reflects the influence of the cognitive-code theory of learning, which may be contrasted to the behavioristic theory of learning. Behavioristic theory is reflected in the methods of audiolingualism, where students hear a stimulus and then are told to respond by mimicing or memorizing the stimulus. In cognitive-code learning, emphasis is placed upon the student's mental powers to make hypotheses about the language he is learning. In SW, students are motivated to think and say the appropriate sentences to accompany actions under the guidance of the teacher. Perhaps the most remarkable characteristic of SW, according to Earl Stevick, who has used and observed this method in teaching, is "the keen attention with which the student watches the actions and listens to the utterances of the teacher and his fellow students, as he strives to grasp the meaning as well as the form of these utterances."

In summary, the Silent Way holds much promise as another effective method of teaching language where students are encouraged to employ their cognitive powers of language acquisition to extract hypotheses from the language data which are presented to them. The learner employs the target language to communicate immediately. Since the teacher speaks only once, students are forced to turn to their colleagues for support or confirmation. In Gattegno's words, in the Silent Way "teaching is subordinated to learning."

*   *   *

Each of these methods and techniques can be employed at various times by one teacher with a single group of students. Just as students have "favorite and idiosyncratic" strategies for learning, teachers, too, may have "favorite" strategies of teaching. Some prefer the methods with more teacher involvement, while others would find methods that encouraged their students to participate more to their liking. There is no single way, no panacea for good language teaching. For our reader who may wish to learn more about the various approaches, methods, and techniques for teaching and learning languages, we have listed references on language teaching at the end of this chapter.

PUBLIC PARTICIPATION

Suggestions for learning a foreign language are not limited only to methods and techniques that can be employed in a classroom. The day is over when knowledge (or the opportunity to acquire knowledge) is the privilege only of those who can afford to attend college or enroll in adult education programs. Today, with more emphasis upon traveling, there are many opportunities to learn and employ foreign languages. For these reasons language training, we feel, ought not to be exclusively tuned to the utilitarian uses of languages, as if languages were useful only for Foreign Service officers and international business managers. Language can be used both as a practical tool and as an effective instrument of communication between and among peoples.

Fortunately, we feel, in contrast with the era of the 1930s and the last half of the 1960s, there appears today evidence of resurgent citizen interest in learning and promoting the use of foreign languages, despite the evidence of our colleges and universities. Classes for adult learners, at both commercial schools like Berlitz and adult continuing education centers, are expanding. And today it is not necessary to leave the United States in order to participate in diplomacy or to speak a foreign language. The United States Travel Service, for example, seeks out and maintains contact with volunteer citizen groups interested in providing hospitality and assistance to foreign travelers.

In a small Iowa town a group of citizens, cooperating with the local hotels and Chamber of Commerce, holds coffee get-togethers for foreign tourists who stop there. If a tourist with a language difficulty signs in at Washington's Statler-Hilton Hotel, a clerk hands him a card that says in 32 languages: "I speak____and I require an interpreter." The hotel then provides an interpreter from its staff or furnishes the name, address, and telephone number of one. That Americans maintain a posture of great friendliness to people from other areas is attested by Mr. Voit Gilmore, at one time Director of the U.S. Travel Service, who has remarked, "People want to do something for their country. They want to be hospitable." But most of us can do little more than exchange glances.

Moreover, a most welcome type of "hot line" for language-distressed visitors in the United States has recently been established by the Travel-Lodge motel chain. A toll-free number reaches Shawnee Mission, Kansas, where the reservation central for Travel-Lodge is located. German, Japanese, French, and Spanish are used most. A wide range of "emergencies" have been attended to, some trivial, others serious. Among the most amusing, perhaps, was a call on behalf of a Spanish-speaking woman in Chicago's enormous O'Hare International Airport, who was unable to locate the ladies' room. An upset Bolivian father reported his daughter to have been bitten by a squirrel. A German gentleman had been enticed to watch someone flip pennies and had been relieved of his wallet. A concerned Frenchman requested to know what precautions should be taken on his trip west in case of an attack from an Indian reservation.

And a few years ago, Lois Hallin in "They Talk Your Language" (*Parade*, April 30, 1972) described a Language Bank that was developed in Seattle, Washington, an international crossroads city and port, at the suggestion of the U.S. State Department and assisted by the Foundation for International Understanding Through Students. Aimed at assisting visitors and others who are "language stranded," 350 volunteer interpreters in 80 languages and major dialects are made available around the clock by the King County Medical Telephone Exchange. A wealth of human interest stories have been accumulated in the several years of operation of the project. The Language Bank has explained the techniques of operating a kidney machine in both Portuguese and Mexican Spanish, interpreters have been supplied at murder trials, and bilingual baby-sitters have been furnished for mothers and fathers in a state of utter exhaustion and frustration.

AND WE MAY CONCLUDE THEN . . .

In summary, although recent research in linguistic and psychological theory cannot support a language teaching technology, we do suggest that research can provide useful directions for the language teacher. We do believe that we would do well to reappraise the way languages have been taught, to question whether certain teaching practices and strategies lead and encourage students to learn and to use a second language. We know that we must provide an environment in which students can give free rein to the creative impulses of language, to be encouraged to be as spontaneous as children learning their first language. We must be certain to expose our students to as much language as we can, for as long as we can, and encourage them to use the language and recognize the fact that language learners will need to make errors in order to learn.

From "Facts and Fantasies About Language," our first chapter, to "The X, Y, Z's of Language Learning: Bilingual and Second Language Education," our last, we have run the gamut. Perhaps then it is fitting to end this chapter, and our text, with a comment that we heard recently from one of our colleagues: that the future will be assured not on the athletic field or through physical fitness programs—however necessary these are—but in classrooms where science, mathematics, the humanities, and foreign languages all are taught. Echoing this, we might paraphrase King Lear and say: "Let us mend our foreign speech, lest it may mar our national fortune."

XIII. QUESTIONS AND ACTIVITIES

1. What are some of the philosophical differences between FLES (Foreign Languages in the Elementary.School) and Bilingual Education?

2. What are the three areas of current research in developmental psycholinguistics? How does this research affect language teaching?

3. Examine any language teaching textbook. Can you tell anything about what the author thinks language is?

4. Visit a foreign language class. Is the class conducted in the target language or in the native language of the student? Do the students do most of the talking or do the teachers?

5. Ask one of the foreign language teachers at your school what he/she feels should be the goal(s) of a language class. Compare his/her answer with your own.

6. Compare the features of Audiolingual, Situational Reinforcement, The Silent Way, and Community Language Learning. How might one be viewed to have certain advantages over the other?

XIII. FOR FURTHER REFERENCE

Alatis, James. 1976. "The Past as Prologue." *TESOL Quarterly* 10:7-18.

Altman, Howard B., ed. 1972. *Individualizing the Foreign Language Classroom*. Rowley, Mass.: Newbury House.

Anthony, Edward M. 1963. "Approach, Method, and Technique." *English Language Teaching* 17:63-67.

Applegate, Richard B. 1975. "The Language Teacher and the Rules of Speaking." *TESOL Quarterly* 9:271-381.

Asher, James J., Jo Anne Kusudo, and Rita de la Torre. 1974. "Learning a Second Language Through Commands: The Second Field Test." *Modern Language Journal* 58:12, 24-32.

Asher, James and R. Garcia. 1969. "The Optimal Age to Learn a Foreign Language." *Modern Language Journal* 53:334-341.

Bailey, N., C. Madden, and Stephen D. Krashen. 1974. "Is there a 'Natural Sequence' in Adult Second Language Learning?" *Language Learning* 24:235-43.

Bloom, Lois. 1970. *Language Development: Form and Function in Emerging Grammars*. Cambridge, Mass.: M.I.T. Press.

Bowerman, M. 1973. *Learning to Talk: A Cross-linguistic Study of Early Syntactic Development, with Special Reference to Finnish*. Cambridge: Cambridge University Press.

Brown, H. Douglas. 1975. "The Next 25 Years: Shaping the Revolution," in Marina K. Burt and Heidi C. Dulay, eds.: *New Directions in Second Language Learning, Teaching and Bilingual Education*. Washington, D.C.: Teaching of English to Speakers of Other Languages.

Bruck, Margaret, Wallace E. Lambert, and G. Richard Tucker. 1974. "Bilingual Schooling Through the Elementary Grades: The St. Lambert Project at Grade Seven." *Language Learning* 24: December, 183-204.

Burt, Marina K. 1975. "Error Analysis in the Adult EFL Classroom." *TESOL Quarterly* 9: 53-63.

Chomsky, Noam A. 1960. "Linguistic Theory," in Robert Mead, Jr., ed.: *Northeast Conference of the Teaching of Foreign Languages: Working Committee Reports*.

_____. 1959. "Review of Verbal Behavior by B. F. Skinner." *Language* 35:26-58.

Cordasco, Francesco. 1976. *Bilingual Schooling in the United States*. New York: McGraw-Hill Book Company.

Curran, C. A. 1961. "Counseling Skills Adapted to the Learning of Foreign Languages." *Bulletin of the Menninger Clinic* 25:78-93.

Diller, Karl C. 1971. *Generative Grammar, Structural Linguistics, and Language Teaching*. Rowley, Mass.: Newbury House.

_____. 1975. "Some New Trends for Applied Linguistics and Foreign Language Teaching in the U.S." *TESOL Quarterly* 9:65-73.

Dulay, Heidi C. and Marina K. Burt. 1975. "Creative Construction in Second Language Learning and Teaching," in *New Directions in Second Language Learning, Teaching and Bilingual Education*. Washington, D.C.: TESOL.

_____. 1972. "Goofing: an Indicator of Children's Second Language Learning Strategies." *Language Learning* 22:235-52.

Edmonds, Marilyn H. 1976. "New Directions in Theories of Language Acquisition." *Harvard Educational Review* 46: May, 175-97.

"Effective Teaching—Enthusiastic Learning." 1976. Silver Spring, Md.: Institute of Modern Languages.

Ervin-Tripp, Susan. 1974. "Is Second Language Learning Like the First?" *TESOL Quarterly* 8: 111-127.

_____. 1968. *Becoming a Bilingual*. ERIC Report No. ED 018 786.

_____. 1973. "Structure and Process in Language Acquisition," in Anwar Dil, ed: *Language Acquisition and Communicative Choice*. Palo Alto, Calif.: Stanford University Press.

Falk, Julia S. 1973. "Native Language Acquisition: What Children Learn"; Learning: Past and Present"; "Foreign Language Learning: Present and Future," in *Linguistics and Language*. Lexington, Mass.: Xerox.

Fishman, Joshua. 1976. *Bilingual Education*. Rowley, Mass.: Newbury House.

_____ et al, eds. 1968. *Language Problems in Developing Nations*. New York: John Wiley.

_____. 1972. *The Sociology of Language*. Rowley, Mass.: Newbury House.

Forum Staff Article. 1974. "Current Trends in Language Teaching." *English Teaching Forum* January-March, 1-7.

Frank, Majorie. 1975. "From Theory to Practice: Situational Reinforcement." Silver Spring, Md.: Institute of Modern Languages.

Gaarder, A. Bruce. 1976. "Linkages between Foreign Language Teaching and Bilingual Education," in James Alatis and Kristie Twadell, eds.: *English as a Second Language in Bilingual Education*. Washington, D.C.: Teaching English to Speakers of Other Languages.

Gattegno, Caleb. 1972. *Teaching Foreign Languages in Schools: The Silent Way*. 2nd ed. New York: Educational Solutions.

Ginott, Haim. 1972. *Teacher and Child*. New York: Macmillan.

Gordon, Susan and Dorie Anisman. 1973. *SR® Orientation in American English Teacher's Manual*. Silver Spring, Md.: Institute of Modern Languages.

Haskell, John. 1976. "The Silent Way." *TESOL Newsletter* June, 13,20.

Hayes, Curtis W. 1975. "The Rise and Fall of the Foreign Language Teacher, Linguistically," in Hassan Sharifi, ed.: *From Meaning to Sound*. Lincoln: University of Nebraska.

Itard, J. 1962. *The Wild Boy of Aveyron*. New York: Appleton-Century-Crofts.

Jakobovits, Leon A. 1970. *Foreign Language Learning*. Rowley, Mass.: Newbury House.

_____. 1971. "The Psychological Bases of Second Language Learning." *Language Sciences* February, 22-28.

_____ and Barbara Gordon. 1974. *The Context of Foreign Language Teaching*. Rowley, Mass.: Newbury House.

Joos, Martin, ed. 1958. *Readings in Linguistics*. New York: American Council of Learned Societies.

Jorden, Eleanor. 1962. *Beginning Japanese*. New Haven: Yale University Press.

Kearny, Mary Ann. 1969. "Pattern Practice and Situational Reinforcement in Language Teaching." Master's Thesis, Georgetown University.

Kessler, Carolyn. 1971. *The Acquisition of Syntax in Bilingual Children*. Washington, D.C.: Georgetown University Press.

Kettering, Judith Carl. 1975. *Developing Communicative Competence: Interaction Activities in English as a Second Language*. Pittsburgh: University of Pittsburgh.

Krashen, Stephen D. 1976. "Formal and Informal Linguistic Environments in Language Acquisition and Language Learning." *TESOL Quarterly* October, 157-168.

_____. 1973. "Lateralization, Language Learning, and the Critical Period: Some New Evidence." *Language Learning* 23:67-74.

_____ and Herbert W. Seliger. 1975. "The Essential Contributions of Formal Instruction in Adult Second Language Learning." *TESOL Quarterly* 9:173-183.

_____, Victoria Sferlazza, Lorna Feldman, and Ann K. Fatham. 1976. "Adult Performance on the Slope Test: More Evidence for a Natural Sequence in Adult Second Language Acquisition." *Language Learning* 26:145-51.

Lado, Robert. 1958. *English Pattern Practices*. Ann Arbor: University of Michigan Press (English Language Institute).

Lambert, Wallace. 1971. "Motivation," in Earl Stevick, ed.: *Adapting and Writing Language Lessons*. Washington, D.C.: Foreign Service Institute.

_____. 1963. "Psychological Approaches to the Study of Language." *Modern Language Journal* 47:51-62, 114-21.

La Forge, Paul G. 1971. "Community Language Learning: A Pilot Study." *Language Learning* 21:45-61.

Lakoff, Robin. 1973. "The Logic of Politeness; or, Minding Your P's and Q's," in *Papers from the Ninth Regional Meeting, Chicago Linguistic Society*. Chicago: University of Chicago.

Mackey, William F. 1968. *Bilingualism as a World Problem*. Montreal: Harvest House.

_____. 1972. *Bilingual Education in a Binational School*. Rowley, Mass.: Newbury House.

MacNamara, John. 1966. *Bilingualism and Primary Education: a Study of Irish Experience*. Edinburgh: Edinburgh University Press.

McNeil, David. 1970. *The Acquisition of Language: The Study of Developmental Psycholinguistics*. New York: Harper and Row.

Newmark, Leonard C. 1963. "Grammatical Theory and the Teaching of English as a Foreign Language," in David P. Harris, ed.: *1963 Conference Papers of the English Language Section of the National Association of Foreign Affairs*.

Paulston, Christina Bratt. 1974. "Linguistic and Communicative Competence." *TESOL Quarterly* 8:347-62.

_____, Barry Brunetti, Dale Britton, and John Hoover. 1975. *Developing Communicative Competence: Roleplays in English as a Second Language*. Pittsburgh: University of Pittsburgh.

Piaget, Jean. 1955. *The Language and Thought of the Child*. Cleveland, Ohio: World.

Rardin, Jenny. 1976. "A Counseling-Learning Model for Second Language Learning." *TESOL Newsletter* April, 21-22.

Richards, Jack C. 1974. *Error Analysis: Perspectives on Second Language Learning*. London: Longman.

Rubin, Joan. 1975. "What the 'Good Language Learner' Can Teach Us." *TESOL Quarterly* 9:41-57.

Schumann, John H. "Affective Factors and the Problem of Age in Second Language Acquisition." *Language Learning* 25:209-35.

_____. 1972. "Communication Techniques." *TESOL Quarterly* 2:161.

Skinner, B. F. 1957. *Verbal Behavior*. New York: Appleton-Century-Crofts.

Stevick, Earl W. 1974. "The Riddle of the 'Right Method.' " *English Teaching Forum* April-June, 1-5.

_____. 1973. "Before Linguistics and Beneath Method," in Kurt R. Janowsky, ed.: *Georgetown University 24th Round Table on Languages and Linguistics*. Washington D.C.: Georgetown University Press.

_____. 1976. *Memory, Meaning and Method*. Rowley, Mass.: Newbury House.

_____. 1976. "Teaching English as an Alien Language." Paper presented at the Annual TESOL Convention.

Taylor, Barry P. 1975. "Adult Language Learning Strategies and Their Pedagogical Implications." *TESOL Quarterly* 9: 391-99.

Wardhaugh, Ronald. 1969. "TESOL: Current Problems and Classroom Practices." *TESOL Quarterly* 3:105-16.

Weinrich, Uriel. 1967. *Languages in Contact*. The Hague: Mouton.

Appendix:
Languages of the World

The following list of 300 languages was originally designed for a set of language files at the Center for Applied Linguistics. Languages were chosen for inclusion principally as ones in which Americans might have some interest. In a few instances—where the individual languages seemed quite minor for purposes of the listing, but where a considerable interest was apparent—a family of closely-related languages appears as a single entry; the notable cases are Iroquois and Polynesian.

NAME OF LANGUAGE

Many languages are known by more than one name, and it is an impossibility to make a list such as this entirely satisfactory from that point of view. In the particular case of Bantu languages, which normally employ a "language prefix," the prefix has been included beginning with a small letter, and the name is alphabetized according to the capitalized letter which begins the stem of the word.

WHERE SPOKEN

The places "where spoken" are put in order of size of the groups of speakers thought to be found there. For many widely dispersed languages, only a few of the places where they are known to be spoken are listed.

MILLIONS OF SPEAKERS

The figures given are attempts to calculate the sizes of population in 1976, using these languages *as their first language*, allowing for expected growth in numbers since the time of a census or other base data. In many instances the figures represent risky extrapolations from rather shaky estimates made some time ago. Even in countries which have taken a language census in relatively recent years, the data published often leave considerable problems of interpretation. Most figures in the millions are to the nearest million, and above 100,000,000 to the nearest five million.

NAME OF LANGUAGE	WHERE SPOKEN	FAMILY	MILLIONS OF SPEAKERS
Achinese	Sumatra	Malayo-Polynesian	2.0
Achooli-Luo	Kenya, Uganda, Sudan	Nilotic (Chari-Nile)	3.6
Afrikaans	South Africa	Germanic (Indo-European)	5.2
Akan (Twi-Fante)	Ghana	Guinean (Niger-Congo)	4.4
Akha	Yunnan (China), Burma, Thailand	Tibeto-Burman	0.7
Albanian	Albania, Yugoslavia, Italy, Greece	Albanian (Indo-European)	3.6
Amharic	Ethiopia	Semitic (Afro-Asiatic)	8.4

NAME OF LANGUAGE	WHERE SPOKEN	FAMILY	MILLIONS OF SPEAKERS
Amoy	Fukien and Kwangtung (China), Formosa, Thailand	Chinese (Sino-Tibetan)	39.0
Anyi-Baule	Ivory Coast, Ghana	Guinean (Niger-Congo)	2.0
Arabic	Northern Africa, Middle East	Semitic (Afro-Asiatic)	130.0
Araucanian	Chile	Araukan	0.44
Armenian	Armenia (USSR), Middle East	Armenian (Indo-European)	4.5
Assamese	Assam (India)	Indic (Indo-European)	10.4
Avar	Caucasus (USSR)	Northeast Caucasic	0.42
Awadhi (Eastern Hindi)	Uttar Pradesh (India)	Indic (Indo-European)	43.0
Aymara	Bolivia, Peru	Kičua-Aymara	1.7
Azerbaijani	Iran, Soviet Azerbaidzhan	Turkic (Altaic)	10.0
Balante	Guinea-Bissau	West Atlantic	0.22
Balinese	Bali, Lombok	Malayo-Polynesian	2.5
Baluchi	Pakistan, Iran, Afghanistan	Iranian (Indo-European)	2.5
Banda	Central African Republic, Congo	Eastern (Niger-Congo)	1.1
Bari	Sudan	Nilotic (Chari-Nile)	0.34
Bariba	Benin (Dahomey)	Voltaic (Niger-Congo)	0.29
Bashkir	Bashkir ASSR* (USSR)	Turkic (Altaic)	1.0
Basque	Spain, France Western U.S.A.	(Isolate)	1.1
Karo Batak	Sumatra	Malayo-Polynesian	0.4
Simalungun Batak	Sumatra	Malayo-Polynesian	0.8
Toba Batak	Sumatra	Malayo-Polynesian	1.6
Beja	Sudan, Ethiopia, Egypt	Cushitic (Afro-Asiatic)	1.02
Belu	Timor	Malayo-Polynesian	0.42
iciBemba	Zambia, Zaire	Bantu (Niger-Congo)	2.2
Bengali	Bangladesh, West Bengal (India)	Indic (Indo-European)	125.0
Bete	Ivory Coast	Guinean (Niger-Congo)	1.2
Bhojpuri	Bihar and Uttar Pradesh (India), Nepal, Mauritius	Indic (Indo-European)	41.0
Bicol	SE Luzon (Philippines)	Malayo-Polynesian	3.2
Bini (Edo)	Mid-Western State (Nigeria)	Guinean (Niger-Congo)	0.97
Boro (Kachari)	Assam (India)	Tibeto-Burman (Sino-Tibetan)	0.56
Breton	NW France	Celtic (Indo-European)	1.2
Buginese	Celebes, Borneo	Malayo-Polynesian	3.2
Bulgarian	Bulgaria, Yugoslavia, Greece	Slavic (Indo-European)	8.1
Buriat	Buriat ASSR* (Siberia, USSR)	Mongol (Altaic)	0.33

NAME OF LANGUAGE	WHERE SPOKEN	FAMILY	MILLIONS OF SPEAKERS
Burmese	Burma, Bangladesh	Tibeto-Burman (Sino-Tibetan)	23.0
Byelorussian	Byelorussia (USSR)	Slavic (Indo-European)	10.0
Cakchikel	Guatemala	Mayan	0.54
Cambodian	Cambodia, Thailand, Viet Nam	Mon-Khmer	8.4
Cantonese	South China	Chinese (Sino-Tibetan)	55.0
Catalan	NE Spain, Balearic Islands, Sardinia, France, Andorra, Argentina	Romance (Indo-European)	6.2
kiChagga	Tanzania	Bantu (Niger-Congo)	0.80
Chamorro	Guam	Malayo-Polynesian	0.05
Chechen	Caucasus (USSR)	North-Central Caucasic	0.64
Cheremis	Mari ASSR* (USSR)	Finnic (Uralic)	0.64
Cherokee	Oklahoma, North Carolina	Iriquoian	0.01
Chocktaw	Oklahoma, Mississippi	Muskogean	0.01
chiChopi	Mozambique	Bantu (Niger-Congo)	0.40
Chuvash	Chuvash ASSR* (USSR)	Turkic (Altaic)	1.8
Circassian	Caucasus (USSR), Turkey, Syria, Jordan, Israel	Northwest Caucasic	0.62
ciCokwe	Angola, Zaire, Zambia	Bantu (Niger-Congo)	1.23
Cree-Montagnais	Canada, U.S.	Algonquian	0.06
Creek	Oklahoma, Florida, Alabama	Muskogean	0.01
Créole French	Haiti, Lesser Antilles, Mauritius & other Indian Ocean Islands	Romance (Indo-European)	6.5
Crioulo	Cape Verde Islands, Guinea-Bissau, Senegal	Romance (Indo-European)	0.25
Czech	Czechoslovakia	Slavic (Indo-European)	10.1
Dagomba	Ghana	Voltaic (Niger-Congo)	2.0
Dan	Ivory Coast, Liberia, Guinea	Mande (Niger-Congo)	0.41
Danish	Denmark, Germany	Germanic (Indo-European)	5.3
Dinka	Sudan	Nilotic (Chari-Nile)	1.8
Duala	Cameroun	Bantu (Niger-Congo)	0.85
Dusun	Sabah (Malaysia)	Malayo-Polynesian	0.26
Dutch	Netherlands, Belgium, Canada, France	Germanic (Indo-European)	20.0
Efik	South-East State (Nigeria)	Guinean (Niger-Congo)	3.0
English	North America, British Isles, Australia, New Zealand, South Africa	Germanic (Indo-European)	275.0
Eskimo (Inupik)	Greenland, Canada, Alaska	Esquimo-Aleut	0.065
Eskimo (South Alaskan)	Alaska, Siberia	Esquimo-Aleut	0.02
Estonian	Estonia	Finnic (Uralic)	1.2

NAME OF LANGUAGE	WHERE SPOKEN	FAMILY	MILLIONS OF SPEAKERS
Ewe-Fon	Benin (Dahomey), Togo, Ghana	Guinean (Niger-Congo)	4.5
Fang-Bulu	Cameroun, Gabon, Equatorial Guinea	Bantu (Niger-Congo)	1.7
Fijian	Fiji	Malayo-Polynesian	0.26
Finnish	Finland, USSR, Sweden	Finnic (Uralic)	5.1
Foochow	Fukien (China)	Chinese (Sino-Tibetan)	12.0
French	France, Belgium, Canada, United States, Switzerland	Romance (Indo-European)	58.0
Frisian	Netherlands, Germany	Germanic (Indo-European)	0.47
Fulani	Nigeria, Guinea, Senegal, Mali, Niger, Cameroun	West Atlantic (Niger-Congo)	12.0
Gã	Ghana	Guinean (Niger-Congo)	0.91
Gaelic	Ireland, Scotland	Celtic (Indo-European)	0.22
Galla (Oromo)	Ethiopia, Kenya	Cushitic (Afro-Asiatic)	8.0
luGanda	Uganda	Bantu (Niger-Congo)	2.9
Garo	Meghalaya (India)	Tibeto-Burman (Sino-Tibetan)	0.46
Georgian	Georgia (USSR)	Kartvelian	3.4
German	Germany, Austria, Switzerland, U.S., USSR	Germanic (Indo-European)	105.0
Goajiro	Colombia, Venezuela	Arawakan	0.03
chiGogo	Tanzania	Bantu (Niger-Congo)	1.4
Gorontalo	North Celebes	Malayo-Polynesian	0.35
Gondi	Andhra Pradesh (India)	Dravidian	1.9
Greek	Greece, Cyprus, Turkey	Hellenic (Indo-European)	10.0
Guaraní	Paraguay	Tupi-Guaraní	2.7
Gujerati	Gujarat (India), Bombay, Pakistan, South Africa	Indic (Indo-European)	32.0
ikiGusii	Kenya	Bantu (Niger-Congo)	1.4
Hakka	Kiangsi and Kwangtung (China), Formosa, Hawaii	Chinese (Sino-Tibetan)	24.0
Hausa	Northern Nigeria, Niger, Cameroun	Chadic (Afro-Asiatic)	15.0
ekiHavu	Zaire	Bantu (Niger-Congo)	1.7
Hebrew	Israel	Semitic (Afro-Asiatic)	2.3
ekiHehe	Tanzania	Bantu (Niger-Congo)	1.1
Hindi-Urdu	India, Pakistan, Trinidad, Guyana, Fiji, Mauritius	Indic (Indo-European)	130.0
Hsiang	Hunan (China)	Chinese (Sino-Tibetan)	7.0
Huayhuash (Quecha B)	Peru	Kičua-Aymara	1.7
Hungarian	Hungary, Romania, Yugoslavia, Czechoslovakia	Ugric (Uralic)	14.0
Ibanag	NE Luzon (Philippines)	Malayo-Polynesian	0.62
Icelandic	Iceland	Germanic (Indo-European)	0.22
Igala	Kwara (Nigeria)	Guinean (Niger-Congo)	0.65

NAME OF LANGUAGE	WHERE SPOKEN	FAMILY	MILLIONS OF SPEAKERS
Igbo	East-Central State (Nigeria)	Guinean (Niger-Congo)	8.1
Western Ijaw	Niger Delta (Nigeria)	Guinean (Niger-Congo)	0.33
ciIla-ciTonga	Zambia, Rhodesia	Bantu (Niger-Congo)	0.88
Ilocano	NW Luzon (Philippines), California, Hawaii	Malayo-Polynesian	5.4
Indonesian-Malay	Indonesia, Malaysia, Thailand, Singapore, Brunei	Malayo-Polynesian	22.0
Iroquois	Ontario, New York, Wisconsin, Quebec	Iroquoian	0.01
Ishan	Mid-Western State (Nigeria)	Guinean (Niger-Congo)	0.42
Italian	Italy, U.S., France, Argentina, Switzerland, Canada, Brazil	Romance (Indo-European)	65.0
Japanese	Japan, Brazil, California, Hawaii	Japanese	110.0
Javanese	Java, Malaysia, Surinam	Malayo-Polynesian	60.0
Jwang-Bui	Kwangsi and Kweichow (China)	Tai	9.0
Kabre	Togo, Benin (Dahomey)	Voltaic (Niger-Congo)	0.48
Kabyle	Algeria	Berber (Afro-Asiatic)	1.6
Kachin	Burma, Yunnan (China)	Tibeto-Burman (Sino-Tibetan)	0.60
kiKamba	Kenya	Bantu (Niger-Congo)	1.6
Kannada	Karnatuka (India)	Dravidian	25.0
Kanuri	North-Eastern State (Nigeria) Niger, Chad	Central Saharan	3.9
Kasem	Ghana, Upper Volta	Voltaic (Niger-Congo)	0.3
Kashmiri	Kashmir (India-Pakistan)	Indic (Indo-European)	3.0
Kazakh	Kazakhstan (USSR), Sinkiang (China), Afghanistan	Turkic (Altaic)	6.4
Khalkha	Outer Mongolia, North China	Mongol (Altaic)	2.9
Khasi	Meghalaya (India)	Mon-Khmer	0.5
kiKikuyu	Kenya	Bantu (Niger-Congo)	3.9
Kipsigis	Kenya	Nilotic (Chari-Nile)	0.57
Kirgiz	Kirgizia (USSR), Sinkiang (China), Afghanistan	Turkic (Altaic)	1.3
Kissi	Guinea, Sierra Leone, Liberia	West Atlantic (Niger-Congo)	0.35
kiKongo	Zaire, Angola, Congo	Bantu (Niger-Congo)	4.5
Korean	Korea, NE China, Japan, Siberia, Hawaii	(Altaic ?)	53.0
Kpelle	Liberia, Guinea	Mande (Niger-Congo)	0.52
Krio	Sierra Leone	Germanic (Indo-European)	0.15
Kru-Bassa	Liberia, Ivory Coast	Guinean (Niger-Congo)	1.3

NAME OF LANGUAGE	WHERE SPOKEN	FAMILY	MILLIONS OF SPEAKERS
Kurdish	Turkey, Iran, Iraq, Syria, USSR	Iranian (Indo-European)	9.0
Kurukh	Madhya Pradesh and Orissa (India)	Dravidian	1.4
Lahnda (Western Punjabi)	Pakistan, India	Indic (Indo-European)	15.0
Latvian	Latvia	Baltic (Indo-European)	1.6
Lisu	Yunnan (China), Burma, Thailand	Tibeto-Burman (Sino-Tibetan)	0.50
Lithuanian	Lithuania	Baltic (Indo-European)	3.1
Lolo	Szechuan and Yunnan (China), Burma	Tibeto-Burman (Sino-Tibetan)	4.6
Loma	Liberia, Guinea	Mande (Niger-Congo)	0.29
siLozi	Zambia	Bantu (Niger-Congo)	0.28
chiLuba	Zaire, Zambia	Bantu (Niger-Congo)	3.8
Lugbara	Uganda, Zaire, Sudan	Central Sudanic (Chari-Nile)	0.7
luLuhya	Kenya, Uganda	Bantu (Niger-Congo)	2.0
Macedonian	Yugoslavia, Bulgaria, Greece	Slavic (Indo-European)	2.0
Madurese	Java, Madura	Malayo-Polynesian	7.5
Magahi	Bihar and West Bengal (India)	Indic (Indo-European)	12.0
Maithili	Bihar (India), Nepal	Indic (Indo-European)	20.0
Makassarese	Celebes, Borneo	Malayo-Polynesian	1.6
chiMakonde	Tanzania, Mozambique	Bantu (Niger-Congo)	1.0
iMakua	Mozambique, Malawi, Tanzania	Bantu (Niger-Congo)	5.8
Malagasy	Madagascar (Malagasy Republic)	Malayo-Polynesian	7.5
Malayalam	Kerala (India)	Dravidian	23.0
Maldivian	Maldive Islands	Indic (Indo-European)	0.12
Mam	Guatemala	Mayan	0.42
Mandarin	China, Formosa	Chinese (Sino-Tibetan)	610.0
Mandekan (Bambara-Malinke)	Mali, Guinea, Ivory Coast, Senegal, Gambia	Mande (Niger-Congo)	4.8
Manipuri (Meithei)	Manipur (India), Burma	Tibeto-Burman (Sino-Tibetan)	0.9
Mano	Liberia, Guinea	Mande (Niger-Congo)	0.14
Marathi	Maharashtra (India)	Indic (Indo-European)	52.0
Masai	Kenya, Tanzania	Nilotic (Chari-Nile)	0.54
Mazatec	Mexico	Otomanguean	0.22
kiMbundu	Angola	Bantu (Niger-Congo)	1.6
uMbundu	Angola	Bantu (Niger-Congo)	2.3
Menangkabao	Sumatra	Malayo-Polynesian	4.6
Mende	Sierra Leone	Mande (Niger-Congo)	0.96
Miao	Southern China, Northern Vietnam, Laos	Miao-Yao (Sino-Tibetan)	3.8
Mixtec	Mexico	Otomanguean	0.50
Mon	Burma, Thailand	Mon-Khmer	0.73

NAME OF LANGUAGE	WHERE SPOKEN	FAMILY	MILLIONS OF SPEAKERS
loMongo-loNkundo	Zaire	Bantu (Niger-Congo)	3.2
Mordvin	Mordvin ASSR* (USSR)	Finnic (Uralic)	1.4
Moré	Upper Volta	Voltaic (Niger-Congo)	3.4
Motu	Papua, New Guinea	Malayo-Polynesian	0.01
Nahuatl	Mexico, El Salvador	Uto-Aztecan	1.9
kiNande	Zaire, Uganda	Bantu (Niger-Congo)	0.48
Nandi	Kenya	Nilotic (Chari-Nile)	0.28
Navajo	Southwestern U.S.	Athabascan (Na-Dené)	0.12
Nepali	Nepal, Uttar Pradesh (India)	Indic (Indo-European)	8.0
Newari	Nepal	Tibeto-Burman (Sino-Tibetan)	0.64
Ngadju	Borneo	Malayo-Polynesian	0.17
liNgala	Zaire, Congo	Bantu (Niger-Congo)	1.7
Norwegian	Norway	Germanic (Indo-European)	4.7
Nubian	Sudan, Egypt	Nubian (Chari-Nile)	0.33
Nuer	Sudan, Ethiopia	Nilotic (Chari-Nile)	0.79
Nupe	Kwara (Nigeria)	Guinean (Niger-Congo)	1.75
kiNyamwezi-kiSukuma	Tanzania	Bantu (Niger-Congo)	2.9
chiNyanja	Malawi, Mozambique, Zambia	Bantu (Niger-Congo)	4.9
oruNyoro-runyNkole-ruHaya	Uganda	Bantu (Niger-Congo)	3.2
Ojibway	Canada, Northern U.S.	Algonquian	0.04
Okinawan	Okinawa	Japanese	0.08
Oriya	Orissa (India)	Indic (Indo-European)	22.0
Ossetic	Caucasus (USSR)	Iranian (Indo-European)	0.52
Otomi	Mexico	Otomanguean	0.75
Ovambo (ociKuanyama)	Southwest Africa, Angola	Bantu (Niger-Congo)	0.45
Pampanga	South Central Luzon (Philippines)	Malayo-Polynesian	1.35
Pangasinan	South Central Luzon (Philippines)	Malayo-Polynesian	1.25
Papago	Arizona, Mexico	Uto-Aztecan	0.01
Papiamento	Netherlands Antilles	Romance (Indo-European)	0.22
Pashto	Afghanistan, Pakistan	Iranian (Indo-European)	19.0
Persian-Tajiki	Iran, Afghanistan, Tadzhikstan (USSR)	Iranian (Indo-European)	26.0
Polish	Poland, U.S.	Slavic (Indo-European)	39.0
Polynesian	Polynesia, New Zealand	Malayo-Polynesian	0.48
Portuguese	Brazil, Portugal, Spain, Uruguay, Argentina, Azores, Goa, Madeira	Romance (Indo-European)	125.0
Provençal	Southern France	Romance (Indo-European)	4.0
Punjabi	Punjab (India), Pakistan	Indic (Indo-European)	51.0

NAME OF LANGUAGE	WHERE SPOKEN	FAMILY	MILLIONS OF SPEAKERS
Pwo	Burma	Karen (Sino-Tibetan ?)	0.75
Quechua [A]	Peru, Ecuador, Bolivia	Kičua-Aymara	7.1
Quekchi	Guatemala	Mayan	0.36
Quiché	Guatemala	Mayan	0.84
Rajasthani	Rajasthan (India)	Indic (Indo-European)	26.0
Rif	Morocco	Berber (Afro-Asiatic)	1.05
Romanian	Romania, USSR	Romance (Indo-European)	21.7
Romansch	Switzerland	Romance (Indo-European)	0.10
kinyaRuanda-kiRundi	Rwanda, Burundi, Uganda, Zaire, Tanzania	Bantu (Niger-Congo)	11.1
Russian	USSR	Slavic (Indo-European)	140.0
Sangir	North Celebes	Malayo-Polynesian	0.25
Sango-Ngbandi	Central African Republic, Zaire	Adamawa-Eastern (Niger-Congo)	0.28
Santali	West Bengal and Bihar (India)	Munda	4.2
Sardinian	Sardinia	Romance (Indo-European)	0.92
Sasak	Lombok (Indonesia)	Malayo-Polynesian	1.4
Senari	Ivory Coast	Voltaic (Niger-Congo)	1.04
Serbo-Croatian	Yugoslavia	Slavic (Indo-European)	16.2
Serer	Senegal	West Atlantic (Niger-Congo)	0.62
Sgaw	Burma, Thailand	Karen (Sino-Tibetan ?)	0.9
Shan	Burma, Thailand, Yunnan (China)	Tai	2.1
Shilha	Morocco	Berber (Afro-Asiatic)	2.0
chiShona	Rhodesia, Mozambique	Bantu (Niger-Congo)	4.9
Sidamo	Ethiopia	Cushitic (Afro-Asiatic)	0.96
Sindhi	Pakistan, India	Indic (Indo-European)	9.7
Sinhalese	Sri Lanka	Indic (Indo-European)	10.1
Sioux	Dakotas	Siouan	0.01
Slovak	Czechoslovakia	Slavic (Indo-European)	5.2
Slovene	Yugoslavia, Italy, Austria	Slavic (Indo-European)	2.1
Somali	Somalia, Ethiopia, Kenya	Cushitic (Afro-Asiatic)	4.7
Songhai	Niger, Mali, Upper Volta	Songhai	1.4
Soninke	Mali, Upper Volta, Senegal	Mande (Niger-Congo)	0.9
Spanish	Latin America, Spain, U.S.A.	Romance (Indo-European)	210.0
Sulu	Southern Philippines	Malayo-Polynesian	0.75
Sudanese	West Java	Malayo-Polynesian	16.5
Suppire	Mali	Voltaic (Niger-Congo)	1.1
Susu	Guinea, Sierra Leone	Mande (Niger-Congo)	0.8
siSuthu	South Africa, Lesotho, Botswana	Bantu (Niger-Congo)	6.7
kiSwahili [native]	Tanzania, Comoro Islands, Kenya, Mozambique, Zaire	Bantu (Niger Congo)	2.5
Swedish	Sweden, Finland	Germanic (Indo-European)	8.9
Tagalog	Philippines	Malayo-Polynesian	8.8
Tamazight	Morocco	Berber (Afro-Asiatic)	1.8

NAME OF LANGUAGE	WHERE SPOKEN	FAMILY	MILLIONS OF SPEAKERS
Tamil	Tamil Nadu (India), Sri Lanka, Malaysia, Singapore	Dravidian	47.0
Tarascan	Mexico	Tarascan	0.19
Tatar	USSR (Central)	Turkic (Altaic)	6.4
kiTeke	Zaire, Congo	Bantu (Niger-Congo)	0.76
Telugu	Andhra Pradesh (India)	Dravidian	52.0
Tem (Kotokole)	Togo, Ghana, Benin (Dahomey)	Voltaic (Niger-Congo)	0.21
Temne	Sierra Leone	West Atlantic (Niger-Congo)	0.93
Teso	Uganda, Kenya	Nilotic (Chari-Nile)	1.0
Thai-Lao	Thailand, Laos	Tai	36.0
Thô	Kwangsi (China), Northern Viet Nam	Tai	3.2
shiThonga	Mozambique, South Africa, Rhodesia	Bantu (Niger-Congo)	3.0
Tibetan	Tibet, Bhutan, Nepal, India	Tibeto-Burman (Sino-Tibetan)	4.5
Tigrinya	Ethiopia, Eritrea	Semitic (Afro-Asiatic)	3.4
Tiv	Benue-Plateau State (Nigeria)	Benue (Niger-Congo)	2.7
Totonac	Mexico	Zoque-Maya	0.31
Tuareg (Tamashek)	Niger, Mali, Algeria	Berber (Afro-Asiatic)	0.8
Tulu	Karnataka (India)	Dravidian	1.3
chiTumbuka	Malawi, Zambia, Tanzania	Bantu (Niger-Congo)	0.87
Turkish	Turkey, Bulgaria, Yugoslavia, Cyprus, Greece	Turkic (Altaic)	37.0
Turkmen	Turkmenistan (USSR), Iran, Afghanistan	Turkic (Altaic)	2.6
Tzeltal	Mexico	Mayan	0.18
Tzotzil	Mexico	Mayan	0.22
Uigur	Sinkiang (China), USSR, Afghanistan	Turkic (Altaic)	5.2
Ukrainian	USSR, Canada, U.S.	Slavic (Indo-European)	46.0
Urhobo	Mid-Western State (Nigeria)	Guinean (Niger-Congo)	0.90
Uzbek	Uzbekstan and Tadzhikstan (USSR), Afghanistan	Turkic (Altaic)	11.5
Vai	Sierra Leone, Liberia	Mande (Niger-Congo)	0.28
chiVenda	South Africa, Rhodesia	Bantu (Niger-Congo)	0.44
Vietnamese	Viet Nam, Thailand, Cambodia, Laos, New Caledonia, France, Dakar	Muong	40.0
Visayan	Central Philippines	Malayo-Polynesian	19.0
Votyak	Udmurt ASSR* (USSR)	Finnic (Uralic)	0.75
Welamo	Ethiopia	Cushitic (Afro-Asiatic)	1.18

NAME OF LANGUAGE	WHERE SPOKEN	FAMILY	MILLIONS OF SPEAKERS
Welsh	Wales	Celtic (Indo-European)	0.80
Wolof	Senegal, Gambia	West Atlantic (Niger-Congo)	1.8
Wu	Chekiang (China)	Chinese (Sino-Tibetan)	68.0
Yakut	Yakut ASSR* (Siberia, USSR)	Turkic (Altaic)	0.31
Yao	Southern China, Viet Nam, Laos	Miao-Yao (Sino-Tibetan)	1.2
chiYao	Malawi, Tanzania, Mozambique	Bantu (Niger-Congo)	1.4
Yiddish	U.S., Israel, USSR, Latin America, Canada, Eastern Europe	Germanic (Indo-European)	3.0
Yoruba	Western, Lagos, and Kwara States (Nigeria), Benin (Dahomey)	Guinean (Niger-Congo)	11.5
Yucatec	Mexico, British Honduras, Guatemala	Mayan	0.92
Zande	Zaire, Sudan, Central African Republic	Adamawa-Eastern (Niger-Congo)	2.1
Isthmus Zapotec	Mexico	Otomanguean	0.41
isiZulu-isiXhosa-siSwati (Nguni)	South Africa, Rhodesia, Swaziland	Bantu (Niger-Congo)	12.6
Zyrien	Komi ASSR*	Finnic (Uralic)	0.51

*ASSR—Autonomous Soviet Socialist Republic, a second-level administrative unit, coming under a Union Republic. Each is inhabited by a large ethnic minority.

Index

This index does not include entries from the questions or references at the end of each chapter or from the Appendix. Major topics like "syntax" or "origin of language" are not included if they are clearly identifiable in the Table of Contents.

THE AUTHORS

Curtis W. Hayes, Ph.D. (University of Texas, Austin) is Director of English Language Programs at the University of Texas, San Antonio. As the new co-author for *The ABC's*, Dr. Hayes brings with him an extensive theoretical and practical language background. He has served as a Ford Foundation Fellow, as a consultant for bilingual programs, and as a Fullbright-Hays Professor and Lecturer in Japan, among numerous other positions.

Jacob Ornstein received his Ph.D. from The University of Wisconsin in 1940, and has since come to be one of the most highly regarded scholars in the fields of Bilingualism and sociolinguistics. Now Professor Emeritus at University of Texas, El Paso, Dr. Ornstein continues to devote himself to research and lecturing in those fields. He has authored numerous publications, in addition to having taken government proficiency exams in 25 languages, 7 of which he speaks fluently.

William W. Gage received a Ph.D. in General Linguistics from Cornell University in 1958 and has since had experience working as a supervising linguist in intensive Vietnamese courses at Cornell and as Research Linguist at the Center for Applied Linguistics in Arlington, Virginia. At present he is a consultant to the Center, where he works on a variety of projects and pursues his special interest, organizing information about the languages of the world.